HABSBURG'S LAST WAR: THE FILMIC MEMORY (1918 TO THE PRESENT)

Other Titles In This Series:

Changing Addresses: Contemporary Austrian Writing
Edited by Johann Holzner, Alois Hotschnig

Jägerstätter
by Felix Mitterer
Translated by Gregor Thuswaldner

University of New Orleans Press
Manufactured in the United States of America

ISBN: 978-1-60801-157-5

Cover photo: *Das Attentat - Sarajewo 1914* ("*The Assassination - Sarajevo 1914*," A/CZ/GER 2014)

Book and cover design by Alex Dimeff

FWF Der Wissenschaftsfonds.

THE UNIVERSITY *of* NEW ORLEANS
CENTER AUSTRIA

Ludwig Boltzmann Institute
Research on Consequences of War

UNIVERSITY OF NEW ORLEANS PRESS
unopress.org

HABSBURG'S LAST WAR: THE FILMIC MEMORY (1918 TO THE PRESENT)

Cinematic and TV Productions in the Neighbouring Countries and Successor States of the Danube Monarchy: Austria, Czechia-Slovakia, Germany, Hungary, Italy, Poland, Romania, Russia, Serbia, Slovenia

Hannes Leidinger, editor
Günter Bischof, series editor

ACKNOWLEDGEMENTS

These essays contain the results of the scholarly research project "Moving Images of Habsburg's Final War." The main objectives of research was to investigate in-depth the filmic memory of Austria-Hungary´s WWI experience, the analysis of cinematic and TV productions in the successor states of the Danube Monarchy: Austria, Czechia-Slovakia, Hungary, Italy, Poland, Romania, and Slovenia, as well as the World War I ally Germany and the erstwhile antagonists Russia and Serbia from 1914 to the present. The larger project will also produce a history of film in Austria-Hungary (1914–1918) and a filmography of movies produced in the Habsburg Monarchy during World War I.

The Austrian Science Fund (FWF) has kindly financed this project (FWF P 25685-G23), including the printing costs of the volume. Center Austria at the University of New Orleans would like to thank the scholars involved in the peer review process of these essays for their suggestions and improvements of the texts. Tobias Auböck (located in Hamburg, Germany) brought the footnotes into alignment. Gertraud Griessner kept Center Austria going while Günter Bischof worked on this volume. Center Austria would like to thank its principal sponsors—the Austrian Marshall Plan Foundation and the Austrian Ministry of Science, Research and Economy, both in Vienna—for their ongoing support of its programs. The Center Austria series, Studies in Central European History, Culture & Literature, is the perfect venue to publish this volume on the history of film and its role in the formation of memories of World War I in the succession states of the Habsburg Monarchy. At UNO Press Abram Himelstein and George Kroening ("G.K.") Darby were instrumental in shepherding this volume towards publication. Ella Pfalzgraff copy-edited the volume and Alex Dimeff designed it (including the cover).

In Vienna, Karin Moser from the University of Vienna has been instrumental in assisting the editor in bringing this volume together and also found the picture for the cover. In the Hungarian National Film Archive of Budapest, Dorottya Szörényi's crucial help in coordinating the "Austro-Hungarian cooperation" was indispensable for the realization of the project's objectives. Furthermore, the editor would like to express his appreciation to the entire project team. Karin Almasy, Enikö Dácz, Karin Moser, Verena Moritz, Thomas Ballhausen, Francesco Bono, László Deák-Sárosi, Aleksandar Erdeljanović, Márton Kurutz, Piotr Szlanta, Václav Šmidrkal, and Philipp Stiasny supported him with good cheer and professional advice throughout the research and completion of this volume. Thanks to all of them for the timely submission of their essays and their willingness to make late revisions along the lines of the peer reviewer's suggestions. Last but not least, the editor would like to thank his wife Verena and daughter Lena for the mental support during the exhausting project work.

Vienna/New Orleans, August 2017

CONTENTS

ESSAYS

IMAGES

ESSAYS

POSTMATTER

PREFACE

Günter Bischof

With the exception of the artistic and intellectual flowering of the "*fin-de*-siecle Vienna," the Habsburg Empire ("Austria-Hungary" since 1867) has received little attention by scholars in the Anglo-American scholarly world.[1] Its role during World War I has long been neglected.[2] The Habsburg Empire has not had a good reputation in the Anglo-American world. Little expertise existed at American universities on East-Central European history prior to World War I – and many of the British experts were anti-Habsburg. Small wonder then that President Woodrow Wilson got bad advice about the future of this region for the Paris Peace Conference in 1919.[3] His selective principle of "self-determination" – not enforced in the South Tyrol question and the entire

1 Carl Schorske, *Fin-De-Siecle Vienna: Politics and Culture* (New York: Knopf, 1980).

2 Notable recent exceptions are Maureen Healy, *Vienna and the Fall of the Habsburg Empire: Total War and Everyday Life in World War I* (Cambridge: Cambridge UP, 2004; Pieter Judson, *The Habsburg Empire: A New* History (Cambridge, MA: Harvard UP, 2016), ch. 8; Geoffrey Wawro, *A Mad Catastrophe: The Outbreak of World War I and the Collapse of the Habsburg Empire* (New York: Basic Books, 2017); John Deak, "The Great War and the Forgotten Realm: The Habsburg Monarchy and the First World War," in: *Journal of Modern History* 86 (June 2014), 336-380.

3 Nicole M. Phelps, *U.S. –Habsburg Relations from 1815 to the Paris Peace Conference* (Cambridge: Cambridge UP, 2013), 219-274.

colonial world – led to the "Balkanization" of the region after the war. Democracy took a hold only in Czechoslovakia; the rest of the new states in East Central Europe quickly succumbed to authoritarian forms of government. "Triumphant in 1918, it was virtually extinct twenty years on," Mark Mazower has observed: "Maybe it was bound to collapse in a time of political crisis and economic turmoil," he adds, "for its defenders were too utopian, too ambitious, too few."[4]

Denounced before and during the war as a "prison of the peoples" ("*Völkerkerker*") by the constituent ethnicities of the empire, most of the new nation states ("successors" to the Habsburg Monarchy) fared considerably worse after the war – rid of the Emperor in Vienna, they soon had to contend with Hitler in Berlin and then Stalin in Moscow. Both the remaining democracies and the newly formed authoritarian regimes on the political right were first occupied and dominated by German National Socialism in the course of World War II and then taken over Stalin's Soviet Union and oppressed for another two generations during the Cold War. Only after the collapse of communism and the end of the Cold War in 1989/90 did they escape totalitarian oppression. Their "transition regimes" regained their national independence, elected democratic governments, and joined "the West" (with NATO and European Union membership).

The succession states saw the end of the war 1918 as the great "rupture." National historiographies (especially in Czechoslovakia and Yugoslavia) have usually focused on the "break" with Austria-Hungary at the end of war and ignored the many continuities with the Habsburg Empire that existed in their new states on the

4 Mark Mazower, *Dark Continent: Europe' Twentieth Century* (New York Vintage, 1998), 5.

local level.[5] Pieter Judson has stressed in his recent work how the Habsburg Empire collapsed in 1918 due to stress of war rather than the internal ethnic tensions as historians have emphasized for so long.[6]

The essays in this volume deal with cinematographic representations of World War I in the various succession states of the Habsburg Monarchy (plus Germany and the Soviet Union). The frequent regime changes in the region during the twentieth century figure front, line and center in film making. These essays reflect starkly how much the predominant ideologies of the various regimes affected artistic expression and World War I memory in these succession states. So, for example, Yugoslav Communists insisted that Slovene film makers continue with the perception of the Habsburg Monarchy as "prison of the peoples", despite their quasi-"incarceration" by Tito's Communist regime in Yugoslavia; film makers in Fascist Italy in the 1930s were not allowed to paint an image of Austria as an "enemy" during World War I due to Mussolini's alliance with the authoritarian Dollfuss regime at the time.

These essays on the representation of World War I in the film-making of the various succession states provide a very useful comparative perspective of how artists (writers and film makers) responded to this "crisis of civilization" that was World War I. For one, many World War I films produced in these countries have

5 Claire Morelon, "Introduction," in: Paul Miller/Clarie Morelon, eds., *"As If There Had Been No Revolution At All": Continuity and Rupture With the Habsburg Empire, 1914 to Today* [forthcoming].

6 Pieter Judson, "'Where our commonality is necessary…': Rethinking the end of the Habsburg Monarchy," *Austrian History Yearbook* 48 (2017): 1-21; this text is based on his "Kann Lecture" at the University of Minnesota-Twin Cities.

been lost. It is striking that "escapist" melodramas most often seem to have been the likely vehicle for film makers (based on novels) to address the turmoil and trauma of the war and thus shape the postwar memory. Rarely did films deal with the actual military history of the war (battles, larger strategic issues), or the war crimes committed by the belligerents, but with the human drama encountered by civilians in the hinterland. Most of the succession states produced documentaries too, if news clips were available in their national archives (that was not always the case as Habsburg censors may not have wanted to document the "national" existence of the Monarchy's diverse constituent parts). Most of the succession states did not have the means to produce Hollywood style dramatic feature films *a la* "All Quiet on the Western Front." Some "succession states" like post-Yugoslav Slovenia did not have any film industry at all in 1918; others like Czechoslovakia had well-developed native private film production companies -- nationalized under the Communist regime after World War II. In almost all of the countries under review here, World War II eclipsed World War I in importance and the film industry produced World War II movies after that war and often ignored World War I.

So the trajectories of film productions about World War I through the various post-World War I periods (Interwar, 1918-1938; World War II, 1938-1945; Cold War, 1945-1989/90; post-Cold War transition regimes, 1990 till today) are very different from country to country. Austria's well established film industry had to build an identity for the new state that many considered "not viable" after the war. Sentimental films about the Habsburg family were designed to suppress the harsh realities and traumas of the war. The new Republic of Czechoslovakia stressed the role of the Czech Legion in World War I to build Czechoslovak national identity around the heroic role of the legionnaires. The foundation myth of the new Polish state was also build on the Polish legionnaires who fought the invading Red Army in 1920/21. In a similar fashion, Yugoslav cinema after World War II concentrated on the heroic role of the partisan resistance against the Nazis in the Balkans.

In some of the countries under review in this volume, the 100th anniversary of World War I in 2014 produced a new wave of films and documentaries on the war. In the case of Slovenia, national television produced the first 5-part documentary series on World War I in the Slovenian region. The Isonzo battles (esp. Kobarid/Caporetto) and the end of the war were at the center of these documentaries, but one segment also dealt with the Eastern front in Galicia, where Slovenes fought in great numbers in 1914/15. In Austria, too, many new films on World War I were produced and shown in 2014 – here too, the state television network ORF played a crucial role.

This volume stands at the beginning of writing the history of World War I films in the succession countries of the Habsburg Monarchy. The rate of production may have varied in various succession states, but the scholarly interest may likely be stirred with this volume.

New Orleans, August 2017

INTRODUCTION

Hannes Leidinger

It was Samuel Hynes who suggested, in his fascinating study on English war culture, *A War Imagined*[1], that the popular memory of the "Great War" from 1914 to 1918 has been recalled and influenced through the written word.[2] Apart from this estimation, analyses of different "cultures of memory" clearly show that there was a plethora of individual and collective forms of recollection such as—among many others—war memorials, remembrance days or other (frequent) commemorative events.[3]

But keeping in mind the growing importance of cinematography since the 1890s and above all during "Europe's seminal catastrophe" after the shots rang out in Sarajevo, it should be taken into consideration what Michael Paris, the editor of the 1999 omnibus volume *The First World War and Popular Cinema*,

1 Titles of scientific publications or printed sources (journals, novels, and so forth) are written in italics throughout the volume "(with the exception of the index)". This applies also to film titles and technical or specialized terminology. Film titles in italics with quotation marks are British or American release titles.

2 Cf. Samuel Hynes, *A War Imagined: The First World War and English Culture* (London: Pimlico, 1990).

3 On Austria for instance: Oswald Überegger, *Erinnerungskriege: Der Erste Weltkrieg,* Österreich *und die Tiroler Kriegserinnerung in der Zwischenkriegszeit* (Innsbruck: Wagner, 2011); Werner Suppanz, Österreichische *Geschichtsbilder: Historische Legitimationen in Ständestaat und Zweiter Republik* (Böhlau: Vienna, 1998).

stated: The "filmic image was equally, if not more, influential for reconstructing that memory. And film continues to provide the dominant popular national interpretation of that War for most people, simply because of the ability of film to reach a far greater public than the printed word," for instance, "not just with the initial exhibition of a film, but through subsequent release, through television screenings," through videos and DVDs respectively.[4]

About a decade later, David Williams wrote detailed explanations on the topic, when he turned to "new sciences" in the process of modernization, "swiftly undermining the verbal epistemology of the ancients." Referring to the first intellectual encounters with cinematography, he quoted a French journalist who got the following impressions: "Already, words are collected and reproduced; now life is collected and reproduced." Thereby, photographs only "fixed a particular past moment," while "cinematic images seemed rather to reproduce actuality, to invade the present." Thus, the strangely invasive power of "moving pictures" overturned familiar notions of temporality. The result was "a relentless telescoping of time in which the boundaries between past and present appear to dissolve."[5] The phenomenon of "(filmed) time and space being rendered apparently simultaneous in the present"[6] fostered the equating of history and its imagination, much to the chagrin of critical commentators. But at the same time, this cinematic visualization of the past secured the box office success of various "movies."

---

4 Michael Paris, "Introduction," in *The First World War and Popular Cinema*, ed. Michael Paris (Edinburgh: University Press, 1999), 2.

5 David Williams, *Media, Memory, and the First World War* (Montreal: McGill-Queen's University Press, 2009), 109.

6 Ibid.

Against this backdrop, an ever-growing number of scholars stressing the central role of the Great War in shaping the twentieth century also started to recognize the meaning of "moving images" to explain or (re-)construct history. Yet this scientific turn was not self-evident even a few decades ago. Michael Paris, focusing on the respective film productions in Austria, Britain and the Dominions, France, Germany, Italy, Poland, Russia, and the United States, was still surprised that—according to the significance of the theme—historians have devoted comparatively little attention to films" about World War One. There was an earlier interest in contemporary footage and particularly cinematic propaganda in the course of the European and global military hostilities up to 1918.[7] But post-1918 productions still received scant attention around 2000.[8]

Nevertheless, Paris—figuring as a kind of a pioneer in the field of research—was more optimistic at the end of the introduction of his collective volume: "Excellent national studies have started

---

7 Cf. M.L. Sanders and Philip M. Taylor, *British Propaganda during the First World War* (London: MacMillan, 1982); Nicholas Reeves, *Official British Film Propaganda during the First World War* (London: Croom Helm, 1986); Larry Ward, *The Motion Picture Goes to War: The United States Government Effort during World War I* (Ann Arbor: University of Michigan Press, 1985). Later on see also for instance: Leslie Midriff DeBauche, *Reel Patriotism: The Movies and World War I* (Wisconsin: University of Wisconsin Press, 1997); Ulrike Oppelt, *Film und Propaganda im Ersten Weltkrieg: Propaganda als Medienrealität im Aktualitäten- und Dokumentarfilm* (Stuttgart: Steiner, 2002); Philipp Stiasny, *Das Kino und der Krieg: Deutschland 1914–1929* (München, 2009). For Russia, including a chapter on film: Hubertus F. Jahn, *Patriotic Culture in Russia during World War I* (Ithaca: Cornell University Press, 1995)

8 Paris, "Introduction," 2–3.

to emerge," Paris remarked.[9] Equally, experts began to explore what might be considered key films, like "*All Quiet on the Western Front*".[10] And even Paris´s innovative attempt to present a synthesis or a comparative analysis of different countries was no flash in the pan: At least the filmic memory of the First World War in France, Great Britain, East and West Germany, as well the USA, anchored an anthology, edited by Rainer Rother and Karin Herbst-Meßlinger, as a central theme.[11] Specialists for various areas of study like philology, literary criticism, cultural and media sciences, publishing studies, ancient, modern, contemporary and art history also cooperated in 2008 to connect film analyses with a broader understanding of memorial culture.[12]

---

9 Ibid., 2. See also: Karel Dibbets and Bert Hogenkamp, eds., *Film and the First World War: Papers from the Fifteenth Conference of the International Association for Media and History* (Amsterdam: Amsterdam University Press, 1995); Andrew Kelly, *Cinema and the Great War* (London: Routledge, 1997); Peter C. Rollins and John E. O'Connor, *Hollywood´s World War I: Moving Picture Images* (Bowling Green: Kentucky University Press, 1997).

10 For example: Modris Ekstein, "War, Memory and Politics: The Fate of the Film *All Quiet on the Western Front*," *Central European History* 13 (1980); Andrew Kelly, *Filming* All Quiet on the Western Front (London: I. B. Tauris, 1998)

11 *Der Erste Weltkrieg im Film*, ed. Rainer Rother and Karin Herbst-Meßlinger (München: edition text + kritik, 2009); cf. Hubertus F. Jahn, *Patriotic Culture in Russia during World War I.*

12 Barbare Korte, Sylvia Paletschek, and Wolfgang Hochbruck, eds., *Der Erste Weltkrieg in der populären Erinnerungskultur* (Essen: Klartext, 2008). Regarding cultures of memory in general, among others: Aleida Assmann, *Erinnerungsräume: Formen und Wandlungen des kulturellen Gedächtnisses* (München: Beck, 1999). With respect to World War I above all: Jay Winter, *Sites of Memory, Sites of Mourning: The Great War in European History* (Cambridge: Cambridge University Press, 1995); Jay Winter, *Remembering War: The Great War between Memory and History in the Twentieth Century* (New Haven: Yale University Press, 2006).

Apart from these new trends, Austria—with the exception of one article in Michael Paris's book—was hardly ever in the focus of such scholarly endeavours, though this was not a foregone conclusion. Obviously, the legacy of the Habsburg monarchy was crucial for filmmaking all through the decades of the twentieth century. The old emperor Francis Joseph I as a symbol of the durability and decrepitude of the Danube monarchy has become an icon even before the "birth of moving images." The years preceding the bloodshed of 1914 and the following years strengthened the trend. At that time, Francis Joseph "did not mind being on film at certain events," as the important expert of language, culture, and (Austrian) film, Robert von Dassanowsky, put it.[13] But, according to Dassanowsky, it was exactly the same aged emperor who "flatly rejected" even requests of famous directors "to film him and members of the imperial family for a 'patriotic film' that might be viewed as commercial and political exploitation."[14] Posterity had to accommodate the threads again, which has torn the First World War. With Karl Ehmann as the "venerable monarch" in the Jakob and Louise Fleck 1933 production *Unser Kaiser* (*Our emperor*), the embodiment of the collapsed Habsburg state reappeared as an "obvious attempt to define sovereign Austrian identity along nostalgia for Kakania and as romanticized biopic positioned against the Pan-German threat of the nascent 'Third Reich.'"[15]

But all of this, and especially the "old man of Schönbrunn," centered around the idea of a peacetime "World of yesterday" before 1914. The Habsburg legacy did not fit in with the images and imaginations of war, the more so because the Dual Monarchy

---

13 Robert von Dassanowsky, *Austrian Cinema: A History* (Jefferson, North Carolina: McFarland & Company, Inc., Publishers, 2005), 20.

14 Ibid.

15 Ibid., 49.

resembled the invention of the operetta, the theater, and the novel, as Philipp Stiasny tries to point out in his introductory remarks to his article of this volume. These artistic influences were especially suited to the requirements of cinematic entertainment. Hence, and in line with Stiasny, the "old monarchy" of the "Casa de Austria" was "never only a historical and geographical, but rather an emotional region and era" of "longing" and cliques of amusement.[16]

Most of the time, "Vienna, the wine, and the waltz," as well as the sentimental film in the regional setting of the Alps and the Danube regions, stood for the perfect antipode of "trenches, night patrols in barbed wire and disfigured landscape with ruins, shell-holes and craters filled with water," sceneries which became symbols of a First World War being equated with the pictures of "*All Quiet on the Western Front*".[17]

Such characteristics of many comparable movies refer also to another explanation for the disappearance of Austria-Hungary in films about World War One: The Habsburg army fought on other fronts, operated in other communication and occupation zones, was involved in mobile warfare, contrary to the trench warfare in France.

Under such circumstances, an approach to "Habsburg´s last war" above all in post-1918 feature films, but also in nonfiction productions and TV documentaries respectively, appears to be futile. And this seems to be even more true because of the dissolution of the empire, losing—as sometimes claimed—its relevance to posterity. Furthermore, the impact of the Second World

---

16 See Philipp Stiasny's contribution in this volume.

17 Pierre Sorlin, "Cinema and the Memory of the Great War," in *The First World War and Popular Cinema*, ed. Michael Paris (Edinburgh: University Press, 1999), 5–26, here: 20–21.

War superseded the events of 1914 to 1918 nearly completely, for instance with regard to the "partisan theme" in Successor States and Neighboring Countries of Austria-Hungary becoming part of the "Soviet Bloc" after 1945. Thus, even some of the authors in the present book have to admit that their topic—the First World War particularly in connection with Austria-Hungary—is at best a sideshow of the development of cinema, television or media in general and, the more so, of historiography in general.

To put it pointedly: Is it worth mentioning the theme at all?

The answer is clearly yes, for several reasons.

First of all, it goes without saying that Successor States of the Danube monarchy like Austria and Hungary, which once formed the nucleus of the Habsburg empire, could not fully ignore what they mostly considered an era of "defeat, humiliation, disruption and catastrophe," not even in the sphere of arts and entertainment. There were always enough relevant productions to be taken into account.[18]

Second, instead of a complete disappearance of "old Austria's final chapter" in film productions, an ideologization took place: In this sense, it was the theming of the topic by different parties, social forces and milieus as well as changing regimes from the immediate revolutionary consequences of the First World War to the rise of fascism, the establishment of totalitarian rule, the Cold War, and the impact of the fall of the Iron Curtain. In this connection, among other aspects, left or right wing cultures of remembrance left their traces in the "moving images" of various historical periods. For example, opposing perspectives in this regard are sometimes based on the contradiction between the integration of amusing entertainment with "Austrian charm and

18 See the following articles of László Deák-Sárosi, Márton Kurutz, and Hannes Leidinger.

good vibrations" in military genres and topics centered around the "Death of the Double-headed Eagle" on the one side, and the presentation of the Habsburg monarchy as a decadent and decayed, aristocratic and "bourgeois" empire doomed to fail, or even as a malicious and bellicose rogue state in (pacifistic) discourses with more or less communist or (left) socialist viewpoints, on the other.[19]

Third, from a national (or nationalist) position, a fragmentation manifested itself in the tendency to replace the Habsburg monarchy by its provinces or crown lands with specific ethnic composition and frictions (like Galicia, with its additional significant "Jewish character"), by legionaries fighting for their "real" and often alleged "ethnically homogeneous future fatherland," but also by certain regions and front lines like Transylvania or the Isonzo valley representing the increased military use of some peoples of the Dual Monarchy, exceptional territorial claims or the "extraordinary will" to defend not so much the multi-ethnic empire as a whole but the "actual (national) home."[20] Additionally, it is necessary to broach aspects and narratives like these also in terms of memorial cultures, long-term developments, and current situations. Therefore, one has to remember the changing perspectives of Austro-Italian relationships in the course of the twentieth century, as well as, for example, Czech-Hungarian, Romanian-Hungarian or Croatian-Serbian controversies up to the present.[21]

---

19 Among other presentations: Statements of Enikö Dácz and Aleksandar Erdeljanović in their present articles.

20 Cf. Expositions of Karin Almasy, Francesco Bono, Enikö Dácz, Václav Šmidrkal, Philipp Stiasny, Piotr Szlanta,

21 In this connection see the respective articles of Francesco Bono, Enikö Dácz, László Deák-Sárosi, Aleksandar Erdeljanović, and Márton Kurutz.

Yet apart from key items and research questions already mentioned, but also apart from aspects such as the (dis)ability of international observers and especially filmmakers to differ between German and Austrian movies or the German-Hohenzollern empire and the Habsburg monarchy mainly dominated by German-speaking elites, there is also a fourth topic focus which should not be neglected: the reasons for the absence of special themes, in the concrete case of the First World War, generally, or the Dual Monarchy and Habsburg's last war specifically. Gaps like that require different explanations and perspectives. Hence, and notwithstanding the already addressed "fragmentation" of Austria-Hungary, these scientific approaches referring to a "history of the absent" or "the void" at all tend to tackle new scientific realms of investigation.[22]

This deliberation ties in with a more fundamental problem of "hauntology" as an "ontological dysfunction": The presence of being is replaced by a deferred or absent non-origin, represented by the figure of the "ghost," which is neither present nor absent, neither absent nor alive—or by the idea of the transformation of the deceased or the perished into a specter. At the same time, the post-imperial notion of "Kakania"—as a proper example in this sense—goes hand in hand with the discussion about the "cinematographization of the world": Moving images shaping "realities" and "public opinion" waver between (the performance of) "authenticity" and "fabricated forgery of events," between realistic "news" or propagandist messages and "cinema as a shore of oblivion, a point or rest," or, to be even more concrete, between the experience and frequent reinterpretations of the traumatizing mass killing of war and the "inner cinematic phenomenon," its (changing) techniques, "patterns of performances and perceptions."

22 Most of all in the present chapter of Verena Moritz and partly also in the article of Enikö Dácz.

Thomas Ballhausen tries to focus on these facets in his postscript of this omnibus volume with many further thoughts, additional suggestions, and final remarks on the (film) archive as a (constantly re-arranged) material basis, surrounded by receptions, re-presentations, re-assessments, and re-uses of sources and narratives.

On this occasion, I would like thank all the contributors of the present collective work, particularly for their readiness to embark on an intellectual journey leading to sideshows of historical research work and sometimes to unusual interpretation approaches. Karin Almasy, Enikö Dácz, Karin Moser, Verena Moritz, Thomas Ballhausen, Francesco Bono, László Deák-Sárosi, Aleksandar Erdeljanović, Márton Kurutz, Piotr Szlanta, Václav Šmidrkal, and Philipp Stiasny made the effort to analyze different perspectives of Austrian, Czech-Slovak, German, Hungarian, Italian, Romanian, Russian, Serbian, and Slovenian cinema and television on the relevant themes, fictional and non-fiction film productions. Depending on different source situations and varying national preconditions, the authors decided to elucidate various time spans, single film productions and special research questions. Some were able to give historical-cross sections and overall views from 1918 to the present,[23] whereas others focused on the interwar era[24] or the post-1945 period[25] as well as on the centennial commemoration of the outbreak of the First World War in 2014

23 Above all the chapters written by Václav Šmidrkal and Hannes Leidinger and with some focal points in different eras also the expositions of Verena Moritz and Piotr Szlanta.

24 See the contributions of Francesco Bono, Márton Kurutz, and Philipp Stiasny

25 Cf. Articles of Enikö Dácz, László Deák-Sárosi, and Aleksandar Erdeljanović

and the respective feature films and TV documentaries.[26] Parts of the texts mirror controversial national, individual, and ideological stances differing also—at least in a few cases—from the editor's standpoint. Yet it was not the intention of the volume to smooth down deviations like that. The multitude of viewpoints reflects obvious internal controversies within Central, East and East-Central or South-East European societies as well as diverse (national) narratives in the countries covered, all of them once part or neighbor of the Habsburg empire.

One might criticize that the national perspectives and structure of this book prolongs traditional historical perceptions being highly questioned by new and fashionable trends of "transnational studies" and a *histoire croisée.* According to that, it has to be stressed that the Habsburg empire, its decline, dissolution, and aftermath is probably not the best research-objective for "transnational phenomena." But, of course, perhaps the opposite is also true (referring sometimes to an arbitrariness of too far-reaching theories and—much more likely—to ubiquitous fashionable terms). Maybe epistemological deliberations on the subject have to be continued, though it could also be argued that the present volume, with its table of contents and national views offers comparisons and insights beyond "ethnic spheres," patriotic narratives, ideological priorities, and state borders.

In any case, the authors of the volume know very well that it is only the moderate beginning of a synthesis in the field of film studies and historiography in general, based on closer cooperation between the Successor States and the adjacent countries of the former Danube monarchy.

26 The text of Karin Almasy and Karin Moser right at the front.

HABSBURG'S LAST WAR IN AUSTRIAN FILMS, 1918 TO THE PRESENT

Hannes Leidinger

Introduction

This article is devoted to a key issue, a question, which was formulated in an exemplary manner by the editor of the Viennese specialist journal, *Meteor*, and publisher of several books on film and media, Franz Marksteiner. In a 1999 omnibus volume, *The First World War and Popular Cinema*, Marksteiner asked: "Where is the war in all of these films? These films have such titles as *Kaiserball* (*The Emperor's Prom*), *Kaiserwalzer* (*The Emperor's Waltz*), *Kaisermanoever* (*The Emperor's Maneuver*), *Der Kaiser und das Waeschermaedel* (*The Emperor and the Washergirl*), *Die Deutschmeister* (*The German Masters*), *Hoch Klingt der Radetzkymarsch* (*Lofty Sounds: the Radetzky March*). The heroes of these movies are decorated officers and dashing soldiers, all able to win the hearts of the ladies. Established comedians and the figure of the Emperor were given much artistic freedom in their appearances. The Emperor enters the scene mainly when it is necessary to disentangle misunderstandings and give the plot a direction, a function that his authority and narrative role allows. But where is the war?"[1]

---

1 Franz Marksteiner, "Where is the War? Some Aspects of the Effects of World War One on Austrian Cinema," in *The First World War and Popular Cinema: 1914 to the Present*, ed. Michael Paris (New Brunswick: Rutgers University Press, 1999), 247–260, here: 254.

Desirable Pictures

As a matter of fact, the existence of so many *Kaiserfilms*[2] refers to the importance of the Habsburg monarchy and even of the Habsburg myth for the construction of a national Austrian identity, particularly after 1945. Robert von Dassanowsky, professor for German language, literature and film, as well as director of the film faculty at the University of Colorado, made conclusions similar to those of Marksteiner in his landmark studies. He included more movies than Marksteiner, stressing the fact that in particular the rival directors Ernst Marischka and Franz Antel followed an international trend, namely the strong desire of the whole Western world to take refuge "from the Cold War in royal romance, through works on Iran's Queen Soraya and Britain's Princess Margaret, and that ultimate overlap between cinema fantasy and monarchical pomp, the wedding of Hollywood star Grace Kelly to Prince Rainier III of Monaco."[3]

2 Another early example of this genre is Jakob and Louise Fleck's *Unser Kaiser* (*Our Emperor*, 1933). Against the backdrop of Hitler's assumption of power in Germany, the movie brought the icon of the lost empire, "his majesty Franz Joseph," to sound film. This "romanticized biopic" was an "obvious attempt to define sovereign Austrian identity along nostalgia for a benevolent symbol of a great polyglot empire." It "positioned itself against the pan-Germans of the past and the newsreel image of the Austrian who had become German chancellor of a 'new empire' (the 'Third Reich') in the present"; Robert von Dassanowsky, *Austrian Cinema: A History* (Jefferson, NC: McFarland & Company, 2005), 49.

3 Robert Dassanowsky, "Finis Austriae, vivat Austria: The Re/Vision of 1918 in Austrian Film," in Österreich *1918 und die Folgen. Geschichte, Literatur, Theater und Film: Austria 1918 and the Aftermath. History, Literature, Theatre, and Film*, ed. Karl Müller and Hans Wagener (Vienna: Böhlau, 2009), 179–196, here: 189.

Austria's filmmakers helped to satisfy some of this "global craving for escapism," more specifically the escape into the world of the rich, powerful, and famous, all the more so since they found the perfect preconditions to do so. The Viennese cliché—waltz, wine, and operetta—was significant for cinematic entertainment not only under Nationalist Socialist rule, but even before, in the interwar period. Apart from that, directors at this time capitalized on a measured wave of nostalgia for the imperial past. Some of the last silent films took a bittersweet look back at the Habsburg's epochs in the manner of fanciful Cinderella-like romances such as *Erzherzog Johann* (Archduke Johann) and *Erzherzog Otto und das Wäschermädel* (Archduke Otto and the Washergirl). Images of the *Biedermeier* era and the Congress of Vienna, like the 1931 Universum Film (UFA) production "*Congress Dances*" strengthened the filmic impression of the better "world of yesterday," as defined by Stefan Zweig. Not accidentally, Franz Antel decided to release a color remake of "*Congress Dances*" in 1955, thirteen years after the Goebbel's propaganda approached the congress theme with its own Viennese comedy *Wiener Blut*, starring Theo Lingen and Hans Moser, the latter in his famous curmudgeon manner. But whatever Antel achieved with his contribution to the filmic image making of the Second Republic, it was Ernst Marischka who took the cake with his *Sissi* trilogy about the young imperial couple Franz Joseph and Elisabeth, "Sisi," the latter up to the present taking the form of Romy Schneider in the minds of many viewers. By incorporating most of the popular film formulas of the 1950s, Marischka's royal melodrama became "one accomplished package": It utilized Austrian and Bavarian landscapes for *Heimatfilm* images, presented two romantic figures of Habsburg history and recalled the "elegant orchestration of the Viennese Film," thereby creating a visually pleasurable pseudohistory that also served

Austrian public images after a decade of Allied occupation in many ways.[4]

Therefore, it is not a surprise that even at the beginning of the twenty-first century Austrian politicians "are committed to conveying such an image of the country. Some of them mention the imperial past, particularly, as Franz Marksteiner wrote in 1999, "when topics involving the European Union's eastern expansion are on the agenda. The potential rejoining of countries which 'once had belonged together'", Marksteiner noted, "repeatedly brings the former Austro-Hungarian Empire onto the floor for consideration as a model for a united Europe."[5]

Dassanowsky, on the other hand, emphasizes most of all that film images and in particular *Kaiserfilms* were crucial for the Austrian search for identity. The pre-1914 Habsburg world, with its intellectual/creative energies "was a safe and positive image to evoke" and, parallel to that, a convenient opportunity to supersede the German nationalist tendencies and the Anschluss movement as well as the (Austrian) responsibility for totalitarian rule, terror, and holocaust.[6]

Preconditions

But the war did not only disappear due to the republic's peculiarities of commemoration and self-representation; it even inherited difficult contemporary footage of the First World War itself. Apart from censorship and the reluctance of military commands of the Habsburg army to permit access of (private and civilian) cameramen to the combat zones, the "total and industrialized war" of "masses," of millions of mobilized subjects, in huge

4 Ibid., 188 and 189.

5 Marksteiner, "Where is the War?", 248.

6 Dassanowsky, "Finis Austriae, vivat Austria," 187 and 188.

"front regions" could hardly be captured by motion pictures. The real fighting scenes were rare, according to the specialist magazine *Der Kinematograph*, which stated as early as August 1914: "The modern battlefield presents communities living in the near vicinity with hardly anything that one could call recognisable. The distances are immense, the gunners along the front lines barely visible."[7] Doubting the value of depictions showing "storming troops" shot from "safe distance" and confronted with the risks of filming in the course of bloody hostilities, cameramen orientated themselves by the slogan "To be seen is to be dead" and resorted to re-enactments of "heroic fighting" beyond the trenches, in communications zones or "in the comfort of a prepared studio."[8] The results, however, were hardly impressive. Spectators expressed their "indescribable disappointment" and ridiculed newsreels and other nonfiction movies with "faked combat scenes."[9]

---

7 Quoted in: Thomas Ballhausen, "Between Virgo and Virago: Spatial Perceptions and Gender Politics in Austrian Film Production, 1914–1918," in *Gendered Memories: Transgressions in German and Israeli Film and Theater*, ed. Vera Apfelthaler and Julia B. Köhne (Wien: Turia + Kant, 2007), 147–159, here: 150.

8 Anton Kaes, *Shell Shock Cinema: Weimar Culture and the Wounds of War* (Princeton: Princeton University Press, 2009), 28–29.

9 Among others: Hannes Leidinger, "Visualisierung des Krieges: Die Ostfront in österreichisch-ungarischen Fotografien und Filmproduktionen," in *Jenseits des Schützengrabens: Der Erste Weltkrieg im Osten. Erfahrung - Wahrnehmung - Kontext*, ed. Bernhard Bachinger and Wolfram Dornik (Innsbruck: StudienVerlag, 2013), 451–465, here: 457; Rainer Rother, "The Experience of the First World War and the German Film," in *The First World War and Popular Cinema: 1914 to the Present*, ed. Michael Paris (New Brunswick: Rutgers University Press, 1999), 217–246, here: 222.

With the continuance of the bloodshed and a growing war-weariness, the short bloom of moving images of military operations came almost to a complete halt anyway. Professionalized propaganda organizations focused on the "home front," as well as on the supply and relief activities for suffering compatriots, wounded or disabled soldiers, war orphans and widows in particular. In the end, even these themes were replaced by the overwhelming majority of pure entertainment films. In this respect, the Habsburg Empire followed international trends. Only a small part of the British and French productions depicted the ongoing fighting,[10] and the tendencies were apparent: Between August and December 1914, 50 of 106 Russian films dealt with the armed conflict and its consequences, but in 1916, the subject amounted only to 13 of 500 productions at all.[11] The Western, Austrian part of the Dual Monarchy came up with the following figures: 26 and 17 percent of the domestic movies could be characterized as more or less "war related" in 1915 and 1916, while within the last two years of the European "seminal catastrophe," only about ten percent of 142 movies referred to current developments on the front lines or at least in the hinterland.[12]

---

10 Gerhard Paul, "Krieg und Film im 20. Jahrhundert: Historische Skizzen und methodologische Überlegungen," in *Krieg und Militär im Film des 20. Jahrhunderts*, ed. Bernhard Chiari, Matthias Rogg, and Wolfgang Schmidt (München: Oldenbourg, 2003), 3–78, here: 8.

11 Hannes Leidinger, "`Die vaterländische Pflicht an der visuellen Front`: Bildberichterstattung und Bildpropaganda in Österreich-Ungarn unter besonderer Berücksichtigung der `östlichen Kampfschauplätze` 1914–1918," in *Erster Weltkrieg: Globaler Konflikt - lokale Folgen. Neue Perspektiven*, ed. Stefan Karner and Philipp Lesiak (Innsbruck: StudienVerlag, 2014), 321–332, here: 324.

12 Quantitative analysis of: Österreichische *Spielfilme. Band 1: Spielfilme 1906–1918*, ed. Anton Thaller (Vienna: filmarchiv austria, 2010), 514–517.

The war itself receded into the background until 1918. This applies especially to the Habsburg Empire and the battlefields of its army. And, even more than before the armistice(s), the Balkan and the Russian fronts were marginalized, in retrospect, by the effective presentations of the "trench-war in the West." The fighting of imperial and royal troops against the Italian forces in the Alps and at the Isonzo river was—surprisingly enough—no exception. Though much more important for the Austrian historical memory, it was not the film industry of the smaller Alpine Republic that broached the topic of the armed confrontation with the "arch-enemy in the south" more intensively. For many decades, nothing changed in this respect.[13]

Embarrassments and Provocations

Apart from this kind of a "double suppression" of the "Habsburg's last war" in filmic representations before and after 1918, the Second World War figures as a "third wave of supersession." After 1945, the positive image-making with a more or less sentimental pseudohistory led to the neglect of many topics. Amongst them was above all the cleansing of National Socialist taint in traditional genres of Austrian film. But according particularly to the importance of cinematic constructions of the national identity in the Second Republic, the respective focus resulted also—for instance—in the avoidance of 1918, along with 1938–1945, in many movies. To create too many links between the endeavors toward a unification with Germany, with the so-called "Great Brother" in the aftermath of WWI and the incorporation of the Austrian "corporate state" into the Third Reich in 1938, was considered too "embarrassing" and too "compromising." And not even this: From 1918 onwards, any other (even ephemeral) hint

13 Leidinger, "Visualisierung des Krieges," 464–465.

to the traumatic loss of the Empire, the preceding bloodshed and the role of the Viennese court and government in the process of unleashing the First World War seemed to be an unacceptable provocation, at least for the conservative elites (particularly) of the (First) Republic, being still loyal to the imperial dynasty or tending toward a Habsburg nostalgia in the form of a "backward reason of state."[14]

Film projects dealing with tragic moments at the eve of World War One, like the death of Rudolf, the heir to the throne, and Mary Vetsera in Mayerling, or the case of Alfred Redl, the high-ranking Austro-Hungarian army officer spying (above all) for the Russians, led to protests. Not only monarchists, but also many former imperial soldiers and civil officials, did not want to face this dark chapter of history. In this connection, the Austrian memory of World War I was obviously a factor interfering with their labile identity. After 1918, to most Austrians, the events of 1914 to 1918 "were reminders of a latent multiculturalism in a republic attempting to solidify national identity as '*Deutschoesterreich*'," Dassanowsky writes. And he continues: "Moreover, a cinematic treatment of the Austrian war experience" could not be sold abroad. "German audiences were uninterested in re-experiencing the disaster of its ally, and other Central European nations were suspicious of any film from Austria dealing with the war as being revanchist or Habsburg-restoration propaganda."[15]

And even the fact that National Socialists demonized the *Casa d'Austria* did not really change the situation, due to the ambiguity

14 Hannes Leidinger, "Verzerrung und Ausblendung," in *Habsburgs schmutziger Krieg: Ermittlungen zur* österreichisch-ungarischen *Kriegsführung 1914–1918*, ed. Hannes Leidinger, Verena Moritz, and Karin Moser (St. Pölten: Residenz, 2014), 223–234, here: 225.

15 Dassanowsky, "Finis Austriae, vivat Austria," 180.

of some co-productions overshadowed by Berlin's interests and the following post-1938 *Tendenzfilme*, (films with clear political orientations), like *Wien 1910*, or the mainstream productions of the Goebbels entertainment industry, with its inclination for the well-established stereotypes of the "Waltzing Vienna." It goes without saying that the hostilities and mass killings of the more than four years up to 1918 were not in harmony with the post-1945 concept of an intact world long gone with a good old "Kaiser" in a historical fairyland.[16]

Metaphorical Narratives

Notwithstanding the mentioned and basically convincing arguments being presented by several scholars, it is, however, useful—and even indispensable—to trace some different interpretations, simply because significant details do not fit with the general narrative, aspects which are revealing from different point of views.

According to Anton Kaes and his influential study about the so-called "Shell Shock Cinema," the hostilities of 1914 to 1918 and the traumatic experiences in the combat zones could hardly be expressed with words or presentations, especially in a more or less "realistic" form. Therefore, as Kaes put it, "prominent examples" of post-1918 movies articulated "an indirect, but more poignant understanding of trauma than many traditional war movies. German Films for instance, like *Nosferatu*, *The Cabinet of Dr. Caligari*, *Die Nibelungen*, and *Metropolis*, translated military aggression and defeat into domestic tableaux of crime and horror," melodrama, myth, or science fiction.[17] Apart from the tendency to reflect the First World War in other periods and

16 Ibid., 184–186.

17 Kaes, *Shell Shock Cinema*, 3; Philipp Stiasny, *Das Kino und der Krieg: Deutschland 1914–1929* (München: edition text + kritik, 2009), 15.

through suggestion, symbolized, for instance, also by Michael Kertész's (later Hollywood's Michael Curtiz) cinematic treatment of Arthur Schnitzler's play *Der junge Medardus* (1923), presenting a war-torn Vienna during Napoleon's occupation,[18] this trend was particularly mirrored by the Austrian horror movie *Orlac's Hände* (*The Hands of Orlac*) of 1924. The film centers around a piano player losing his hands due to a train accident and getting transplanted new hands from a murderer and robber. Henceforth dominated by a strange, criminal spirit, Orlac literally becomes the embodiment of bodies dismembered by the industrial war and its destructive potential, resulting in injury and wide-spread dying-off.[19]

Controversies and Patriotic Objects

Interpretations insinuating a loss of individual coherence or control and by the way focusing on a key issue of the long Fin de Siècle from about 1870 to at least 1930,[20] namely the dissolution of the self, prevailed particularly in German and Austrian post-1918 productions. Contrary to that, "naturalist" approaches to the events on the battlefields up to 1918 existed only in foreign productions and led to many controversies. Against the backdrop of an intensified remembrance of WWI around 1930, the Vienna premiere and subsequent screenings of the US-adaptation of Erich Maria Remarque's "*All Quiet on the Western Front*" caused

18 Dassanowsky, "Finis Austriae, vivat Austria," 179.

19 Elisabeth Büttner and Christan Dewald, *Das tägliche Brennen: Eine Geschichte des* österreichischen *Films von den Anfängen bis 1945* (Salzburg: Residenz 2002), 355–356. Cf.: *Gothic Crime: Essays und Materialien zu Orlac's Hände*, ed. Armin Loacker and Thomas Ballhausen (Wien: filmarchiv austria, 2013). See also Thomas Ballhausen's article in this volume.

20 Büttner and Dewald, *Das tägliche Brennen*, 355–356.

protest and violent disturbances by conservative, right-wing circles, and National Socialists. The Hollywood sound film, based on Remarque's novel and directed by Lewis Milestone, was even banned in Austria in the beginning 1930s because of ongoing conflicts and the government's aim to limit the influence of the movie to the audience.[21]

While members of the Christian Social and the Pan German parties criticized the sobering effect of Milestone's movie, and while the oppositional Social Democrats organized trips to the neighbouring Czechoslovakian cities to see the film, another movie, directed by Luis Trenker and Karl Hartl, met with a much more positive response among anti-Marxist groups: The German and French production *Berge in Flammen* (*Mountains on Fire*) from 1931, presenting the war in the Alps fought by Austrians and Italians from 1915 onwards and thus turning away from the frequently depicted Western front to the combat zones of the Habsburg army, was a heroic, patriotic answer to Remarque and was well received by the National Socialists and later on in the Third Reich.[22]

Though aiming at the same "positive meaning" of the war being a necessary "sacrifice for the fatherland" and an individual test of strength and courage, comparable movies of the rival "Austrofascist" or Austrian corporative state were rare.[23] Only Major Karl Wratschko offered a message to the veterans of the

---

21 Dassanowsky, "Finis Austriae, vivat Austria," 181.

22 Verena Moritz, "Krieg," in *Kampfzone Kino: Film in* Österreich *1918–1938*, ed. Verena Moritz, Karin Moser and Hannes Leidinger (Wien: filmarchiv austria, 2008), 255–277, here: 271.

23 Just like *Mountains in Flames*, the German movies *Drei Kaiserjäger* (1933) and *Standschütze Bruggler* (1936) praised patriotism and camaraderie at the Italian or Alpine front.

Habsburg army, praising the troops of the Kaiser for the "glorious" fighting in Galicia, Serbia, Tyrol, and elsewhere in his film *Schulter an Schulter* (*Shoulder to shoulder*).[24] Lasting roughly an hour and integrating some non-fiction, contemporary footage of the war, *Schulter an Schulter* was significant for the authoritarian Viennese government of the 1930s to reconcile the country with its own (Habsburg) past, while at the same time stressing the importance of the German character of Austria. Correspondingly, Wratschko's work did not question the German-Austrian brotherhood in arms, (from 1914 to 1918), notwithstanding the difficult relationship between Vienna and Berlin in the eve of the Anschluss.[25]

Sideshows and Marginal Notes

However, *Schulter an Schulter* was an exception in the long run, and World War I was destined to figure as a marginal note in the Austrian film productions. Unlike in Germany— with its UFA trend—a kind of a mental (re-)armament did not take place in

---

24 Another approach to the theme dated back to 1930, when Franz Pollack presented *Der letzte Kampf der Donaumonarchie* (alternative titles: *Unter den Bannern Alt*-Österreichs or *Licht* über Österreich). Yet film viewers of the Austrian government reacted cautiously and were divided: Some critics reproved clichés and kitschy scenes. Others complained about the arbitrary assignment of documentary footage. Definitely, Pollak's film was not able to shape Austria's visual memory of the last war of the Habsburg monarchy and its fighting force; Cf. Verena Moritz, "Krieg," 259.

25 Karin Moser, "Visuelles Erinnern: Der Erste Weltkrieg im österreichischen Film- und Fernsehschaffen," in *Habsburgs schmutziger Krieg: Ermittlungen zur* österreichisch-ungarischen *Kriegsführung 1914–1918*, ed. Hannes Leidinger, Verena Moritz, and Karin Moser (St. Pölten: Residenz, 2014), 235–253, here: 240 and 241.

Austrian film studios.[26] By 1928, Hans Otto Löwenstein, former head of the film department of the Austro-Hungarian War Press Office in 1917–18, and also responsible for the first Alfred-Redl feature in 1925, remade cinematography pioneers Louise and Anton Kolm's 1915 *Der Traum eines* österreichischen *Reservisten* (*The dream of an Austria reservist*). But Löwenstein's attempt to "launch a Great War genre in film analogous to the popular war and imperial collapse novels of the era"[27] remained an exception. In turn, the Austrian movie *Die große Liebe* (*The great love*), being Otto Preminger's first directorial effort and starring Attila Hörbiger, stressed the fate of those returning from Russian captivity, but the misery of war and its consequences are not connected with political messages, social critics, or martial gestures. Rather, "virtues of Christianity" turn out to be the "true answers" to the manifold loss of home and family.[28]

In the following decades, the filmic depiction of "Habsburg's final war" continued to be a sideshow of the national movie industry, especially after 1945, for example as the background for military slapstick comedies and—close to that—the Austrian "humorous" version of Jaroslav Hasek's *The Good Soldier Svejk.*[29]

Apart from that, the First World War was just one chapter of TV family stories such as *Der Engel mit der Posaune* (1948) or the serial *Ringstraßenpalais* deploring the "pity of war" but at the

26 Cf. Dassanowsky, "Finis Austriae, vivat Austria," 180.

27 Dassanowsky, *Austrian Cinema*, 37.

28 Moser, "Visuelles Erinnern," 239; Dassanowsky, *Austrian Cinema*, 44–45. Returnees figured prominently also in the German movies *Der Mann aus dem Jenseits - Feldgrau* (1926) and *Heimkehr* (1928).

29 Moser, "Visuelles Erinnern," 242. Cf. Václav Smidrkal's article in this volume, as well as the interwar production *Schwejk in Zivil* (1928) or the German-Russian cooperation *Mikosch rückt ein*.

same time keeping an extensively positive image of the Danube monarchy. This applies also to Fritz Kortners's movie *Sarajewo/ Um Liebe und Tod*, evoking compassion for the heir to the throne and—more than that—for his wife, the warm-hearted (future) mother of the empire.[30]

Turning Points

Nevertheless, in the 1960s there were first signs that things might change: Michael Kehlmann deconstructed the epic nostalgia of the *Kaiserfilms* in his 1964 black and white television treatment of Joseph Roth's *Radetzkymarsch*. His focus was "on the role of the static patriarchy, the unyielding social order" and an empty military code of honour as well as "his cinematic visions on the corruption and fall of the monarchy." Nearly at the same time, Edwin Zbonek worked on his film adaptation of Franz Theodor Csokor's 1936 play *3. November 1918*. This production turned out to be an intimate and neo-realistically tinged demolition of the fairytales promoted by the grand costume epics of the 1950s. Zbonek's movie, released in 1965, portrayed the growing nationalist divergences of a group of Austro-Hungarian soldiers in a convalescent home at the end of the Great War. It failed, however, to inspire a new wave, a *noveau vague*, of Austrian movies "to span the wide cleft between the dead commercial cinema and the isolated Actionist" experimental film of the 1960s. In many ways, Csokor's play "was far more attuned to the imperial mourning of the Austrofascist period in which it was written, than to reception at the height of the Cold War."[31]

Besides, apart from their readiness to present more problematic facets of the Danube monarchy, not only Csokor, but also Roth, failed

30 Dassanowsky, "Finis Austriae, vivat Austria," 189.

31 Ibid., 190 and 191.

to question many of the Habsburg myths. Therefore, it was not the filmic treatment of this literature, but a new perspective on Austria-Hungary and World War I as a consequence of a changing culture of recollection in the 1970s and 1980s, that led to more critical narratives. Thus, the TV serial *Alpensaga* (1976–1980) offered an unvarnished interpretation of the Austrian province as a homefront full of troubles and populated by poor peasant families, run and managed by women after their men were drafted into the army and oppressed by the same forces in times of destitution and requisitions.[32]

Notwithstanding TV productions like that, it was above all the re-assessment of the role of Austrians during the Second World War and the Third Reich, as well as the debate about the responsibility of Austrians for terror, war crimes, and genocide under National Socialist rule, that brought about a more fundamental change in the way Austrian history was presented in movies.[33] Accordingly, younger filmmakers concentrated on the "deceptive splendour" of the remote imperial past as well. More than anyone else, Austrian director Peter Patzak tried to establish a sort of a contrast with his 1990 movie *Himmel unter Steinen*. This work is probably the most remarkable attempt of an Austrian artist to present the Serbian assassin of the Habsburg crown prince Franz Ferdinand and his wife, Gavre Princip, not as an instrument of "dark powers" and impersonal social structures, but as an individual in a special milieu beyond the traditional national stereotypes and clichés surrounding the so-called "gravedigger(s) of the Dual Monarchy."[34] Yet the

32 Moser, "Visuelles Erinnern," 248–249.

33 Cf. Österreich *und der Große Krieg: Die andere Seite der Geschichte*, ed. Klaus Amann and Hubert Lengauer (Wien: Brandstätter, 1989), Klappentext 1.

34 *Gavre Princip - Himmel unter Steinen* (1990). Regarding Patzak's Film, see also Karin Moser's contribution to this omnibus volume.

reactions of the audience, as well as the reviewers, to Patzak's perspective were mixed. This reflected the polarized debate about the Habsburgs and their "final war" in the different political and ideological camps.[35] Controversial approaches to Austria-Hungary and its role in the First World War also particularly characterized Austrian TV documentations relevant to theme in 2014, albeit with a dwindling intensity of emotions. Yet the vast majority of the productions offered a more detailed and balanced interpretation of the four years of bloodshed.[36]

Conclusion

From this point of view, dealing with the dark chapters of two World Wars—at least after the death of the contemporaries, eye-witnesses, victims, and perpetrators—signals a kind of normalization of the relationship between the Austrians and their past. This process started in the 1960s and continued during the "Kreisky years," with the chancellors' will to rapprochement between the church, the conservatives, the former ruling dynasty, and the "leftist camp" in the Alpine republic. It was eventually accelerated in the context of the "Waldheim case" and the commemoration of the Anschluss in 1988.

Above all before that period, as long as critical analyses of Austria-Hungary were generally precarious, "Habsburg's final war"

35 *Die Presse*, Oct. 8, 1990; cf. *Die Furche*, Oct. 18, 1990, and *Arbeiter-Zeitung*, Oct. 24, 1990, 26.

36 Cf. *Das Attentat - Sarajewo 1914* (2014), and above all: *Kaiser Franz Joseph* (2006), *Menschen & Mächte: Kaiser Franz Joseph und der Erste Weltkrieg* (2008); *Der stille Berg* (2014); *Die Macht der Bilder: Lüge und Propaganda im Ersten Weltkrieg* (2014). See also the critical review of Kurt Mündl's production *Sarajewo - Das Attentat* (2014) in: Moser, "Visuelles Erinnern," 247.

was hardly ever mentioned or only grazed by referring particularly to the beginning and the end of the hostilities in 1914 and 1918.[37] Even this, however, could mostly only happen when the beginning and the end of the First World War was integrated in interpretations and depictions of a Habsburg myth, of the mourning with regard to the downfall of the "world of yesterday."

In any other case filmmakers anticipated troubles. The trauma of 1914–18, Robert von Dassanowsky stated, "would hardly be a topic that would fit" into "formulaic structures aimed at international box-office successes. Even the official state film, *1. April 2000* (1952), an all-star historical-musical-comedy pageant film framed by a futuristic science fiction plot that attempts to plead an end to Austria's Allied occupation to the world, halts its review

37 Moser, "Visuelles Erinnern," 245. As an early example see also *Die Brandstifter Europas* (*The Arsonists of Europe*, 1926). Besides—and apart from Fritz Kortner's *Sarajewo/Um Liebe und Tod*—the continuing occupation with a more or less fictional Redl-genre should not be disregarded in this connection. Cf. Karl Anton's Czech production *Der Fall des Generalsstabs-Oberst Redl* (1931), Erich Engel's *Hotel Sacher* (1939), as well as Franz Antel's *Spionage* (*Espionage*, 1955), and István Szabó's *Oberst Redl* (1985).

Apart from Edwin Zbonek's film adaptation of Franz Theodor Csokor's *3. November 1918*, the collapse of the Habsburg monarchy and the birth of the republic is—among other examples—also depicted in the anti-revolutionary production *Kampf der Gewalten* (*Battle of Powers*) of 1919 or—to give a recent, more metaphoric example—Stefan Ruzowitzky's *Die Siebtelbauern* (1998). Ruzowitzky's work obliterates "the symbolic imperial father or grandfather figure of Emperor Franz Joseph as idolized by Habsburg Myth literature." Therefore, the film deals with the idea of a fatherless society in the years of rupture, upheaval and disorientation; Dassanowsky, "Finis Austriae, vivat Austria," 193–195.

of Austria's benevolent nature through history" with Emperor Franz Joseph and Empress Elisabeth: The "twentieth century is ignored and neither world war is evoked."[38]

For one or another group of spectators, the last war of the Austro-Hungarian army seemed to be an embarrassment or a provocation. This was due to the intransigent attitudes of the political camps, the conservative "backward reason of state" and the weakness of the Social Democrats to influence the Austrian historiography for many decades. Furthermore—as Dassanowsky put it—the Austrian republic's difficult and problematic search for its own homogeneous national identity played an essential role.

38 Dassanowsky, "Finis Austriae, vivat Austria," 187; Dassanowsky, *Austrian Cinema*, 149. Contrary to Franz Joseph and significant for the role of the First World War in Austrian films, the Emperor Charles was not able to reappear on stage. According to contemporary spectators, the 1921 movie *Kaiser Karl* was presented too early: A few years after the collapse of the Monarchy and faced with Habsburg's restoration trials in Hungary, Austrian reviewers considered themselves incapable of making "objective judgments." The situation did not change for many decades. The beatified emperor remains controversial even to this day; Verena Moritz, "Vergangenheitsbewältigung," in *Kampfzone Kino: Film in* Österreich *1918–1938*, ed. Verena Moritz, Karin Moser and Hannes Leidinger (Wien: filmarchiv austria, 2008), 141–172, 144.

REMEMBERING WORLD WAR I IN 2014:

FILMS AND TV PRODUCTIONS IN AUSTRIA AND A NEW PATH OF VISUAL MEMORY

Karin Moser

For decades, World War I has been less interesting for movie and TV productions in the German-speaking area, whereas in the United Kingdom, Canada, Australia, and New Zealand, the memory of the Great War has quite a long tradition, in film and also in the visual culture. In Austria and in Germany, the Second World War and the Shoah dominated documentary films and movies.[1] In Austria, however, this subject matter has been addressed only since the 1970s. Before that, the Austrian victim-myth made it impossible to discuss the participation of Austrians in crimes during the era of National Socialism.

The 2014 memorial entailed substantial changes in visual memory.Movie and TV productions reflected the First World War in partly similar, partly quite different ways when compared to the prior visual memorials. Those films will shape a new kind of collective memory.

1 Barbara Korte, Ralf Schneider, and Claudia Sternberg, *Der Erste Weltkrieg und die Mediendiskurse der Erinnerung in Großbritannien: Autobiographie - Roman - Film 1919–1999* (Würzburg: Königshausen & Neumann, 2005), 2.

Commemorative cultures are always based on identity-building contents—contents traditionally transmitted and consolidated. Naturally, cultures of memory are never totally homogenous. There always exists various parameters of remembrance that are competing and that are changing permanently.[2]

However, a common place of experience and expectation connects people and creates collective memory. Concerning Austria, the public broadcaster Österreichischer Rundfunk (ORF) is—especially because of the Film Funding Act—still decisive for film productions.[3] Movies and TV programs produced or co-produced by the ORF are therefore essential for the Austrian culture of memory. They represent the current opinions and values of this memorial community. Hereafter, tendencies of this actual visual commemorative culture are highlighted.

Questions of guilt

"A period of violence started. And this period has left deep scars in the history of our continent." –Jean-Paul Bled[4]

Who is to blame for the outbreak of World War I? This is one of the central questions that is raised and answered, at least in many of the films released in 2014. The response is difficult and easy at the same time; difficult, because of the complex alliance system in Europe at

2 Astrid Erll, *Gedächtnisromane: Literatur* über *den Ersten Weltkrieg als Medium englischer und deutscher Erinnerungskulturen in den 1920er Jahren* (Trier: WVT, 2003), 6.

3 Karin Moser, "Kinowelten: Eine Filmgeschichte," in *Streitbare Brüder:* Österreich *: Deutschland. Kurze Geschichte einer schwierigen Nachbarschaft,* ed. Hannes Leidinger, Verena Moritz, and Karin Moser (St. Pölten: Residenz, 2010), 209–213.

4 Jean-Paul Bled in the film documentary *Der Weg in den Untergang,* directed by Robert Gokl and Leo Bauer (2014).

that time and because of the variety of national demands and independence efforts, especially in the Austrian-Hungarian monarchy. Film documentaries like *Der Weg in den Untergang,* (directed by Robert Gokl and Leo Bauer) describe the circumstances surrounding the start of the War in a clear, neutral way, accompanied by statements of Austrian, German, British, French, Serbian, and Bulgarian historians. Graphic cards, animated photos, re-enactment scenes, and contemporary film clips try to illustrate by means of these visually appealing images a complex political system. The "expert part" of these films is unemotional and sober as possible and tries to give answers through facts, particularly concerning the question of guilt.[5]

While in previous Austrian documentary films the role of Emperor Franz Joseph with regard to the beginning of the Great War was now and then indifferent or even pro-Habsburg, in 2014 there are no more "excuses" about his old age or his mental confusion. No one talks about his supposed "love of peace." Even the relieving question, "Was he misinformed or ill advised by his brain trust?", isn't raised anymore. All experts, all voiceovers, agree unanimously that Franz Joseph wanted war.[6] Some documentarians, (notably *Kaiser*

5 The same strategy is presented in Andreas Novak's documentary *Kaiser Franz Joseph und der Erste Weltkrieg* (2014).

6 The only exception is *Sarajevo: Das Attentat*, a film "documentary" directed by Kurt Mündl. This film seems to be a propaganda film for royalists. Without any kind of critical grappling with the role of the Emperor, the successor to the throne, and the military brain trust, this film provides nostalgic kitsch and old-fashioned clichés. In addition to that, contemporary film clips, feature films, and photos are cited incorrectly. Cf.: Karin Moser, "Visuelles Erinnern: der Erste Weltkrieg im österreichischen Film- und Fernsehschaffen," in *Habsburgs schmutziger Krieg: Ermittlungen zur* österreichisch-ungarischen *Kriegsführung 1914–1918*, ed. Hannes Leidinger, Verena Moritz, Karin Moser, and Wolfram Dornik (St. Pölten: Residenz, 2014), 247–248.

Franz Joseph und der Erste Weltkrieg, directed by Andreas Nowak), explain the Emperor's psyche and attitude: In his view, declaring war was a matter of honor. Nobody doubts that the emperor, as well as the majority of his advisory team, opted for the war, regardless of the consequences. They knew, as well as all sovereigns of the continent did, that there would be a European and even a global armed conflict. "The responsibility for the war was located in Vienna and Berlin" states the German-British historian John C. G. Röhl in *Der Weg in den Untergang*.

While film documentaries try to explain the outbreak of the War in a more or less unemotional way, feature films are more focused on evoking emotions or capturing moods.[7] The Austrian/German/Czech film production *Das Attentat: Sarajevo 1914*, (2014, directed by Andreas Prochaska), tries to capture the general mood of melancholia, the farewell of an era and first of all a wartime spirit. The main character is Leo Pfeffer, an examining magistrate who is ordered to clarify the background of the assassination of the Austrian heir to the throne, Franz Ferdinand. It soon becomes clear that the head of the government and the military forces demand only one single unambiguous result: The attack was planned and supported by the Kingdom of Serbia. A casus belli should be legitimized, but Leo Pfeffer is interested in the truth. While in film documentaries of 2014, the general opinion is that unlucky coincidences ended in the assassination, in this political thriller a new kind of conspiracy theory is presented:

---

7 Moods are long-winded, vaguer interpreted, while emotions are more influenced by experiences and are related to actions, objects or persons. Cf.: Carl Plantinga, *Moving Viewers: American Film and the Spectator's Experience* (Berkeley: University of California Press, 2009), 54–61. Gerhard Roth, *Fühlen, Denken, Handeln: Wie das Gehirn unser Verhalten steuert* (Frankfurt am Main: Suhrkamp, 2001), 269–270.

All information engenders the suspicion that political forces at the top of the Austrian monarchy at least enabled the attack. Pfeffer confronts the political leaders with unpleasant questions: Why did only thirty-six policemen protect the route of the convoy of Franz Ferdinand? How can they explain the absence of army and gendarmerie? Why was the route of the convoy published in the newspapers? Additional examinations of Pfeffer are thwarted, witnesses disappear, and Pfeffer is threatened and blackmailed. The mood of insecurity, fear, and aggression is imparted through stylistic means. The basic note of color is blue; a cold atmosphere is created. Typical thrill elements, like changing effects of light and shadow and the interchange of focus (Pfeffer sharply defined, his opponents blurred) produce a feeling of generalized insecurity—the insecurity of a disappearing (outdated) world, the unrest at the beginning of a war.

Thus, the film evokes emotions at various sensual levels and communicates messages in direct and subliminal ways. High-ranking representatives of the Austrian-Hungarian Ministry of War were aware of the power of visual propaganda. The wartime propaganda transported enemy images, mythical hero images, and announced victories. Film documentaries of the memorial year unmasked the work of the propaganda departments. *Die Macht der Bilder. Lüge und Propaganda im Ersten Weltkrieg* (2014, directed by Günter Kaindlstorfer) takes a look backstage: Production conditions, censorship regulations, the fakeness of re-enacted combat scenes are discussed, and the presentation of a "clean" visualized war, without dead bodies, injured soldiers, poison gas attacks, etc. is critically examined. The nearly idyllic and glorious presentations of war in the contemporary films of the Austrian-Hungarian monarchy are contradicted by photographs demonstrating the cruelties of war. Especially the topic of war crime is no longer a taboo; many film productions of 2014 focus on crimes against the civil population, especially in Serbia and Galicia. Thousands of people were accused of spying without any evidence, expelled and even executed. Film documentaries like *Kaiser Franz Joseph und der Erste Weltkrieg* or *Die Macht der Bilder* apply new animation technologies to visualize the atrocities of World War I. By zooming in on the pictures of executions and dwelling for some seconds on the faces and dead bodies of older men, women, and even children, the gruesome fate of thousands of people and the feeling of lawlessness becomes tangible.

Documentary movies of 2014 finally reflected the disappearance of old resentments toward Serbs passed on for a long time. Peter Patzak's feature film *Gavre Princip: Himmel unter Steinen* was attacked even in 1999 by an Austrian newspaper. Director Patzak presented on the one hand occasionally brutal-acting Austrian-Hungarian law enforcers, and on the other hand a sensible, clever, and fragile assassin having grown up in poverty. The Austrian daily paper *Kronen Zeitung* headlined "Peter Patzak Honored Murdering Boy" and insinuated treason.[8] At that time, the Serbs were still considered an enemy by some people. Nowadays, documentaries also include the Serbian side. In *Der Weg in den Untergang*, not only do Austrian and Serbian historians and scientists give differing views of the conflict, the Serbian remembrance of The Great War is even a central part of the film. Two musicians play old Serbian melodies composed during World War I. In history lessons, Serbian pupils learn about

8 Peter Patzak quoted this headline in an interview ("Patzak setzt Mörderbuben ein Denkmal"). Cf.: Andreas Ungerböck, Karin Moser, Roman Scheiber, "Ich habe mit der Spitzhacke hineingeschlagen, alles war Stein" in *Peter Patzak: Filmemacher, Autor, Maler*, ed. Karin Moser and Andreas Ungerböck (Wien: filmarchiv austria, 2009), 34.

the successful battles of the Serbs and about the massacre of Šabac in August 1914, where the civil population was murdered by soldiers of the Austrian-Hungarian army. At the mass grave, the son of a survivor tells the young people about the crime and asks them to preserve the memory of the victims.

But concerning war crimes, one question is missed: Is there also an individual kind of guilt? What about the guilt of the single soldier? Only in one documentary—*Krisen, Morde, Bürgerkriege* (2014, directed by Andreas Nowak and Wolfgang Stickler)—this topic briefly sketched: In 1918, a commission of lawyers started to examine "breaches of duty" during the War. The investigations considered revising bad treatments and punishments by soldiers, death penalties and executions. But the commission was interfered with; records disappeared and were kept under lock. War crimes against the civil population were, at least, not sanctioned. The leaders of the old system, (for example, military personnel, but also lawyers), who still filled important positions after 1918, had no interest in critical approaches to the "last chapter" of the monarchy and its army. Traditional mentalities, resentments, and enemy images prevailed in the long run.

Furthermore, nearly all the films produced in the memorial year carry the message that World War I was a prelude to World War Two. Potential for violence increased, and the use of weapons of mass destruction became habitual. Above all, the rise of fascist and racist ideas is discussed: Resettlements of people in order to create "ethnic pure" territories at the Eastern border (*Kaiser Franz Joseph und der Erste Weltkrieg*), anti-Semitic attacks especially in the East (*Die Macht der Bilder*), using the Jews as scapegoats for losing the war and the social crises after World War I (*Krisen, Morde, Bürgerkriege*). Feature films also refer to anti-Semitism: The examining magistrate Leo Pfeffer (*Das Attentat: Sarajevo 1914*) is attacked because he is a Croatian Jew. In the biopic drama, *Clara Immerwahr*, (2014, directed by Harald Sicheritz) the husband of the main character, a leading chemist, is mocked and called an "artificial Aryan."

Several films—documentaries as well as features—end with a view toward poverty, suffering, economic crises, and remilitarization after World War I, as well as the atrocities of World War II. Often, the number of victims are compared: violence leads to more violence. There is always an invitation to reflect.

Personalization

"*What is heroism? There are no heroes!*" –Franz Künstler, survivor of World War I[9]

Various studies show that documentaries with biographical background generate more interest. Personal access seems to be more attractive to the audience.[10] Anecdotes, peculiarities, and family history make political, economic, and social facts digestible to viewers. Thus film documentaries nowadays tend to use typical feature film styles and elements. And as Robert A. Rosenstone ascertained: "Film insists on history as the story of individuals, either men or women (but usually men) who are already renowned, or men and women who are made to seem important because they have been singled out by the camera."[11]

9 Statement of Franz Künstler (soldier of World War I) in the film documentary *Kaiser Franz Joseph und der Erste Weltkrieg*, directed by Andreas Nowak (2014).

10 Sönke Neitzel, "Der Erste Weltkrieg in den Geschichtsdokumentationen des ZDF," in *Der Erste Weltkrieg im Film*, ed. Rainer Rother, Karin Herbst-Messlinger (Munich: edition text + kritik, 2009), 224.

11 Robert A. Rosenstone, "The Historical Film: Looking at the Past in a Postliterate Age," in *The Historical Film: History and Memory in Media*, ed. Marcia Landry (New Brunswick: Rutgers University Press, 2001), 50–66.

As a matter of fact, films about World War I released in 2014 also focused on personal biographical elements and stories.[12] Two productions deal with the life stories of important, confident women who fought against conventional patriarchal structures, misogyny, and war. The dull and underwhelming biopic film *Eine Liebe für den Frieden*, (2014, directed by Urs Egger) is less focused on the strong character and work of Nobel Peace Prize Winner Bertha von Suttner. On the contrary, her relationship to Alfred Nobel dominates the story, narrated in a dime novel style. In the end there remains only one question among the audience: How intimate was their relationship?

Clara Immerwahr, on the other hand, succeeds in presenting a rich and complex picture of a highly intelligent, spirited Jewish woman who is ultimately ruined by a patriarchal militant system. She attained an admission to study at the university level, was the first woman with a degree in chemistry in Germany, and worked together with her husband Fritz Haber at the technical university of Karlsruhe. The film impressively shows how Clara is more and more restricted by conventions, male chauvinism, (even from her husband), and by the political system. We sense that she is more and more cornered by the expressive play of Katharina Schüttler, by narrowing camera angles, by alternating light and shadow and dark color patterns. Clara publicly condemned the use of poison gas and shot herself in protest.

Movies are fiction, and in order to attract the public interest, dramatization and emotionalizing strategies are utilized. Highlighting positive and negative characteristics of the protagonists and creating popular and unpopular figures provide

12 This of course also includes *Das Attentat: Sarajevo 1914*. Here the story is narrated from Leo Pfeffer's point of view.

orientation to the audience and specify the interpretation.[13] Regarding the Great War, family stories are very popular to evoke empathy. The year 1914 marks the dramatic turning point and offers extensive personal emotional referents. Everybody is affected by the conflict, suffers deprivations, and loses relatives in the War. Contemporary personal family stories (such as the experiences of grandparents and great-grandparents) are in this manner connected to fictitious dynasties. Big politics changed the life of every single person. After 1945, the rare Austrian feature films that refer to World War I mostly center around these kinds of family stories.[14] In 2014, one production picked up this type of plot: *Der stille Berg*, (2014, directed by Ernst Gossner) focuses on an Austrian-Italian family and the conflict in the Dolomite Alps. During a wedding party, the message of the outbreak of war is transmitted. Exactly in this moment, a wedding photo is shot. The shocked faces of the guests are freeze-framed on the picture. Henceforth, the family is divided. Friends and relatives find themselves confronting each other as enemies. The War is a severe test for relationships, whether between lovers, relatives, or friends. The exceptional situation intensifies positive and negative traits. The popular figures act as opponents of war, the negative characters serve as denunciators (an envious Austrian teacher) and fanatical warmongers (a narcissistic Italian commander). The central Austrian-Italian lovers survive the War and dream of a new life in the New World: America.

Broadcasting companies and film production companies tend to focus on interesting, now and then ambivalent, historical persons for the sake of popularity. The whole story of historic

---

13 See also the theoretical explanations of Sönke Neitzel concerning TV documentaries: Neitzel, *Geschichtsdokumentationen*, 219, 232.

14 Moser, "Visuelles Erinnern," 241–245.

events is structured around one or several "persons of interest."[15] In *Der Weg in den Untergang*, the central figure is General Oskar Potiorek, military governor of Bosnia-Herzegovina. His role at the beginning of the War and during the conflict, as well as his character, are closely examined. The circumstances that lead to World War I are explained, but the plot always returns to Potiorek. We learn from commentary that Gavrilo Princip wanted to kill him (instead of Sophie Chotek) and Franz Ferdinand. Re-enactment scenes emphasize the information we get about Potiorek. His reaction to the assassination attempt is demonstrated in the facial expression of the actor playing the part of Potiorek. He always tries to divert attention from his failures in guarding the convoy of Franz Ferdinand and Sophie. For this purpose, he blamed and attacked the government circles in Serbia and constantly demanded an act of reprisal. The first attack against Serbia commanded by Potiorek in August 1914 is accompanied by his diary entry: "Today my war started!" Again and again, we see the artist performing his part, writing letters, looking contemplative and grave through the window of his office. (He never talks.) His face is spotlighted to be able to observe mimic art in every detail. Blurred colors, brown, green and grey shades generate the idea of a historical atmosphere. In contrast to Potiorek, his "enemies," the Serbs, are presented in contemporary film clips or animated sceneries. The Serbian people are portrayed in a human, fun-loving, and peaceful way; scenes of everyday life, of family celebrations, contradict the picture of a violent ethnic group spread by the propaganda. The filming in the Šabac of today—with the pupils and the son of the survivor of the massacre—affirm this impression. The spectators are motivated to build a positive relationship with the Serbs and to adopt a more distanced attitude to Potiorek and thus to the leaders of the Austrian-Hungarian monarchy.

---

15 This reflects the experiences of the author (who is also scriptwriter) with broadcasting companies (ORF, Arte) and film production companies.

Nowadays, sovereigns are certainly no longer the central figures of memorializing art. Film documentaries maybe still pretend to have the story of a monarch in focus by choosing a sovereign-oriented title, but the voices of the people have become more and more important. In *Kaiser Franz Joseph und der Erste Weltkrieg*, we still find generally known icons of the Emperor (the huntsman, the old, quirky ruler) whose honor dictated that he start the War. But we have counterparts: Fairly old Austrian and Italian soldiers describe the unvarnished truth of wartime experiences, for example, how dead bodies of troopers were used by the Italians to cover and protect them from bullets. The Austrian soldier describes the physical reactions to a gas attack: burning in his nose and throat and the blinding of comrades.

The 2014 film documentary *1918: Ende und Anfang* (2014, directed by Robert Gokl) is completely dominated by voices, voices of the rulers and the people.[16] The so-called "communicative memory" has an important role in films released in the memorial year, although 100 years have passed. The "communicative memory" is linked to a personal horizon of experience and therefore dependent on contemporary witnesses. But also their direct descendants are carriers of this memory if they experienced real daily life contact to them. So personal conversations, but also personal letters and diary entries of the contemporary witnesses, are parts of the "communicative memory."[17]

16 Not one single expert (e.g. a historian) takes part in this film documentary.

17 According to the cultural scientist Jan Assmann, the "collective memory" is composed of the "communicative memory" and the "cultural memory." The "cultural memory" is fare abstracted from the personal carriers of memory (contemporary witnesses, for example) and is shaped by the meanings and values of the present society. Cf.: Jan Assmann, "Kollektives Gedächtnis und kulturelle Identität," in *Kultur und Gedächtnis*, ed. Jan Assmann, Tonio Hölscher (Frankfurt am Main: Suhrkamp, 1988), 9–19.

In *1918: Ende und Anfang*, interviews from earlier years, sometimes decades-old, are reused to give people a voice. Sound recordings of Emperor Karl I, Empress Zita, and Heinrich Schuhmann, the personal cinematographer of Karl, represent the perspective of the dynasty. Through the personal statements and reactions of the first-person witnesses, we get an impression of the attitude to life in these days during and after World War I. One woman—incited by the filmmaker—starts to sing the old hymn of the Emperor. Another lady explains that there was never enough food, but she wanted her father to eat more. So whenever she finished half of her meal, she pretended to have had enough. Such little personal stories evoke empathy, here for a girl who loves her father. A soldier speaks to the different treatment of ordinary soldiers and officers: People fighting at the front nearly starved, receiving substandard food, while the military leaders without combat mission had four meals during the day. An audio recording of Karl I during the War provides another image: In his propaganda statement, the Emperor presents an ideal of a united Austrian-Hungarian army full of fighting spirit and confidence. His personal cinematographer Heinrich Schuhmann describes a totally different situation, which gives the impression that Karl officially played a role but in reality was shocked by the experiences on the battlefields. Once, they came to a place where a whole regiment was exterminated. The Emperor started to cry, prayed, and wanted to end the War.

The stories give insight into a time of misery, hunger, fear, and insecurity.[18] After the war, nobody knew what the future will bring, the old familiar system having ended. This atmosphere is

---

18 Even the recording of Empress Zita gives an impression of end time, being left alone. She describes the last hours in Schloss Schönbrunn and how the guards disappeared little by little—only their weapons were left in a corner.

captured by interviews and sound recordings, while the re-enactment scenes of the war failed.[19]

In a quite personal view, the programs on World War I were designed by the nine federal studios of the Austrian broadcasting station ORF. The story of the Great War was focused on local history. Television broadcasts gave an insight into living conditions of the rural population, showed aspects of the daily life of women in the regions during the War, reported about one of the worst prisoner-of-war camps in Salzburg, and presented the works and destinies of Styrian artists (painters and photographers) who had been in service for the propaganda department.[20] Diary entries, letters, photos, and souvenirs provided by the general public helped to create a folk, popular memory. The audience was invited to become a producer themselves by adding their family memorabilia.[21] By sharing their memories with others, they start to recreate the commemorative culture.

---

19 We see pictures of dead soldiers, which are interrupted by shots with a handheld camera. These scenes demonstrate an escape on the battlefield accompanied by dramatic piano sounds. The whole sequence is constructed and artificial.

20 Pressemappe ORF: Gedenkjahr 2014. 100 Jahre Erster Weltkrieg, 2014, 29–33, March 15, 2016, http://programm.orf.at/dateien/55545_100_Jahre_Erster_Weltkrieg.pdf.

21 This tendency in program design (inviting the population to add their family stories and souvenirs) has been apparent for several years. Cf.: David Williams, *Media: Memory, and the First World War* (Montreal: McGill-Queen's University Press, 2009), 279.

Global emotions

"It was possible for us to travel from the Atlantic to the Bosporus in a few days. [...] Anything was possible; we only had to desire it hardly."[22]

The reminiscence of the First World War is nowadays a global phenomenon. No longer do individual nations have their more or less self-contained memory; different aspects and views are demanded, and they are already standard, in the cinematic reappraisal as elsewhere. The common (especially European) remembrance was obvious in numerous com memoration ceremonies also broadcasted on television.[23] Moreover, almost all the documentaries from 2014 (such as *Kaiser Franz Joseph und der Erste Weltkrieg* or *Der Weg in den Untergang*) pictured World War I as a global, and not only European, conflict.

The 2014 three-part TV documentary series *Der taumelnde Kontinent,* (2014, directed by Robert Neumüller and based on the eponymous book by Philipp Blom) also followed a pan-European perspective but concentrated on the period before 1914. Political, economic, technical, social, and cultural evolutions in Germany, France, Austria-Hungary, the United Kingdom, and Russia are presented as connected. The variations in experience, positive and negative, at the beginning of the modern age is revealed. Industrialization, motorization, freedom of movement, consumer

22 *14 Tagebücher des Ersten Weltkriegs*, directed by Jan Peter (2014), Part I, opening comment.

23 This involves, for example, intercultural and international concerts in remembrance of the victims of World War I: "Europe Sings: Opening of the Wiener Festwochen" or "Memorial Concert 1914–2014 in Sarajevo." Pressemappe ORF: Gedenkjahr 2014. 100 Jahre Erster Weltkrieg, 2014, March 15, 2016, 26, http://programm.orf.at/dateien/55545_100_Jahre_Erster_Weltkrieg.pdf.

culture, trends in sexual liberation, the women's movement, political mass movements, eugenics and anti-Semitism are exemplified by more or less well-known personalities. The message of *Der taumelnde Kontinent* is that European nations had already been interlinked before 1914, intellectually, mentally, but also culturally and economically. Every action of a nation or a country affects the rest of the continent.

Connection instead of disconnection is the guiding principle of the films broadcasted in 2014. Again and again, personal writings are used to show similarities of experience of the "enemies." Based on diaries and letters from 35 countries, the 2014 international large-scale production *14 Tagebücher der Ersten Weltkriegs*, (2014, directed by Jan Peter) recounts the history of the Great War through the individual fates of participants known through pictures and writings. The experience of war is portrayed through the point of view of female and male soldiers, nurses, children, female workers, journalists, housewives, and artists. The starting commentary of every episode appeals to a sense of collective community. This strong community is presented by emotional attachment. Emotions, fears, and privations are the same in Austria-Hungary or Serbia, in France or Germany. Re-enactment scenes, letters, and documentary footage are skillfully connected and convey an atmospheric picture from the outbreak of the War, from the front lines, from those who stayed at home, and from the end of the struggle. Psychic and physical exertions, longing for family and for lovers, and fear of death are the essence of writings left from the War. The presented individuals have more in common than they have differences. By connecting individual war experiences, the idea of global emotions is demonstrated.

The director of *14 Tagebücher der Ersten Weltkriegs*, Jan Peter, explained in an interview that this series is a kind of new genre. He named it "documentary feature film" (*Dokumentarischer*

Spielfilm).[24] Actually, Peters arranged a play of the senses in an impressive manner: On the one hand, the spectator starts to have a personal relationship with the portrayed characters, as we learn about their life journey, their family environment, and their motives to fight, to help, to survive. Close-up shots of the faces of the actors let us observe their emotions in detail. By combining their writings with re-enactment scenes and documentary film footage, the senses of the audience are activated: We seem to hear, smell, and even feel what happened to them.

In one of the eight episodes, wounds and disability are the central topics. A fifteen-year-old Cossack woman, Marina Yurlova, is wounded. The army doctor decides to amputate one of her legs. Through her writings, and through the re-enactment scenes, we become aware of her panic, fear, despair, and her struggle for the preservation of her leg. At least she succeeds; we hear actors reading out lines of letters written by soldiers who lost limbs: They feel incomplete, useless, and are afraid of their future. They see no more sense in life. They describe in a comprehensive way their pains and the sense of still feeling the lost limb. Voices of "nurses" report about terrible cries of pain and the permanent smell of blood ("I live in a world of bandages and blood!"). Sounds and smells in some sequences become dominant. For an example, in picturing gas attacks, commentary and pictures are skillfully connected. Re-enactment parts are interrupted by documentary film material and combined with lines from letters. The voices of the soldiers of the past report of the smell of chlorine, the painful irritations of the throat, the impossibility of breathing. In such a way, the War is perceptible in its diversity of terror and violence. The senselessness of the War is strikingly illustrated.

24 *Making of 14 Tagebücher des Ersten Weltkriegs*, directed by Reinaldo Pinto Almeida.

The documentary film series *14 Tagebücher der Ersten Weltkriegs* is significant for the development of Austrian and probably also European filmmaking. Large-scale productions can only be financed in a cooperative effort between several countries. The microcosm of a state or nation is no longer in focus; on the contrary, the global importance of events has to be presented. But film producers are also interested in utilizing current political and social attitudes. Therefore, the film productions on the occasion of the 100-year anniversary reflect social values and norms of a dominant memorial community. Present demands of this community determine how the history of the Great War has to be read.[25]

Broadcasting companies, film producers, and (also political) funding institutions, as well as sponsors, develop an extended visual memory and affect the current and future commemorative culture sustainably. The message is clear: World War I was a global phenomenon and is a memorial for the whole of Europe. Mutual understanding is demanded; the political and military forces of all involved countries are to blame for the outbreak of war. The horrors of the First World War were the beginning of a long, painful process characterized by setbacks, leading to a European policy of agreement and peace. Thus film and television prepare a culture of memory apart from the mostly nation-focused historiography.[26]

---

25 Siegfried J. Schmidt, *Die Welten der Medien: Grundlagen und Perspektiven der Medienbeobachtung* (Braunschweig: Vieweg, 1996), 65.

26 Cf.: *Salzburger Nachrichten*, March 21, 2016, http://www.salzburg.com/nachrichten/oesterreich/politik/sn/artikel/1914-national-er-blick-auf-krieg-dominiert-95878/.

THE FIRST WORLD WAR IN THE CZECH AND SLOVAK CINEMA[1]

Václav Šmidrkal

Introduction

In a speech broadcast from the Vítkov National Memorial in Prague on October 28, 2014, the ninety-sixth anniversary of Czechoslovakia's declaration of independence, Colonel Jaroslav Vodička, Chairman of the Czech Union of Freedom Fighters (Český svaz bojovníků za svobodu), urged the Czech government to fund a new feature film about the Czechoslovak Legionnaires. He said, "we lack a film in our cinema that would show the audience the heroic campaign of the Legionnaires and their fundamental influence on the recognition of Czechoslovakia. It is one of the brightest points in our modern history, deserving of a high-quality film adaptation. It would be a great thing for 2018's hundredth anniversary of the end of the First World War and would pay tribute to our brave ancestors."[2] In the history of

1 This study was supported by the Charles University Research Centre program No. 9 (UNCE VITRI).

2 Speech by the President of the ČSBS, Jaroslav Vodička, given October 28, 2014 at Vítkov in Prague, accessed July 27, 2017, http://www.ceskenovinky.eu/2014/10/29/projev-predsedy-csbs-jaroslava-vodicky-predneseny-dne-28-rijna-2014-na-prazskem-vitkove/.

post-1989 Czech liberal democracy, this was rather unprecedented lobbying on the part of a veterans' organization for the involvement of the Czech state in a film production. The producers as well as their supporters stressed the point that such a film would be instructive and help strengthen the national identity. The last film solely devoted to the Legionnaires, *Zborov*, was made in 1938, and it soon became outdated after Germany's dismemberment and occupation of Czechoslovakia. Surprisingly, despite the large number of historical films made in the Czech lands every year since 1989, the theme of the First World War has for the most part not returned to the Czech cinema.[3] A 1993 Slovak-Czech television co-production, *Anjel milosrdenstva/Anděl milosrdenství* (*Angel of Mercy*), which was already in production before 1989, was one exception. Another was a Czech romantic drama about a returning First World War veteran, *Hlídač č. 47* (*Guard No. 47*, 2008, directed by Filip Renč), which was a remake of a film directed by Josef Rovenský and Jan Sviták in 1937. Otherwise, both the Czech and Slovak cinemas showed little interest in the topic. It was only with the coming of the centennial of the First World War that a need was felt to come to terms with this war from the perspective of contemporary

3 Jaroslav Sedláček, *Rozmarná léta českého filmu* (Praha: Česká televize, 2012); Jan Čulík, *A Society in Distress: The Image of the Czech Republic in Contemporary Czech Feature Film* (Brighton: Sussex Academy Press, 2014); Sune Bechmann Pedersen, *Reel Socialism: Making Sense of History in Czech and German Cinema since 1989* (Lund: Lund University, 2015); for an overview of Czech historiography of the First World War, see Ota Konrád, "Von der Kulisse der Nationalstaatsgründung zur Europäisierung der Forschung: Die tschechische Historiographie zum Ersten Weltkrieg," In *Die Habsburgermonarchie 1848–1918, Bd. XI/3: Bewältigte Vergangenheit? Die nationale und internationale Historiographie zum Untergang der Habsburgermonarchie als ideelle Grundlage für die Neuordnung Europas*, eds. Helmut Rumpler, Ulrike Harmat (Wien: ÖAW, forthcoming).

hegemonic discourse, which resulted in a new film project about the Czechoslovak Legionnaires' adventures in Russia.

Yet, previous political regimes sought to establish a useful and meaningful relationship to the First World War through its cinematic representations, and filmmakers repeatedly showed interest in this turning point of Czech and Slovak history. This chapter gives an overview of the First World War as represented in Czech and Slovak feature films from 1918 until today. It identifies the cinematic interpretations of the war as filtered through the hegemonic ideology of each distinctive period. I use the term "hegemony" in Antonio Gramsci's sense, meaning the dominant ideology of an existing social order, which is projected upon history. For my analysis, I created a list of Czech and Slovak films dealing with the First World War, drawing upon existing film catalogues[4] and secondary literature.[5] My intention here is not to give an exhaustive

4 *Český hraný film* [Czech Feature Film], 6 vols. (Prague: Národní filmový archiv, 1995–2010); Renáta Šmatláková, *Katalóg slovenských celovečerných filmov* [Catalogue of Slovak Feature Films] *1921–1999* (Bratislava: Slovenský filmový ústav, 1999).

5 Jiří Rak, "Obraz vzniku Československa v české filmové tvorbě dvacátých let," *Filmový sborník historický* 2 (1991): 9–19; Květa Kořalková, "Film Zborov ve společenském a politickém kontextu přelomu roku 1938 a 1939," *Filmový sborník historický* 2 (1991): 39–55; Tomáš Lachman, "Legionářská tematika v hraném filmu první republiky aneb Od Československého Ježíška ke Zborovu," In *Film a dějiny*, ed. Petr Kopal and Petr Blažek (Prague: Nakladatelství Lidové noviny, 2005), 209–218; David Zima, *Reflexe první světové války v kinematografii: Audiovizuální válečná tvorba Německa, Ruska a Československa v letech 1914–1939.* Západočeská univerzita v Plzni, Master thesis, 2013; David Zima, "Interpretace první světové války v československé meziválečné kinematografii," in *České, slovenské a československé dějiny 20. století IX.*, ed. Tomáš Hradecký, Pavel Horák, Pavek Boštík a kol. (Ústí nad Orlicí: Oftis, 2014), 181–196; Michal Kšiňan and Juraj Babják, "La mémoire de la Grande Guerre en ex-Tchécoslovaquie," *Matériaux pour l'histoire de notre temps* 113-114 (2014): 15–24.

account of all such films, but to point out the hegemonic influences upon Czech and Slovak depictions of the First World War.

The Battle for a Czechoslovak Nation-State (1918–1939)

Despite a variety of genres, topics, and treatments, the hegemonic view of the First World War underlying the interwar Czechoslovak cinema was that of a resounding victory by the Czechoslovak Legionnaires. The War was seen in terms of anti-Habsburg resistance, leading to the breakup of Austria-Hungary and the creation of new nation-states. The soldiers who defected from the Austrian-Hungarian military and voluntarily enlisted in the Czechoslovak legions in Russia, France, and Italy enjoyed a privileged status in interwar society, and their reputations were particularly exalted in their public representations. To a significant extent, it was the former Legionnaires themselves who promoted their own importance and historicized their experiences in literature, drama, and film.[6]

Unlike in Slovakia, where in the interwar period only one full-length feature film was made, the Czech lands had a fast-developing film industry that produced a large number of films.[7] Although filmmaking was a loosely-regulated private business, it did not exist only to seek profit. In the wave of enthusiastic patriotism

---

6 Ivan Šedivý, "Die Tschechoslowaischen Legionäre: ein historischer Mythos des 20. Jahrhunderts," In *Mythen und Politik im 20. Jahrhundert: Deutsche - Slowaken - Tschechen* (Essen: Klartext, 2013), 91–99; Dalibor Vácha, "Výstavba moderního československého mýtu: Legionáři a legionářská literatura jako jeden z jeho základních kamenů," In *Čas optimismu a ctižádostivých naději: prezentace a reprezentace české vědy a kultury v prvním desetiletí samostatného státu (1918–1920)*, ed. Dagmar Blümlová (České Budějovice: Jihočeské muzeum v Českých Budějovicích, 2009), 357–378.

7 Václav Macek and Jelena Paštéková, *Dejiny slovenskej kinematografie* (Martin: Osveta, 1997).

that crested after 1918, film producers manifested their loyalty to the new state by their eagerness to shoot films on themes from national history. The historical film was believed to be a top artistic genre, a magnificent spectacle contributing to the building of the Czechoslovak nation-state by promoting the approved view of key events in Czech and Slovak national history.[8]

Nevertheless, in the 1920s, Czechoslovak films were marked by a "pettiness" that did not allow them to withstand the test of time.[9] Film was still understood as a fairground attraction, a commodity, or an educational tool, and the artistic ambitions of authors remained low. Moreover, the interwar state was rather reluctant to develop a comprehensive film policy that would support steady conditions for domestic film production that might have increased the artistic level of films. It took years before the state began to protect its small domestic market from an overwhelming influx of U.S. and German films by regulating film imports and introducing systematic state aid for production of domestic films.[10]

---

8 Jiří Rak, "Úvahy o národním charakteru českého filmu po roce 1918," *Iluminace* 1, no. 1 (1989): 30–42; Ivan Klimeš and Jiří Rak, "Idea národního historického filmu v české meziválečné společnosti," *Iluminace* 1, no. 2 (1989): 23–37; Ivan Klimeš and Jiří Rak, "'Husitský' film - nesplněný sen české meziválečné kinematografie," *Filmový sborník historický* 3 (1992): 69–109.

9 Luboš Bartošek, *Náš film: kapitoly z dějiny (1896–1945)* (Prague: Mladá fronta, 1985), 67.

10 Gernot Heiss and Ivan Klimeš, "Kulturindustrie und Politik: Die Filmwirtschaft der Tschechoslowakei und Österreichs in der politischen Krise der Dreißiger Jahre," in *Obrazy času: Český a rakouský film 30. let / Bilder der Zeit: Tschechischer und österreichischer Film der 30er Jahre*, ed. Gernot Heiss and Ivan Klimeš (Prague: NFA and Österreichisches Ost- und Südosteuropa-Institut - Außenstelle Brünn, 2003), 392–483; for a more detailed account, see Ivan Klimeš, *Kinematografie a stát v českých zemích 1895–1945* (Prague: FF UK, 2016).

The democratic Czechoslovak state did not shrink from controlling public discourse by censoring potentially subversive attacks against the new order and unwanted representations of history. Censorship imposed by the Ministry of Interior followed political criteria and was slow to adapt to the specific needs of art films.[11] For example, there was no place in the Czechoslovak interwar cinema for a positive appraisal of the Habsburg monarchy or its legacy because that would contest the official mainstream narrative about an Austria-Hungary that oppressed the Czechs and Slovaks and was doomed to downfall.

The state sought to build a new national identity by supporting an interpretation of history that would help to cement the contemporary social order. Stories that challenged the prevailing hegemonic view were marginalized, either through censorship or negative reviews. For example, *Šachta pohřbených idejí* (*The shaft of buried ideas*, 1921, directed by Rudolf Myzet and Antonín Ludvík Havel), showed First World War-era miners in the Ostrava region from a socialist perspective. The film was censored before it was released. If a film did not provoke the attention of the censors, it could be still marginalized by negative reviews from exponents of the then-current hegemonic view. *Jménem Jeho Veličenstva* (*In the name of his majesty*, 1928, directed by Antonín Vojtěchovský), was based on the true story of an infantryman, Josef Kudrna. It illustrated the brutality of the Austro-Hungarian military machine, which sentenced Czech soldier Kudrna to death because he opposed the maltreatment of the troops by their officers. The film drew criticism from right-wing army officers such as Rudolf Medek because it championed

11 Heiss and Klimeš, "Kulturindustrie und Politik," 396–398; Zima, *Reflexe*, 136–137.

an act of insubordination that did not have a clear basis in the cause of an independent Czechoslovakia.[12]

The early Czechoslovak films celebrated the victory of the Entente, cherished the heroism of the Czechoslovak Legion, and defamed the previous imperial order. The determination of private producers to combine both profit and patriotism resulted in a popular genre of romantic drama that stressed the passions and sudden turns in the intimate lives of ordinary people, played out against the background of the First World War. The film *Za svobodu národa* (*For the freedom of the nation*, 1920, directed by Václav Binovec), was based on the true story of a Legionnaire, Jiří Voldán, who fought on all three fronts, but after his return to Czechoslovakia had to go on to Slovakia to fight the Hungarian Bolsheviks. *Legionář* (*Legionnaire*, 1920, directed by Rudolf Měšťák), was a similar romantic drama set against the background of the First World War with a Legionnaire in the lead role. *Za čest vítězů* (*In honor of the victor*, 1921, directed by Antonín Ludvík Havel and Julius Lébl), dealt with the post-war demobilization and reintegration of a Legionnaire into civilian society. *Pražské děti* (*Prague children*, 1927, directed by Robert Zdráhal), was a love story on the home front between Jiří and Anna, whose brother, given up for dead, joyfully returned home as a Legionnaire.

Unlike the aforementioned romantic dramas, which coupled sentimentality and patriotism, attempts to give the Legionnaires' story a more overtly nation-building frame could result in an almost *agitprop* style. *Za Československý stát* (*For the Czechoslovak*

---

12 Martin Zückert, "Antimilitarismus und soldatische Resistenz: Politischer Protest und armeefeindliches Verhalten in der tschechischen Gesellschaft bis 1918," In *Glanz, Gewalt, Gehorsam. Militär und Gesellschaft in der Habsburgermonarchie (1800 bis 1918)*, ed. Laurence Cole, Christa Hämmerle, and Martin Scheutz (Essen: Klartext, 2011), 218.

state, 1928, directed by Vladimír Studecký), was made with the support of the Ministry of National Defense for the tenth anniversary of Czechoslovakia's independence. It tells the story of three brothers who bravely fight with the Czechoslovak Legions in Russia, France, and Italy and whose sons also become soldiers when they grow up.[13]

Films based on an already successful novel or stage play, or ones written by an experienced screenwriter, were more likely to avoid an overdose of didacticism. The leading writer-Legionnaires, acknowledged for their poems, novels, and dramas, participated in the adaptation of their works for the screen. Rudolf Medek's *Plukovník Švec* (*Colonel Švec*, (1929, directed by Svatopluk Innemann), shows the Legionnaires enduring a crisis of confidence caused by Bolshevik agitation, which leads their commander, Colonel Josef Jiří Švec, to commit suicide. *Třetí rota* (*The third company*, 1931, also directed by Innemann), brought to the screen a digest of Josef Kopta's numerous literary works reflecting his overall experience with the Czechoslovak Legion in Russia. František Langer's *Jízdní hlídka* (*Mounted patrol*, 1936, directed by Václav Binovec), tells the story of a mounted patrol of Legionnaires in Siberia that is stranded in a solitary house and bravely fights against a Bolshevik horde. Interestingly, due to a rapprochement in Czechoslovak-Soviet relations in the 1930s, the Bolsheviks are not demonized in this film. The stress is on timeless military values and the patriotism of the Czechoslovak Legionnaires, rather than their anti-Bolshevism.

Generally, the introduction of sound and the gradual professionalization of the film industry had a positive effect on the quality of films. However, the limited availability of capital meant

13 Jiří Rak, ed., "Rudolf Medek: Za československý stát," *Iluminace*, no. 1 (1993): 117–122.

that the stories of the Legion, typically taking place on the Russian front, eschewed grandiose battle spectacle in favor of wartime chamber drama. The directors sometimes got around this problem using documentary footage from the war, as in the film *Poručík Alexander Rjepkin* (*Lieutenant Alexander Rjepkin*, 1937, directed by Václav Binovec), which is a chamber drama about a Czech Legionnaire who is captured and taken to an Austrian army hospital, where he has to pretend he is a Russian soldier in order to avoid a court-martial.

As international tensions grew in the late 1930s, efforts to mobilize for defense and prepare for a war with Nazi Germany also grew in Czechoslovakia. Using heroic motifs from the First World War was one way to motivate the Czechoslovak population to increase their readiness. The Ministry of National Defense cooperated with filmmakers on such productions. The last of these films was *Zborov* (1938, directed by J. A. Holman and Jiří Slavíček), which depicts a legendary 1917 battle where the Legionnaires distinguished themselves and that was seared in the public memory of interwar Czechoslovakia.[14] The film presents patriotic values that were outdated after the Munich Agreement, the creation of a truncated second Czechoslovak Republic (1938–39), and the occupation of the Czech lands in 1939.

Despite the higher artistic quality of these films, none of them qualified for the all-time "honor roll" of Czech films. Forbidden during the Nazi occupation, they never returned to movie screens. Unlike many comedies from the 1930s and early 1940s, which have gained "retro" popularity and are retained in the collective memory, the Legionnaire films were replaced by a new generation of war movies.

---

14 Cf. Jan Galandauer, *2. 7. 1917 - bitva u Zborova: česká legenda* (Prague: Havran, 2002).

During the Nazi occupation of the Czech lands between 1939 and 1945, the Czech cinema industry did not stop producing films, but none of them focused on the conflicts from the First World War. The intention of the Nazis to shoot a new version of *Colonel Švec* that would make use of the Legionnaires' popularity and recast them as fighters against Bolshevism, rather than fighters against Germans, did not materialize.[15]

Beyond Regimes: The Good Soldier Švejk

Despite changing hegemonic views of the history of the First World War that corresponded to different political regimes, Jaroslav Hašek's *The Good Soldier Schweik* is an evergreen that strikes a chord with audiences under different circumstances. The satiric mockery of militarized Austrian society embodied by the conscripted dog thief and pub idler, Josef Schweik (Švejk), deconstructs features that are intrinsic to every military machine. Not surprisingly, the interwar Czechoslovak military and the Legionnaires rejected the mindset Švejk reflected.[16]

The Legionnaires took up arms against their enemies and risked their lives at the warfront. They were an example of civic duty fulfilled. By contrast, Josef Švejk undermined state power with an exaggerated yet subversive obedience to authority. While the organized working class threatened the existing order with revolution, Švejk preferred simply to pursue his illicit trafficking in stolen dogs. Celebrations of the Legionnaires and the proletarian Bolshevik revolution attacked the old regime directly, with a clear didactic purpose. On the other hand, the Švejkian style employed

15 Bartošek, *Náš film*, 348.

16 Cf. Sebastian Paul, "Die Rezeption des Švejk in der Ersten Tschechoslowakischen Republik: Eine Neubewertung und systematische Einordnung," *Zeitschrift für Ostmitteleuropa-Forschung* 63, no. 2 (2014): 249–278.

entertaining satire that exposed, step-by-step, the "rotten" foundations of the Austrian empire, without proposing any better alternative; it considered all systems to be more or less the same.

All attempts to adapt Hašek's novel for the screen had to cope with the problem of Hašek's narrative style, which was essential to the novel's comic effect because it was in reality a bunch of unrelated stories. Silent film versions with subtitles or puppet films with a narrator were more likely to succeed than live-action feature films with sound. The first attempt to adapt the novel for screen was a three-part series of silent films from 1926 with Karel Noll as Švejk: *Dobrý voják Švejk* (*Good soldier Švejk*), *Švejk na frontě* (*Švejk at the front*) by Karel Lamač, and *Švejk v ruském zajetí* (*Švejk in Russian captivity*) by Svatopluk Innemann. Those films were edited together in 1930 by Martin Frič into one single film, *Osudy dobrého vojáka Švejka* (*Good soldier Švejk's fate*). Shortly thereafter, Frič shot a re-make with sound of *Dobrý voják Švejk* (*The Good Soldier Schweik*), with a new cast, in 1931.

During the Second World War, the film *Švejk bourá Německo* (*Švejk destroys Germany*, released in English as "*Schweik's New Adventures*," 1943, directed by Karel Lamač), was shot in exile in Britain. It transported the character of Švejk into the anti-Nazi resistance in Germany. After the war, a full-length puppet film, *Dobrý voják Švejk* (*Good Soldier Schweik*, 1954), directed by Jiří Trnka, was considered a successful adaptation of Hašek's novel because its narrator (beloved Czech actor Jan Werich) commented in the author's own words on the action played by the puppets.

The newest, and until today, most popular, adaptation was filmed by Karel Steklý. It was shot in color and divided into two parts. *Dobrý voják Švejk* (*The Good Soldier Schweik*, 1956) tells Švejk's story up to when he and First Lieutenant Lukáš are sent to war. *Poslušně hlásím* (*I Dutifully Report*, 1957) covers their war exploits. Rudolf Hrušínský, in the role of Švejk, brilliantly interpreted his character. He became the ultimate version of Švejk on the screen, just as Josef Lada's illustrations have become iconic of the book in print. Steklý did not reduce Hašek's criticism of Austro-Hungarian bourgeois society and its military to a shallow lithographic poster, nor did he abuse it with a display of degraded humor. He picked out key stories from the novel and chained them together into a storyline. Despite rather negative reviews that considered these films to be mere shadows of the novel, and not particularly creative in transferring it to the screen, this film adaptation scored high box office numbers and became popular abroad.

A follow-up to these films was the Czechoslovak/Soviet co-production *Bol'shaya droga/Velká cesta* (*The great journey*, 1962, directed by Yuri Ozerov), which counted on common knowledge of Švejk's story in both countries. This comedy about Jaroslav Hašek's adventures in Russia during the First World War included an allusion to Steklý's film in the character of the soldier Strašlipka, supposedly the model for the literary Švejk, played here by Rudolf Hrušínský.[17] Despite its mythologization of the Bolshevik revolution and the ideological filter through which the story is told, the film is an almost post-modern culmination of the Švejk film adaptations.

The Cradle of a Popular Pro-Communist Revolt (1945–1989)

The reconstitution of Czechoslovakia and its society after 1945 made the Second World War into a new foundational watershed that assumed the role in the national psyche played earlier by the First World War. Unlike in Western Europe, where both world wars still remain deeply anchored in the collective memory, in East-Central Europe, the First World War was overwhelmed by

17 N. Sumenov and O. Sul'kin, *Yuri Ozerov* (Moscow: Iskusstvo, 1986), 78.

the memory of the Second.[18] The Second World War provided a legitimizing historical narrative for communist power as well as a bottomless well of inspiration for filmmakers, while cinematic depictions of the First World War were far less frequent after 1945. The films that were produced shifted their perspective from that of heroic patriots fighting in the Czechoslovak legions for an independent nation-state to the masses revolting against the existing social order under the influence of the Bolshevik revolution in Russia. The First World War was generally characterized as a springboard for the socialist revolution and for its irresistible spread from Russia across Europe.

In the interwar period, film production was a private business seeking immediate profit, and the state only reluctantly made policy in the field of film production. After 1945, the whole film industry was nationalized in order to create stable conditions. Almost entirely freed from the Scylla of economic pressure, the film industry had to contend with the Charybdis of censorship in all its assorted forms. Despite the intrinsic drawbacks of the state socialist model of the cinema, state ownership allowed Czechoslovak films to achieve unprecedented success and worldwide acclaim in the 1960s. Nationalization also enabled the development of the Slovak film industry in Bratislava and the regular production of Slovak feature films, something that had not existed until then.

The First World War returned to the screen as the feature films of the first half of the 1950s sought to retell important events in Czech and Slovak national history in accord with their new Marxist-Leninist reinterpretations.[19] The First World War itself

18 Cf. Robert Blobaum, "Warsaw's Forgotten War," *Remembrance and Solidarity Studies in 20th Century European History* 2 (March 2014): 185–207.

19 Ivan Klimeš, "K povaze historismu v hraném filmu poúnorového období," *Filmový sborník historický* 2 (1991): 81–86.

was not a key event in this new version of history. However, two films, based on novels, told the story of immediate post-war developments in the organization of the working class and of a stolen chance for a socialist revolution in early Czechoslovakia. The first of the films that popularized the Communist Party's pre-history on the big screen was *Anna Proletářka* (1952, directed by Karel Steklý). This was a socialist-realist adaptation of a 1928 novel of the same name by Ivan Olbracht. Whereas Olbracht combined the genre of women's fiction and political agitation, in his film version Steklý de-emphasized the former and magnified the latter in order to underline the communization of the working-class movement. In the film and the book, Anna, a submissive country girl working as a servant for a rich Prague family, was transformed into a self-confident urban proletarian determined to shoot down the bourgeoisie. The story on film was deprived of juicy moments depicting male-female relationships, sexuality, and violence, and it stuck to the history of the split in the Social Democratic Party that led to the establishment of the Communist Party of Czechoslovakia in 1921. A clear dichotomy between good and evil, one-dimensional characters, and a trite ending made this film into a lengthy political lecture of substandard quality.

Similar in theme, aesthetic, and even casting was the film adaptation of Antonín Zápotocký's autobiographical novel *Rudá záře nad Kladnem* (*Red glow over Kladno*, 1955, directed by Vladimír Vlček). Zápotocký, who succeeded Klement Gottwald as Czechoslovakia's President in 1953, again told the story of the split in the Social Democratic Party, this time from the perspective of a worker in the Kladno steelworks. The repetition of this story not only served the purpose of presenting the official version of the Communist Party's history but also contributed to Zápotocký's image as a working-class revolutionary leader, a long-time communist politician, and also as a successful writer.

The de-Stalinization of the mid-1950s shifted the focus in film from disciplined rows of workers marching toward unquestioned victory under Bolshevik leadership to unrestrained popular mutinies and social revolts, motivated more by fuzzy discontents than clear-cut ideology. The first Slovak film to deal with the First World War was *Štyridsaťštyri* (*The forty-four mutineers*, 1957, directed by Paľo Bielik). It told the story of a mutiny by soldiers of the 71st Austro-Hungarian Infantry Regiment (most of them were Slovaks from the Trenčín region) in Kragujevac, Serbia in June 1918. This uprising was suppressed by a decimation of the troops in which forty-four soldiers were sentenced to death and executed. What was initially non-ideological opposition to the war became onscreen a social protest by "tinkers against lords," set against the background of the Serbian revolutionary movement.[20]

A similar mutiny by Czech soldiers in Rumburk, Northern Bohemia in 1918 was the subject of the Czech film *Hvězda zvaná pelyněk* (*A star called wormwood*, 1964, directed by Martin Frič), which was more overtly anti-war than revolutionary in the communist sense. The dichotomy between these two concepts is represented by a pacifist, Stanko Vodička, and a revolutionary, František Noha. A group of Austrian-Hungarian prisoners of war return home from Russia, tired of war, and mutiny against their forced re-enlistment into the military machine. Under the leadership of the utopian pacifist Vodička, they seize the town of Rumburk and march toward Nový Bor, where their mutiny is put down and its leaders are sentenced to death. The film eschews over-ideologization and focuses on the human face of the soldiers, who simply long desperately for civilian life at home, for which they are willing to risk their lives.

20 Macek and Paštétová, *Dejiny*, 168–170; Petra Hanáková, *Paľo Bielik a slovenská filmová kultúra* (Bratislava: Slovenský filmový ústav, 2010), 144–150.

The Czechoslovak New Wave and historical films of the 1960s liberal era generally preferred themes that had been twisted or concealed after 1945, such as the Second World War and the early communist era. In the Czech lands, the First World War was not among those themes, but it remained important in Slovak cinematography, filling a gap in the national *historiophoty* (a term coined by Hayden White) as a catalyst for the Slovak's revolt against their national and social oppressors. In 1966 a classic Slovak novel, *Živý bič* (*The Living Whip*), by Milo Urban, was adapted for a two-part television series by Martin Ťapák, and it was also released on film for screening in cinemas. It showed the transformation during the war of docile, rural Slovak people into rebels who liberated themselves from the "yoke of Magyar administrators and Jewish businessmen" in a violent uprising initiated by the returning soldiers.

The artistic highlight among Czechoslovak war movies was the Slovak/Italian co-production *Zbehovia a pútnici/Il disertore e i nomadi* (*The Deserters and the Nomads*, 1968, directed by Juraj Jakubisko). It deals with the violence of war, offering three examples of how wars can end: the First, the Second, and an imagined future Third World War. Based in part on Ladislav Ťažký's novelette *Vojenský zbeh* (*The military deserter*), the film was originally shot for television and later remade and released in movie theaters. The first story shows a group of Slovak deserters in revolt against the elite of a village, killing gendarmes and plundering and torturing a rich farmer and his wife. In a torrent of imagination and incredible energy, Jakubisko depicts the brutality unleashed by the deserters, whose wild behavior gradually costs them the support of the local population.[21] Similar in its imagery and its "carnivalization" of war was the story of two veterans and the

21 Cf. Peter Michalovič and Vlastimil Zuska, *Juraj Jakubisko* (Bratislava: Slovenský filmový ústav, 2005).

impossibility of their reintegration into civilian society, depicted in Elo Havetta's film *Ľalie poľné* (*Field Lilies*, 1972).[22]

The most successful period of Czechoslovak cinema that also produced important films about the First World War ended in the early 1970s, when the so-called "normalization" after 1968 caused a U-turn in cultural policy.[23] Across-the-board purges of personnel, bans on completed and unfinished films, and the reideologization of future productions based on a new political consensus reinforced a class-based viewpoint and conservative aesthetics. The three-part TV miniseries and film *Červené víno* (*Red wine*, released in 1972 for television and in 1976 for cinemas), directed by Andrej Lettrich, was a portrait of a wine-making family in southern Slovakia at the beginning of the twentieth century. This film already mirrored the new trend and lacked the vital energy of the 1960s aesthetic. Instead of the wild crowds of returning soldiers, looting and killing in *The Living Whip* and *The Deserters and the Nomads*, *Červené víno* showed soldiers as a disciplined group taking only what ostensibly belongs to them in the sense of "moral economy."

This shift was even more visible in Juraj Jakubisko's monumental epic *Tisícročná včela* (*The Millennial Bee*), a 1983 Czechoslovak/German/Austrian co-production for both television and movie theaters, based on a novel of the same name by Peter Jaroš. The war was again shown as a conflict between a destitute Slovak population that is rushed into war by an inhuman Hungarian- and

22 Jozef Macko, "Karnevalizácia v diele Ela Havettu," in *Elo Havetta (1938–1975)*, ed. Václav Macek (Bratislava: Sovenský filmový ústav, 1990), 61–88.

23 Cf. Štěpán Hulík, *Kinematografie zapomnění* (Prague: Academia, 2011); Paulina Brenn, *The Greengrocer and His TV: The Culture of Communism after the 1968 Prague Spring* (Ithaca: Cornell University Press, 2010).

German-speaking military elite, against which the people cannot rise up in order to stop the pointless slaughter. Small but frequent hints of the Bolshevik revolution surface in the film, such as a red flag that appears in the final scene of a fantasized uprising. The film was a success in the context of the 1980s cinema, but a comparison with Jakubisko's earlier works made in the 1960s, which were subsequently banned, reveals some of its limits.[24]

As already indicated above, a number of films dealing with the topic of the First World War were international co-productions, beginning with 1962's Czechoslovak/Soviet *The Great Journey*. The theme of the First World War lent itself to co-productions that promised synergies in coping with a theme that spanned national borders and required a high level of international cooperation and funding. The majority of these films were made inside the Soviet bloc. There were, however, examples of co-productions across the "Iron Curtain," such the Czechoslovak/Austrian farce *Dýmky/Pfeifen, Betten, Turteltauben* (*The Pipes*, 1966, directed by Vojtěch Jasný), which was based on Ilya Ehrenburg's book *Thirteen Pipes*.[25] The last act of the film, entitled "Saint Hubertus's Pipe," involved a wife cheating on her husband, who had been called up to serve in the military during the First World War.

In the 1970s and 1980s, international co-productions became commonplace, but Czechoslovakia preferred projects that conformed to its redefined, post-1968 ideological consensus. The

---

24 Macek and Paštétová, *Dejiny*, 416.

25 Cf. Pavel Skopal, "'Svoboda pod dohledem': Zahájení koprodukčního modelu výroby v kinematografiích socialistických zemí na příkladu Barrandova (1954 až 1960)," in *Naplánovaná kinematografie: Český filmový průmysl 1945 až 1960*, ed. Pavel Skopal (Prague: Academia, 2012), 102–148; Pavel Skopal, *Filmová kultura severního trojúhelníku: Filmy, kina a diváci českých zemí, NDR a Polska 1945–1970* (Brno: Host, 2014).

Czechoslovak/Soviet co-production *Větrné more/Poputyi veter* (*Windy sea*, 1973, directed by Eldar Kuliev), tells the story of a Russian Bolshevik of Czech origin, Ivan Prokofyevich Vatsek, who organized the retreat of Bolshevik troops from Baku, Azerbaijan to Astrakhan, Russia during the Russian Civil War. Similar in its approach to class conflicts was the Czechoslovak/East German *Ostrov stříbrných volavek/Die Insel der Silberreiher* (*Island of the Silver Herons*, 1976), directed by Jaromil Jireš. The film is set on the home front in a Pomeranian town in summer 1918. It stresses growing class-based antagonisms and defiance of participation in the war. The Czechoslovak/Austrian co-production Šílený kankán/Die Schieber (*Insane Cancan*, 1982), directed by Jaroslav Balík, was a product of its time, depicting a former Austrian-Hungarian officer, Krumka, and his servant Scholef in a decaying, early post-war Vienna, where they take advantage of the general economic misery to run their scams. Emphasizing the "inhuman morality of money"[26] that makes both of them inconsiderately think only of themselves, *Insane Cancan* presents an unconvincing argument for the economic roots of fascism that was a flop with both Austrian and Czechoslovak audiences.

Two high-budget, yet dry and lifeless co-productions, suffered from the problem of being reduced to an illustration of textbook narratives. The Czechoslovak/Yugoslav film *Sarajevský atentát/Atentat u Sarajevu* (*The Day that Shook the World*, 1975), directed by Veljko Bulajić, was an epic reconstruction of the assassination of Austrian Archduke Franz Ferdinand by Serbian anarchists. Admiring the assassins as freedom-fighters for Greater Serbia, the film took an unsurprising approach, marked by conventional portrayals and shallow characterizations. The

26 Ivana Richterová, "Nelidská morálka peněz," *Tvorba*, no. 10 (May 11, 1983).

Czechoslovak/East German/Soviet co-production *Evropa tančila valčík/Europa tanzt Walzer/Evropa tantsevala val'c* (*Europe danced the waltz*, 1989), directed by Otakar Vávra, was similar. It focused on the same period of time, summer 1914, showing the three emperors, Franz Joseph I, Wilhelm II, and Nicholas II, and their ill-fated decision-making that led to the First World War. The film combines a narrative of high-level politics with the story of a Czech archivist working in Vienna. With the help of a "Serbian connection," the archivist manages to shred documents stored in occupied Belgrade that evidenced anti-Austrian agitation by Czech activists. This film is even more didactic than the others and teaches that the First World War paved the way for the Russian revolution and began a new era in human history. It tightly conforms to the then-reigning interpretation of history that was swept away by the flow of events just a few weeks after its release in late 1989.

Probably the most substantial contribution to the theme of the First World War in the 1970s and 1980s was the Czech/Slovak co-production *Signum Laudis* (1980), directed by Martin Hollý. As a study of a fanatic individual obsessed by war, scriptwriters Vladimír Kalina and Jiří Křižan chose a non-commissioned officer, Corporal Hoferik, a horse trader by profession, who became a reliable cog in a monstrous military machinery. Hoferik turns off his ability to think about the meaning of the war and his participation in it, proceeding blindly.[27] His devotion earns him the prestigious *Signum Laudis* medal. Although he tries to appeal to his superiors by enforcing their commands, he finds himself alone and despised by both officers and soldiers. Eventually, he is sentenced to death by the same officers who honored him with

27 *Martin Hollý: život za kamerou*, ed. Richard Blech (Bratislava: Slovenský filmový ústav, 2001), 162–165.

the medal when he proves that he lacks enough cynical flexibility to carry out their most heinous orders. The film does not show any specific battle or real historical characters but focuses on the psychology of a non-commissioned officer who finds himself squeezed between different social groups.

After 1989: A Missing Theme

In reaction to decades of strictly-dictated discourse about history, the post-communist era brought about a re-interpretation of Czech and Slovak contemporary history on the screen, opposed to the previous narratives and aesthetic. In fact, there were more urgent and more attractive historical subjects than the First World War that had been twisted and made taboo during the communist period, which called for preferential artistic treatment. The film industry's most pressing need has been to reject the legacy of the communist past and its historical interpretations, and contribute to the new anti-communist, anti-totalitarian identity of society. Compared to the severe collective traumas experienced by the Czechs from 1938 to 1989, the horrors of the First World War seemed like a healed wound that did not need to be revisited. Moreover, the dramatic potential of the First World War might seem weak because the ethnic, social, and military conflicts provoked by the First World War present themselves in the Second World War in an even more drastic form. The fact that the heroes and victims of the totalitarian regimes were still alive and waiting for an homage played a role as well, while the last Legionnaires had died before the turn of the twenty-first century.

The rushed transformation of the Czech cinema from a state-run nationalized industry into a neo-liberal, market-oriented one has caused a long-term production crisis. The breakup of old industry structures, combined with high production costs and the limited ability of the Czech distribution network to generate revenue, have created a vicious circle of increasingly mediocre productions pandering to popular tastes. Despite occasional successes, such as the Academy Award for Best Foreign Language Film conferred upon *Kolja* (*Kolya,* 1996), directed by Jan Svěrák, the Czech cinema has been looking for a viable organizational model in which public funding could offset the disadvantages of a small national market.[28] The situation became even more serious in Slovakia, where the national cinema broke down after 1989 and yearly output has dropped to a fraction of its average volumes in the 1980s.

Besides the impact of structural changes in the film industry, scriptwriters and audiences have been indifferent to the theme, which has seemingly been exhausted in the previous decades and has lost meaning to society. The Slovak/Czech co-production *Anjel milosrdenstva/Anděl milosrdenství* (*Angel of Mercy,* 1993), directed by Miloslav Luther, was an exception to this. However, that film was in fact connected more with the era before 1989 than with the 1990s. The screenplay was based on Vladimír Körner's novella of the same name, which was published in 1988 and then prepared for film or TV adaptation. Due to political and structural changes in the filmmaking industry, *Angel of Mercy* was finally produced as a Slovak-Czech TV film that also appeared briefly in cinemas. This critically acclaimed chamber drama about an aristocratic widow who wants to expiate the war crimes of her deceased husband by serving as a nurse in a military hospital resembles in its existentialist statement about people rendered inhuman by war to 1980's *Signum Laudis.*[29]

---

28 Cf. Petr Szczepanik a kol., *Studie vývoje českého hraného kinematografického díla* (Brno: Masarykova univerzita, 2015).

29 Vladimír Novotný, *Tragické existenciály Vladimíra Körnera* (Prague: Arsci 2013), 131.

Despite renewed sympathies that appeared for the first Czechoslovak Republic after 1989, which was idealized as a golden age of modern Czech history and the ultimate source of democratic traditions, there was no clear return to the exploits of the Legionnaires and the First World War as the key event that formed the sensibilities of that era. The story of the Legionnaires who fought the Russian Bolsheviks had potential appeal to a society redefining itself by anti-communism, but a need to produce a "Legionnaire film" only arose as the centenary of the First World War in 2014 approached. Despite a declared intention to fortify the national identity by paying homage to the Czechoslovak Legionnaires in Russia and their arduous Siberian anabasis, film producers have had difficulties to find funding for a film with a potential budget of approximately four million euros.

Conclusion

The First World War has gone through several interpretational stages in the Czech and Slovak cinema. In the interwar period, stories highlighting the victorious Czech Legionnaires, their ethos, their nationalism, and their military prowess were emphasized. Other interpretations were marginalized or even forbidden. Unlike the 1920s, when the impact of "big history" on private lives was depicted in silent melodramas, in the 1930s the professionalization of filmmaking and a more active role by the state enabled the production of some high-quality dramatic films. Adaptations of Jaroslav Hašek's *Good Soldier Švejk* for the screen provided a remarkable counter-narrative to the heroism of the Legionnaires. The timeless story of Švejk appealed to audiences in different countries and under different political regimes. After 1945, the Second World War replaced the First World War in its national identity-making function, and cinematic representations of the Second World War far outnumbered those of the First. In the early

1950s, the First World War was depicted mainly as the event that accelerated the formation of an organized working class, inspired by the Russian Bolsheviks. The serried ranks of workers loosened in the films of the late 1950s, to the point that they were replaced by violent mobs in revolt. The filmmakers of the 1970s and 1980s usually did not challenge the new ideological consensus created after 1968. As a result, they at most offered tamer variations on themes already expressed in the 1960s. Many of these films were international co-productions, but that did nothing to dissolve the fossilized aesthetic and ideological attitudes dominant in the Czechoslovak cinema of the time. The almost total failure of the theme of the First World War to return to the screen after 1989 can be explained by the privatization and commercialization of film production and the press of more urgent historical topics. Nevertheless, a more detailed reappraisal of the First World War is expected in 2018 with the production of a new "Legionnaire film."[30]

30 Legionáři – Sibiřská anabáze, accessed July 27, 2017, http://www.legiefilm.cz/.

THE CONTACT ZONE:

IN SEARCH OF THE GALICIAN THEATER OF WAR IN GERMAN CINEMAS OF THE 1920S[1]

Philipp Stiasny

Franz Joseph's Empire can only ever have been an invention of the operetta, of the theater, of the novel, and of the cinema. In Germany, too, it was never only a historical and geographical region and era, but also an emotional one, a place of memory and of longing. This is especially true of the period after the First World War, when films about the Danube, Vienna, and waltzes, complete with dashing lieutenants and jaded princes, jocular musicians and Viennese dames, made up a considerable part of the Weimar Republic's box office offerings and landed high on the popularity charts.[2]

---

1 Many thanks to James Straub for translating the text and commenting on it. Many thanks, too, to Mila Ganeva and Cynthia Walk for their comments and help.

2 Cf. the polls for the most successful films of the season in *Film-Kurier*, no. 85, Apr. 9, 1927 (no. 1: *An der schönen blauen Donau* [*The Beautiful Blue Danube*]); ibid., no. 116/117, May 16, 1928 (no. 3: *Das tanzende Wien* [*Dancing Vienna*]); ibid., special edition, June 1, 1929 (no. 3: *Ungarische Rhapsodie* [*Hungarian Rhapsody*]); ibid., special edition, May 31, 1930 (no. 2 of sound films: *Liebeswalzer* [*Waltz of Love*]); ibid., no. 119, May 23, 1931 (no. 6: *Zwei Herzen im Dreivierteltakt* [*Two Hearts in Waltz Time*]); ibid., no. 118, May 21, 1932 (no. 1: *Der Kongress tanzt* [*Congress Dances*]).

These stories almost always took place before the First World War—in the good old days, before everything fell apart, before the battlefields of Europe drank the blood of millions of people, and the Habsburg dynasty was wiped off the face of the earth, along with the Romanovs and the Hohenzollern. Although people in the 1920s wanted to look back at this era with laughter in one eye and tears in the other and to wallow in memories of a now-defunct multinational state, there was scant interest in films about German-Austrian cooperation and its consequences in World War I. Perhaps people wanted this chapter forgotten. In any case, although the memorialization of the First World War was a hotly debated issue, hardly any of the Weimar Republic's films evoked the battles—often fought beside German troops—of the Austro-Hungarian army in Galicia, in Bukovina or Romania, in the Alps and on the Isonzo, or in the Balkans and in the Carpathians.

One such exception was the hugely popular directorial debut by Luis Trenker, *Berge in Flammen* ("*Mountains on Fire*") from 1931, which depicts the struggle between Austrians and Italians in the Dolomites, complete with spectacular location shooting, in a cross between a thriller and a mountain film.[3]

However, apart from "*Mountains on Fire*", between 1918 and 1933 only two other German productions dealt with the Austro-Hungarian theater of war at some length, *Leichte Kavallerie* ("*Light Cavalry*", 1927, directed by Rolf Randolf) and *Zwei Welten* ("*Two Worlds*", GER/UK 1930, directed by E.A. Dupont). Both of them belong to a small corpus of not exclusively German films set in Galicia that haven't been studied so far. My essay first of all attempts to give an account of the films in question: What narratives

3 *Berge in Flammen* was the fifth most successful film of the 1931–32 season; cf. "1400 Theaterbesitzer haben abgestimmt," *Film-Kurier*, no. 118, May 21, 1932.

do they use in order to speak about the war in Galicia? Are there prevalent patterns, themes, motifs? Are the films in dialogue with each other, or do they stand for themselves? What are the main discourses that the films reflect, produce, partake in? Not least, this essay will try to illuminate some of the contexts of the films' production and their reception by the German press of their day.

The War of the Movie Seats

In the aftermath of the war, not only the production of films about the Austro-Hungarian theater in general and Galicia in particular were insignificant in commercial terms; in fact, this goes for all of German cinema after 1918, including foreign films shown in Germany. Only in the mid-1920s did the production of war films begin getting into gear. This trend was pushed forward by sensational American films like "*The Big Parade*" (USA 1925, directed by King Vidor) and "*What Price Glory?*" (USA 1926, directed by Raoul Walsh). These Hollywood films, the products of massive outlays of technology and capital, had been highly praised in the press for their peerless realism in the portrayal of war. They were also heavily promoted by the production and distribution companies.[4] Nevertheless, these films failed to find much favor with the German cinema audiences. Faced with the choice between viewing the war from an American or German perspective in the movie seats, the public preferred the latter. On the one hand, the choice betrays a preference for a national, and often nationalistic, interpretation of the war, while on the other hand it attests to a domestic preference for domestic films, despite

4 For the role of American war movies within the German film discourse cf. Thomas J. Saunders, "Politics, the Cinema, and Early Revisitations of War in Weimar Germany," *Canadian Journal of History* 23 (1988): 25–48.

American competition and the lack of language barriers in the silent film era.[5]

The German World War films were also shaped by a German perspective. This is evident in the choice of subject matter: melodramatic films, like *Ich hatt' einen Kameraden* (*I Once Had a Comrade*) (1926, directed by Conrad Wiene), about the colonial war in German East Africa, and *Die versunkene Flotte* ("*Wrath of the Sea*"/"When Fleet meets Fleet", 1926, directed by Manfred Noa), on the battle of Jutland, were marked successes at the box office.[6] Other popular films included *Unsere Emden* ("*The Emden*", 1926, directed by Louis Ralph) on the near-mythical Cruiser *Emden* and its privateer voyages in the Indian Ocean, *U9 Weddigen* (1927, directed by Heinz Paul) and *Richthofen, der rote Ritter der Luft* (*Richthofen, the Red Knight of the Skies*, 1927, directed by Desider Kertész) on heroic U-Boat commanders and fighter pilots, *Volk in Not* (*A people in distress*, 1925, directed by Wolfgang Neff) on the war in East Prussia and Hindenburg's victory at Tannenberg, and *Heimkehr* ("*Homecoming*", 1928, directed by Joe May) on German P.O.W.s in Russia and their way back.

In the wake of the scandal surrounding Erich Maria Remarque's bestselling novel *All Quiet on the Western Front* (1929) and numerous other war novels, *Westfront 1918* (1918, directed by G.W. Pabst), among others, focused on trench warfare in northern France and Flanders. Nonfictional films focusing on particular battles and their official interpretation—composed in part with the help of historical film materials, and in part with the help of re-enactments—also

---

5 For the preferences of German audiences cf. Joseph Garncarz, *Hollywood in Deutschland: Zur Internationalisierung der Kinokultur 1925–1990* (Frankfurt am Main: Stroemfeld, 2013).

6 For these and the following titles cf. Bernadette Kester, *Film Front Weimar: Representations of the First World War in German Films of the Weimar Period (1919–1933)* (Amsterdam: Amsterdam UP, 2003).

met with enthusiastic responses: *Die Somme* (*The Somme*) (1929, directed by Heinz Paul), *Douaumont* (1931, directed by Heinz Paul), and *Tannenberg* (1932, directed by Heinz Paul) were all successful. As these titles indicate, producers and filmmakers were generally interested in events from the war that were familiar to the largest possible audience and allowed for a heroic interpretation.

With the exception of East Prussia and the Battle of Tannenberg, none of these films assign the Eastern European theater any particular significance in the progression or outcome of the World War, an observation that points to the German public's increasingly strong focus on the Western Front. The war of attrition and trench warfare became synonymous with the entirety of the First World War and the embodiment of modern warfare at around this time. Even the two-part, chronological Ufa-Kulturfilm *Der Weltkrieg* (*The World War*, 1927/28, directed by Leo Lasko, 2 Parts) references the Gorlice-Tarnów Offensive, the recapture of Lemberg (Lviv), the Serbian Front, the War in the Alps, and overall German-Austrian cooperation only in passing.[7]

Between the Fronts

In comparison to the war on the Western Front and East Prussia, the war in Eastern Europe and especially the war in Galicia appeared neither as lucrative nor particularly appropriate from a national perspective. This was certainly related to the fact that

---

7 *Der Weltkrieg* was made in collaboration with the Reichsarchiv, the State Archive; the film's first part was the fifth most successful film of the 1927–28 season, just behind *Metropolis*; cf. "Das Ergebnis der Abstimmung," *Film-Kurier*, no. 116/117, May 16, 1928. The details on the theatres of war mentioned in the film derive from the surviving one-part version released in 1933. Available as "*Der Weltkrieg: Ein historischer Film*" on http://www.filmportal.de/node/77431/video/1213579.

Galicia no longer belonged to Austria and no longer existed as a unified territory. That the rapid Russian occupation of the country immediately following the beginning of the War and the aimlessness of the Austro-Hungarian army leadership revealed by this situation were linked to traumatic experiences for the majority of the Galician population certainly did not help. The Jewish population of Galicia especially, traditionally loyal to the Emperor and opposing Russian rule, became victims of outbursts of anti-Semitic violence. The Russian Army leadership collectively believed the Jews to be engaged in espionage and ambushes.[8]

Even if the pogroms in the Galician theater during the first weeks of the war resulted from rampant prejudice and the troops' lack of discipline and not the orders of the army leadership, the consequences for the Jewish population were catastrophic: Jews were the victims of humiliation, depredation, pillaging, rape, and even murder. The atrocities in Lemberg on the 27th of September, 1914, three weeks after its occupation, earned the city a sad celebrity, as Cossacks rode shooting through the Jewish quarter and killed fifty people. News of such crimes led half Galician Jews, approximately 400,000 people, to flee to the west. The Eastern European Jews ended up in a long, "forgotten war" between the fronts, as Frank M. Schuster demonstrates in his important book on the topic.[9]

---

8 For this and the following cf. Alexander Watson, *Ring of Steel: Germany and Austria-Hungary in World War I* (New York: Basic Books, 2014), 181–188; and John R. Schindler, *Fall of the Double Eagle: The Battle for Galicia and the Demise of Austria-Hungary* (Lincoln: Potomac Books, 2015).

9 Cf. Frank M. Schuster, *Zwischen allen Fronten: Osteuropäische Juden während des Ersten Weltkriegs (1914–1919)* (Vienna: Böhlau, 2004). In military history, too, the Eastern Front remained a blind spot for a long time. On the German Eastern Front cf. Gerhard P. Groß, ed., *Die vergessene Front – der Osten 1914/15: Ereignis, Wirkung, Nachwirkung* (Paderborn: Schöningh, 2006).

German cinema audiences had already learned of the Galician theater during the World War, through newsreels and propaganda films, though to what extent is impossible to say with certainty based on the currently available and usable sources. Judging from the sparsely surviving editions of the Messter-newsreel, little argues against the idea that footage from Galicia was also shown.[10] This can't, however, be true for the early phase of the war, when the Austro-Hungarian Army suffered terrible defeats and was quickly pushed back by the Russians, leaving Galicia largely to the enemy. Indeed, it is difficult to imagine that the loss of such an important territory could have even been mentioned while the cinema was subject to strict military censorship.

On the other hand, just two weeks after the retaking of the important Galician fortress of Przemysl at the beginning of June 1915, an apparently private film company alluded to the event in advertisements for their film *Przemysl* (1915); the Russian's months-long occupation of Przemysl had led only a few months earlier to the surrender of the entire garrison and the imprisonment of approximately 110,000 Austro-Hungarian soldiers. Shortly thereafter, while fighting was still taking place around Lemberg in June of 1915, another company announced a film entitled *Ansichten aus Lemberg* (*Views from Lemberg*, 1915, produced by Max Löser).[11] The longest film on the topic was

10 Some of these Messter-newsreels include footage of Austro-Hungarian troops and name the Viennese Sascha-Film as the production company of specific segments.

11 For more data cf. "*Przemysl* (1915)," *The German Early Film Database*, http://www.earlycinema.uni-koeln.de/films/view/31884; and "*Ansichten aus Lemberg* (1915)," *The German Early Film Database*, http://www.earlycinema.uni-koeln.de/films/view/17766.

produced by the Freiburg company Expreß-Film in 1916, under the title *Die Durchbruchsschlacht in Galizien* (*The Breakthrough Battle in Galicia*, 1916, 7 reels).[12] All three films have been lost. From 1916–17 on, official propaganda films from the newly founded Bild-und Filmamt (Bufa) appeared on the war in Galicia and the neighboring regions, including the two one-reelers *Die Durchbruchsschlacht in Galizien* (*The Breakthrough Battle in Galicia*, 1917, 1 reel) and *Die Befreiung der Bukowina* (*The Liberation of Bukovina*, 1917, 1 reel).[13] It is unlikely that the fate of Galicia's Jewish population played a significant role in these lost films. Following the logic of other newsreels and propaganda films, the emphasis probably lay on the martial prowess of the army and the destruction of the enemy.

The treatment of Galicia's "forgotten war" begins first in the 1920s, with a meager corpus of films, which were screened in Germany. Like the aforementioned films *Leichte Kavallerie* ("*Light Cavalry*") and *Zwei Welten* ("*Two Worlds*"), "*Surrender*" (USA 1927, directed by Edward Sloman), too, connected the Galician location with the fate of the Jews. Also set in Galica were *Die Beichte des Feldkuraten* (*Confessions of an Army Chaplain*, A 1927, directed by

12 Cf. "*Die Durchbruchsschlacht in Galizien* (1916)," *The German Early Film Database*, http://www.earlycinema.uni-koeln.de/films/view/20791.

13 *Die Befreiung der Bukowina* is available here: *filmportal.de*, http://www.filmportal.de/node/63801/video/1220587. Another subject, titled *Aus der Durchbruchsschlacht in Galizien*, was apparently shot in July 1917 during the Tarnopol Offensive, available as part of the more accurately dated *Messter-Woche 1916*: *filmportal.de*, http://www.filmportal.de/video/messter-woche-1916. After the war, the Reichsfilmstelle (the successor of Bufa) produced the 2-reeler *Von Gorlice-Tarnow bis Lemberg vom 1. Mai bis 25. Juni 1915*, which probably recycled and re-edited older stock material to be shown in the context of military education and gatherings of veterans.

Hans Otto Löwenstein) and, chief among them and most influential, "*Hotel Imperial*" (USA 1927, directed by Mauritz Stiller).[14]

Tarnów on the Pacific

In 1926, the Hotel Imperial lay in Madrid, and the former Galicia was a dream built out of Californian plywood as the film of the same title was shot on the sets of the Pola Negri spectacle "*The Spanish Dancer*" (USA 1923, directed by Herbert Brenon), which were still lying around the Famous Players Lasky (Paramount) lot.[15] In contrast to the American title, "*Hotel Imperial*", the German title, *Hotel Stadt Lemberg*, opened up a very particular field of memory: The former capital of Galicia, Lemberg, was part of the Habsburg Empire until 1918 and after that became part of the newly-founded Republic of Poland.

"*Hotel Imperial*" is a Pola Negri film too. The big-budget American production occupies a special place in the context of this essay, not only because it was the first film shown in Germany after 1918 that took place in Galicia during the war years, but also because it paved the way for thematically related films.

If things had gone according to the wishes of producer Erich Pommer, the film would have been made in Germany, before his short 1926–27 Hollywood intermezzo. Ufa, however, rejected the content,[16]

---

14 The films were also released in Austria: "*Hotel Imperial*" was shown under the title *Hotel Stadt Lemberg*, *Leichte Kavallerie* under the title *Die Spionin* (*The Female Spy*), "*Surrender*" under the title *Ergib Dich, Weib!* (*Surrender, Woman!*).

15 Cf. Kevin Brownlow, *The Parade's Gone By...* (New York: Alfred A. Knopf, 1968), 243.

16 Cf. Roland Schacht, "Das Problem der deutschen Filmproduktion," in *Kunstwart* 40, no. 6 (March 1927): 416. On Erich Pommer and the production of *Hotel Imperial* cf. Wolfgang Jacobsen, *Erich Pommer: Ein Produzent macht Filmgeschichte* (Berlin: Argon, 1989), 79–82.

although it was based on Hungarian author and screenwriter Lajos (in Germany also known as Ludwig) Biró's bestseller *Hotel Stadt Lemberg*, published in German in 1916 by Ullstein-Verlag.[17] In 1917, the novel was re-worked for the theater, and a now apparently lost film version appeared in the last year of the war in Hungary, under the direction of Jenö Janovics.[18] The subject matter proved popular again in 1929, when Jean Gilbert and Ernst Neubach brought *Hotel Stadt Lemberg* to the stage as an operetta.[19] In 1939 and 1943, Biró's story was again adapted for the cinema.[20]

"Hotel Imperial" depicts an episode from 1915, as the Russian Army occupies a large part of Galicia and can only be dislodged by a combined German and Austrian force several months later.[21] Although

---

17 Ludwig Biro, *Hotel Stadt Lemberg*. Translated from Hungarian by Eduard Kadossa (Berlin: Ullstein, 1916). The novel was reprinted numerous times; by 1928, 281,000 copies had been sold.

18 For a short review of *Hotel Imperial* (Hungary 1918, 1,880 m, 6 reels), cf. *Paimanns Film-Liste*, no. 144, Nov. 29–Dec. 5, 1918, 1. In Austria the 1918 film's title was "Hotel Stadt Lemberg." According to Paimann's summary, the story did not differ from the 1927 version.

19 Cf. e.g. the reviews by Edwin Neruda: "'Hotel Stadt Lemberg': Erstaufführung im Theater des Westens," *Vossische Zeitung*, no. 609 (Dec. 27, 1929) and S-e., "Film als Operette: Erstaufführung von 'Hotel Stadt Lemberg,'" *Deutsche Allgemeine Zeitung*, no. 599 (Dec. 27, 1929).

20 Cf. *Hotel Imperial* (USA 1939, Dir. Robert Florey) and *Five Graves to Cairo* (USA 1943, Dir. Billy Wilder); in fact, Wilder, born 1906 in Galicia, and his family emigrated to Vienna during the war. For some time, Wilder's father was a hotel owner.

21 Neither the German version of "*Hotel Imperial*" nor the censorship card with the German intertitles have survived. Therefore, my analysis refers to the American version of which a 35mm print (2,160 m) is held in the Library of Congress (Washington). The film has been released on DVD by Grapevine Video (length: 77 minutes), however, the visual quality of this DVD is poor.

the film takes place between March and May 1915 and the specific location of the story is never given, the literary model provides enough topographical and temporally precise details to deduce that it takes place in Tarnów between November 1914 and May 1915. Biró's opening shows the advance of the Russians to the Dunajec River in Western Galicia following the Battle of Lemberg. In fact, Battle of Lemberg meant a decisive defeat for the Austro-Hungarian Army and resulted in catastrophic losses. The film ends with the Battle of Gorlice-Tarnów, which brought about a turning point in the fortunes of the Central Powers. On the heels of the Battle of Gorlice-Tarnów followed not only the recapture of Lemberg, but of all the Polish territories occupied by Russia. In reference to this latter event, tied as it was to important victories in Germany and Austria, the German distribution earned the subtitle: "The Heroine of Tarnow."[22]

The Lieutenant as Head Waiter

The story follows a noble Austrian Hussar lieutenant, Paul Almasy (James Hall), who's caught behind enemy lines. Pursued by the Russians, Almasy uses his last ounce of strength to flee into the eponymous hotel, where he sinks into a deep sleep. In the hotel, which comes across as extremely provincial despite its name and has no guests, he is hidden by the parlor maid Anna (Pola Negri), the actual hero, the loyal porter Elias (Max Davidson), and the sullen cook Anton, who's in love with Anna. The Russians

22 Apparently, the city of Tarnów was directly mentioned in the German version. At least several critics referred to Tarnów in their reviews. Cf. F.D-S. [Fränze Dyck-Schnitzer], "Hotel Stadt Lemberg," *Berliner Volks-Zeitung*, no. 9 (Jan. 6, 1927), and Willy Haas, "Hotel Stadt Lemberg," *Film-Kurier*, no. 5 (Jan. 6, 1927), reprinted in Willy Haas, *Der Kritiker als Mitproduzent: Texte zum Film 1920–1933*, ed. Wolfgang Jacobsen et al. (Berlin: Ed. Hentrich, 1991), 192–195.

move into the city without resistance, and their General (George Siegmann) makes the hotel his headquarters. Almasy, whose way back to his lines is cut off, finds himself in the middle of enemy headquarters. He remains unrecognized, and Anna passes him off as the Hungarian head waiter; the real head waiter had fled before the advancing Russians. The General is immediately taken with Anna, who attracts him with her genuine and spirited nature. He makes her the lady of the house and outfits her with fashionable clothes and jewelry. Anna goes so far as to encourage the general's amorous advances in order to protect Almasy from the looming threat of imprisonment occasioned by his lack of papers. She convinces the General that the waiter, whom she obviously likes, is indispensable. In the meantime, the General also sends out his best spy, Petroff (Michael Vavitch), on a mission to sniff out information regarding the enemy's troop deployments.[23]

When Petroff returns during a rambunctious Russian festival covered in mud, but apparently successful, Almasy senses danger. Anna gets the General drunk in his room and ensures that Petroff isn't allowed in, while Almasy runs a hot bath for Petroff—before shooting the unsuspecting spy, who finds himself alone with Almasy in the bathroom. He had to do it, he explains to Anna, to save the lives of thousands. Anna takes the initiative, burns Petroff's notebooks and makes it look like the spy committed suicide. As suspicions falls on Almasy and he's threatened with execution, Anna gives him an alibi: he had spent the time period in question with her. The General then flies into a rage, rips off Anna's expensive clothes and casts her out. Almasy escapes the same night and makes his way back to his regiment.

23 In the German version the spy's name is Tabakowitsch—as in Biro's novel.

The great offensive of the Austro-Hungarian army begins the next day and takes the Russians completely off guard. The troops have to pull out in a hurry and abandon the hotel. Shortly thereafter, Almasy enters the city on horseback in his dress uniform alongside the Austro-Hungarian troops, who are greeted enthusiastically by the townsfolk. The soldiers take part in a mass in front of the church; then Almasy is supposed to be honored with a medal for his bravery. From the mass of spectators, he calls Anna forward and introduces her to the Commandant, who greets her like a noblewoman and thanks her for her great service to her country. He grants Almasy a short leave to get his personal affairs in order—that is, to marry Anna.

Transformations and Transgressions

In the film that takes place largely at night, Galicia is primarily represented by the not particularly elegant, somewhat dusty hotel, which seems cut off from the outside world.[24] The wall around the building and the heavy venetian blinds covering the windows only allow glimpses through narrow slits and bars into the threatening outside world, and not many good things make it through the doors. It's the place of the small, cramped rooms, in which the staircase covers the screen and introduces a rare diagonal. It constantly draws attention to the symbolic passage between above and below. In a short period of time, Russians, Austrians, Hungarians, and other unspecified ethnic groups, (female) civilians, and (male) soldiers encounter each other in this space.

24 For a nuanced reading of the film focusing on its director Mauritz Stiller, cf. Arne Lunde, *Nordic Exposures: Scandinavian Identities in Classical Hollywood Cinema* (Seattle: University of Washington Press, 2010), 63–90.

Here, different forms of existence come into contact. Next to the male personnel, Elias and Anton, we meet Anna, whose first scene has her scrubbing the stairs. Later, if she isn't yet a countess, she is nevertheless outfitted like a rich mistress and, finally, in a simple dress, she finds her prince. Anna, too, brings out the sexual motivations of the belligerent men. As she explains to the General, men only make war because their own wives have begun to bore them; men in search of different sexual experiences in the war exercise violence on women.

We meet a noble officer who loses his troops and his military rank, has to disguise himself, suffers under the fear of discovery, and—also in a social sense—transforms into a waiter; a general who first demonstrates independence and a certain masculine strength, and in the end jealousy and overconfidence; a spy who appears in a diverse array of disguises and then, when he tries to climb naked into a bathtub, is shot by another man in disguise. As if he had to protect his true identity, the first thing the murderer does after the crime is to wipe the steam off the mirror and stare in horror at his own reflection; we have already had occasion to witness the nightmares about the war that wake him covered in sweat. Compulsion, and this game of hide-and-seek, characterize Almasy as well as the rest of the film.

The Hotel Imperial is thus a place of transformations, of both the crossing and the blurring of borders, where occupier and occupied live under one roof, and camouflage and masquerades are essential for survival. Not even the hotel's name remains untainted by a loss of meaning and oscillations, because the Habsburg Empire, which the hotel's name obviously points to, fails to protect its subjects from the imperial might of the czar. It seems to express an especially bitter irony when the film equates the invasion or penetration of the various armies—first Russian, then Austro-Hungarian—into the civilian world of the city. It was all the same to the viewer who saw the film in 1927, the year it was released: Both empires, the Austro-Hungarian as well as the Russian, had long since passed into history.

A Desire for Reconciliation?

On the 1 January, 1927, "*Hotel Imperial*" celebrated its premiere in New York, and the film began its run in Berlin only a few days later. The German critics raved about its engrossing drama, the elegant cinematography, and the performance of the actors, with Pola Negri leading the way. At the same time, critics noted a business-minded mixture of romance, adventure, and war.[25] Opinion divided itself according to aesthetic and political sensibilities as to whether or not to criticize *Hotel Imperial* or even flatly dismiss it as a "fairly regular hero film"[26] and a "typically German, Austro-Hungarian film for American palates"[27]—or to greet it as the product of a "pointed desire for reconciliation"[28] and a "worthy and sublime" portrayal of the events of the war.[29] Some saw in "*Hotel Imperial*" mainly an exciting spy movie laden with special effects.[30]

---

25 For a brief overview of the politicized press reception of *Hotel Imperial*, cf. also Saunders, "Politics, the Cinema, and Early Revisitations of War in Weimar Germany," 39–40.

26 Ernst Blass, "Hotel Stadt Lemberg," *Berliner Tageblatt*, no. 14 (Jan. 9, 1927).

27 L.R., "Nationalistische Filme: 'Hotel Stadt Lemberg,'" *Rote Fahne*, no. 5 (Jan. 7, 1927).

28 E.B. [Erna Büsing], "Hotel Stadt Lemberg," *Vorwärts*, no. 14 (Jan. 9, 1927).

29 R., "Hotel Stadt Lemberg," *Neue Preußische Zeitung*, no. 9 (Jan. 7, 1927).

30 Cf. I.E. -L., "Hotel Stadt Lemberg," *Berliner Börsen-Courier*, no. 8 (Jan. 6, 1927); and Dr. Konrad Glück, "Hotel Stadt Lemberg," *Berliner Morgenpost*, no. 6 (Jan. 7, 1927).

"The miracle has happened: the Americans, who were still making anti-German war movies two years ago, have created a counter-example here; a more German-friendly version could hardly be thought of," praised the right-wing, conservative *Börsen-Zeitung*.[31] In the context of the larger controversy surrounding the genre of war films at that time, *Germania*, the journal of the Catholic Centre Party, attacked the film because "all the work spent on peace scatters like so much chaff in the face of these splendidly staged scenes"; thus, for *Germania*, the film is totally unfit to stabilize the will to "No More War!"[32] And in the liberal *Berliner Tageblatt*, they condemn the manner in which "bloody and lewd situations in the guise of a freshly experienced war are exploited for excitement, emotion, and enthusiasm."[33] According to the social-democratic *Vorwärts*, the film "falls radiantly into the commonplaces of the usual militaristic hype" and in so doing alienates those opposed to national military films: "[If] further cinematic illustrations of the reports of the OHL should follow, then we better prepare for the worst."[34]

The clearest is the condemnation from the communist press: "This film about 1915 is filmed in such a way as to give 1915 all honors. Imperial and royal through thick and thin. Exactly as it is, it could have cropped up as in Austro-Hungary and Germany in those days as cheap propaganda. Nothing's missing. Avowals: 'We are good Austrians.' Dream-images of God, Emperor and fatherland. [...] One hardly believes his eyes. More than ten years have passed since

31 Fritz Olimsky, "Hotel Stadt Lemberg," *Berliner Börsen-Zeitung*, no. 8 (Jan. 6, 1927).

32 J., "Hotel Stadt Lemberg," *Germania*, no. 9 (Jan. 7, 1927).

33 Ernst Blass, "Hotel Stadt Lemberg," *Berliner Tageblatt*, no. 14 (Jan. 9, 1927).

34 E. B. [Erna Büsing], "Hotel Stadt Lemberg," *Vorwärts*, no. 14 (Jan. 9, 1927). OHL is short for *Oberste Heeresleitung* (Army High Command).

then—and yet people still dare to bring out such a 'timely' piece of trash that rekindles the hopeless Austro-Hungarian militarism!"[35]

Of the public's reaction after the withdrawal of the Russians, Willy Haas writes in the *Film-Kurier*: "At the entrance of the Austrian troops, thunderous applause rang out and lasted for minutes. But it was no war fever, no nationalism. It was because it achieved a *Bildmusik*, like sunshine blazing forth, exultant and radiant. It's a very particular film: its equal was, in its way, not yet there."[36]

It is worth mentioning that, in contrast to Biró's novel, neither in contemporary reviews nor in the plot of *Hotel Imperial* does it come out that Galicia, where the story takes place, was, among other ethnic groups, home to a significant Jewish population, and that cities like Tarnów and Lemberg were centers of urban Jewish culture.

The Hussar and the Beautiful Jewess

Ten months after the German premiere of "*Hotel Imperial*", two more films that take place in Galicia during the war, now lost, came to German theaters within days of each other in October 1927: *Die Beichte des Feldkuraten* (*Confessions of an Army Chaplain*) and *Leichte Kavallerie* ("*Light Cavalry*"). In the meantime, numerous other big war films celebrated their premiere, which is why one can sense a certain tedium regarding the theme in the Berlin Press in the fall of 1927.

The Austrian film *Confessions of an Army Chaplain*, produced by the Viennese Sascha Film-Industrie after a script by Walter Reisch, plays in Germany with the title *The Court Martial of Gorlice* (*Das Feldgericht von Gorlice*), which specifically places the plot

35 L.R., "Nationalistische Filme 'Hotel Stadt Lemberg,'" *Rote Fahne*, no. 5 (Jan. 7, 1927).

36 Willy Haas, "Hotel Stadt Lemberg," *Film-Kurier*, no. 5 (Jan. 6, 1927), quoted from Willy Haas, *Der Kritiker als Mitproduzent: Texte zum Film 1920–1933*, ed. Wolfgang Jacobsen et al. (Berlin: Ed. Hentrich, 1991), 192–195, here: 195.

geographically. According to the surviving sources, the film depicts the tragic love story of an Austrian officer (Hans Marr) and a Polish countess (Dagny Servaes) who meet again during the war through a present-day frame narrative of the memories of a priest (Ingo Sym).[37] In his function as a military judge, the officer mistakenly condemns a Polish farmer to death for corpse-robbing. He first learns during the Russian attack that the farmer had orders from the Polish countess to bring her daughter to safety—the very same daughter that resulted from the earlier relationship with the officer, of whom the father knows nothing. Although the daughter is brought out of the combat zone early enough, and the Polish farmer escapes the death penalty, the officer and his rediscovered love, the Polish countess, end up Russian prisoners of war and are only reunited—now married—with their child after the end of the war.

No numbers attest to the success of *Confessions of an Army Chaplain* in Germany. Reviews in the Berlin dailies were overwhelmingly negative.[38] The trade journal *Der Film* nonetheless

37 For a summary cf. LBB-Kinoprogramm, "Das Feldgericht von Gorlice," (Bundesarchiv-Filmarchiv, Schriftgutarchiv). In Germany, the film was released by *Messtro-Film-Verleih GmbH*. In Austria, it was also released as *Das Feldgericht von Uszok*, probably hinting to the small town Uschok, South of Przemyśl.

38 Cf. e.g. W.B., "Das Feldgericht von Gorlice," *B.Z. am Mittag*, no. 279 (Oct. 28, 1927); "Das Feldgericht von Gorlice," *Berliner Börsen-Courier*, no. 508 (Oct. 28, 1927); "Das Feldgericht von Gorlice," *Berliner Börsen-Zeitung*, no. 505 (Oct. 28, 1927); R., "Das Feldgericht von Gorlice," *Vorwärts*, no. 514 (Oct. 30, 1927); -ü-, "Das Feldgericht von Gorlice," *Vossische Zeitung*, no. 514 (Oct. 30, 1927); F.D-S. [Fränze Dyck-Schnitzer], "*Das Feldgericht von Gorlice,*" *Berliner Volks-Zeitung*, no. 518 (Nov. 2, 1927). *Der Montag* praised "gripping images from the struggles at the Eastern Front." Cf. "*Das Feldgericht von Gorlice*," *Der Montag (Montagsausgabe des Berliner Lokal-Anzeigers)*, no. 42 (Oct. 31, 1927). The reference to "true images" from the front line may indicate that historical stock footage was edited into the film.

praised the "war scenes" that came across as "not staged [...], but rather real" and drew attention to the fact that this was the first film to treat the Court Martial theme. The film asks, according to the article: "Is the fate of one man important at a time when thousands are dying?"[39]

In contrast to *Confessions of an Army Chaplain*, where apparently nothing hints at the existence of a Jewish population in Galicia, precisely this Jewish population plays a central role in the Phoebus production "*Light Cavalry*".[40] Also for this film, all the information we have is from censorship and press materials, but the relationship to "*Hotel Imperial*", remarked by many critics of the day, is patently obvious, to such an extent

39 The answer of the reviewer was (in German): "Gewiß, der Bauer Wojtech ist unschuldig zum Tode verurteilt. Für uns, die wir den Tatvorgang mitangesehen haben, bedeuten die Indizien, die gegen ihn sprechen und das Kriegsgericht zu seiner Verurteilung veranlaßten, nichts. Aber vorne an der Front kämpfen die Unseren, und unser Herz ist mit ihnen, mag auch das Schicksal dieses Einen noch so furchtbar sein"; Fedor Kaul, "Das Feldgericht von Gorlice," *Der Film (Sonderausgabe: Kritiken der Woche)* (Oct. 29, 1927). The film was banned for young viewers by the Supreme Board of Film Censors, because of "the inappropriate presentation of a trial ending with a death sentence." This, the censors continued, "appears as a heavy burden in a spiritual sense endangering the mental development of young people"; cf. decision of the board of censorship, no. 86, from Jan. 28, 1928 (Deutsches Filminstitut, Schriftgutarchiv), available here: http://www.difarchiv.deutsches-filminstitut.de/zengut/df2tb339z.pdf.

40 The title "Leichte Kavallerie" refers to an operetta of the same title by Franz von Suppé and Karl Costa, written in 1866; it deals with love life in a provincial town in Austria that is affected by the arrival of Hungarian hussars.

that one could employ an expression from the time period and call it a *Neuauflage*, a new edition.[41] The story takes place in Galicia in October 1914, near the Russian border, where in this case no Russian troops, but rather a squadron from the Austro-Hungarian Hussar Regiment Nr. 9, stops in a small village during their advance: The first lieutenant (Alfons Fryland) finds quarters in the estate of the countess Komarôff (Vivian Gibson), lieutenant count Starhemberg (André Mattoni) is lodged in the house of the rabbi Süß (Albert Steinrück), and the Hungarian sergeant Farkas (Fritz Kampers) by the general store owner Moritz Wasserstrahl (Siegfried Arno), an apparently orthodox Jew with *payot* (sidelocks).[42]

As in "*Hotel Imperial*", the encounter between the not-entirely welcome soldiers and civilians is intertwined with struggles for love, jealousy, and espionage: The countess Komarôff, who makes a secret pact with the Russians, manages to seduce the first lieutenant and pump him for information that she sends to the Russian army leadership through her husband (Jack Mylong-Münz), who's living in hiding (and often appears in disguise). At the same time, Starhemberg and Rahel (Elizza la Porta), the Rabbi's charming daughter, fall in love; but the Rabbi cannot stand Rahel's relationship with someone of a different creed, and wants to send her as quickly as possible out of the combat zone to live with relatives in Vienna and protect her (sexual) integrity. Starhemberg, on the other hand, confesses his love and tells

---

41 Cf. F.D-S. [Fränze Dyck-Schnitzer], "Leichte Kavallerie," *Berliner Volks-Zeitung*, no. 494 (Oct. 19, 1927).

42 Cf. the photography of Arno as Wasserstrahl in *Illustrierter Film-Kurier*, no. 688 (1927) (Deutsche Kinemathek, Schriftgutsammlung).

the Rabbi that he feels strong enough to "overcome outmoded prejudices."[43]

The melodramatic entanglements of the officers are contrasted in the film with a comical male duo, played by Fritz Kampers (as Farkas) and Siegfried Arno (as Wasserstrahl). Farkas teases Wasserstrahl by constantly mispronouncing his name (he calls him Wasservogel, Wasserkopf, Wasserkrug). In addition, the Hungarian Farkas is a lady's man; it's he who constantly repeats the verse of the song that gives the film its name: "Today it's her—tomorrow she, / Thus kisses the light cavalry!"[44]

The last third of the film sees events following in rapid succession: Farkas, Wasserstrahl, and the Rabbi learn that the countess Komarôff has betrayed an important order to the Russians, who now want to attack the town. The lieutenant is informed immediately, but the Russians have already cut the telephone lines to the next-closest unit. The squadron is surrounded and threatened with capture. At the last second, Rahel manages to sneak through the enemy lines and bring German soldiers to the rescue; the Russians are forced to retreat, and the victors enter the city to the tune of a march. (At this point, the premiere audience clapped loudly.[45]) The commandant thanks Rahel in grand style

---

43 Quoted from the censorship card for *Leichte Kavallerie*, B. 16777, Sept. 28, 1927 (Bundesarchiv-Filmarchiv, Berlin), Akt 6, Titel 2. At the beginning, Starhemberg apparently falls in love with Rahel's violin playing, which he associates with "so much fervor and desire at the same time"; cf. ibid., Akt 2, Titel 9.

44 Cf. censorship card for *Leichte Kavallerie*, B. 16777, Sept. 28, 1927 (Bundesarchiv-Filmarchiv, Berlin), Akt 3, Titel 13, Akt 5, Titel 3 and 6, Akt 7, Titel 18.

45 Cf. Georg Herzberg, "Leichte Kavallerie," *Film-Kurier*, no. 243 (Oct. 14, 1927). According to *Berliner Volks-Zeitung*, no. 494 (Oct. 19, 1927) the "entry of the victorious army was accompanied by the 'Radetzky-Marsch.'"

for her "decisive and self-sacrificing actions."[46] While she devotes herself to caring for Starhemberg, who was wounded in the battle, Wasserstrahl reports to Farkas to volunteer for military service. Although Wasserstrahl wore the clothing of an orthodox Jew at the beginning of the film, at the end he wears an Austro-Hungarian uniform. The viewer can only presume that this should be read as a renunciation of a tradition-conscious Judaism (that Rahel's father, the Rabbi, stands for) and a pointed identification with the (Roman Catholic) Austrian Empire—even, perhaps, as an act of conversion.

The commonalities between "*Light Cavalry*" and "*Hotel Imperial*" in terms of plot are obvious: They stretch from the love between officer and civilian, a love rendered more complex because of social, religious, and ethnic differences, from the seduction of an officer and the betrayal of a secret, up to the decisive assistance of a woman in the defeat of the enemy and the official recognition of her services at the end. Although the Jewish dimension of Birós's novel comes through only cryptically, if at all, in the film version of "*Hotel Imperial*", it is immediately present in the screenplay for "*Light Cavalry*", by the Bucharest-born Jewish author Emanuel Alifieri. Military success in this latter film depends directly on the dedication of Jewish civilians, which is motivated in turn by a historically conditioned fear of persecution by the Russian Army as well as by romantic relationships that are able to transcend differences between Jewish and Christian beliefs.

Soldiers' Humor and the Pangs of Love

Whether transformations, the crossing and blurring of borders were portrayed in "*Light Cavalry*" as they are in "*Hotel Imperial*" must remain an open question. If we follow contemporary critics,

---

46 Censorship card for *Leichte Kavallerie*, B. 16777, Sept. 28, 1927 (Bundesarchiv-Filmarchiv, Berlin), Akt 7, Titel 14.

the essential difference to the earlier film was that "*Light Cavalry*" possessed neither a unified narrative attitude, nor a unified, appropriate aesthetic mold.

"A war film in a minor key and cushioned very softly. But that shouldn't be a primary criticism, that reports of funny situations, of soldiers' humor, or of seductively illuminated pangs of love, also come from the lines, but rather that this is driven by falsehood, kitsch, and cheap showmanship," writes the *Berliner Tageblatt* after the premiere of "*Light Cavalry*".[47] Hans Sahl, similarly dismayed, condemns the film in the *Börsen-Courier*: In his eyes, the film completely lacks the "terrifying nearness of the war in "*Hotel Imperial*", the oppressively real seriousness" and instead presents "a comfortable mess of feelings and militarism." He continues: "For the German film, the war is still a fun maneuver with colorful flags and agreeable-sounding games." The result is "a shameful film. [...] Everything is seen skewed, incorrectly, un-psychologically."[48]

Compared to such general impressions—in no way shared by all critics—the dissatisfaction of several reviewers with the casting of several roles seems largely secondary.[49] The acting of Albert Steinrück as the rabbi and Siegfried Arno as Wasserstrahl are both, however, positively emphasized.[50] "The milieu of the

---

47 Lo., "Leichte Kavallerie," *Berliner Tageblatt*, no. 490 (Oct. 16, 1927).

48 Hans Sahl, "Leichte Kavallerie," *Berliner Börsen-Courier*, no. 485 (Oct. 16, 1927).

49 The casting of Elizza la Porta as Rahel and André Mattoni as Starhemberg was particularly criticized for the amount of cliché. Cf. e.g. "Leichte Kavallerie," *B.Z. am Mittag*, no. 267 (Oct. 14, 1927); and G.H., "Leichte Kavallerie," *Berliner Morgenpost*, no. 248 (Oct. 16, 1927).

50 Cf. e.g. E.Cz., "Leichte Kavallerie," *Vossische Zeitung*, no. 490 (Oct. 16, 1927); and Hans Sahl, "Leichte Kavallerie," *Berliner Börsen-Courier*, no. 485 (Oct. 16, 1927).

Galician village and especially its Jewish community is painted lovingly and with obvious expertise," praises the *Börsen-Zeitung*.[51]

The "mixture of sentimental, serious, and humorous [aspects]" was simultaneously deemed "skillful" and a recipe for a good box office draw in the countryside.[52] As the secondary plot thread around Farkas and Wasserstrahl shows, the film also wanted to emulate the numerous popular barracks comedies. On that note, Georg Herzberg writes in the *Film-Kurier*: "The author Emanuel Alfieri can be criticized in that he takes the gruesome war and robs it of its horror, turns it into an operetta and sugar-coats it in order to make [the war] carry an entertainment film. These are justified impressions, but no more than Alfieri's response that the vast majority of moviegoers don't think much about it, that they still like soldiers' humor and a tiny bit of the pangs of love, and are completely satisfied if the German troops triumphantly defeat Russia. For that reason, I feel a responsibility to remind critics in their criticisms of the author not to forget the public, who very much like seeing such films, and who, despite everything, don't want to hear anything about pacifism. And about realistic depictions of war, even less."[53]

The Prince and the Beautiful Jewess

Like "*Light Cavalry*", "*Surrender*" avoids such "realistic depictions of war," which first become central, if never completely dominant, modes of the cinematic portrayal of war in the wake of "*The Big Parade*", and in a major way only after "*All Quiet on the Western*

51 Oly. [Fritz Olimsky], "Leichte Kavallerie," *Berliner Börsen-Zeitung*, no. 485 (Oct. 16, 1927).

52 Fedor Kaul, "Leichte Kavallerie," *Der Film, Sonderausgabe 'Kritiken der Woche'* (Oct. 15, 1927).

53 Georg Herzberg, "Leichte Kavallerie," *Film-Kurier*, no. 243 (Oct. 14, 1927).

Front" (USA 1930, directed by Lewis Milestone). As before in "*Hotel Imperial*", a young woman occupies the focal point. And once again the audience encounters romantic entanglements and allegorical elements with regards to Jews and non-Jews, as in "*Light Cavalry*". Critics also pointed to the close connection between "*Surrender*" and "*Hotel Imperial*".[54]

The story is set at the beginning of the war in a small town with a majority Jewish population in the Austrian part of Galicia close to the Russian border.[55] At the river that marks the border between the two empires, Lea (Mary Philbin) meets a Russian called Konstantin (Ivan Mosjukin), and the two get to talking. When Lea's old father, Rabbi Mendel Lyon (Nigel de Brulier), finds the couple holding hands, he attacks Konstantin and accuses him of being an oppressor of the Jews. He demands that Konstantin leave Austrian soil immediately. Konstantin replies, rather arrogantly, that he is not used to following the orders of Jews. A delegation of Russian officers arrives on the scene, and to the surprise of Lea and her father, it is revealed that Konstantin is in fact the commander of a Cossack regiment and a member of the Russian high aristocracy.

54 Cf. e.g. Dr. F.K. [Fedor Kaul], "Opfer," *Der Film (Kritiken der Woche)* (Jan. 21, 1928). Heinz Pol speaks of a "dull extraction" of "*Hotel Imperial*" in H.P. [Heinz Pol], "Opfer," *Vossische Zeitung*, no. 37 (Jan. 22, 1928).

55 Neither the German version of "*Surrender*", released under the title *Opfer*, nor the German censorship card has survived. Therefore, what follows is based on an American DVD-version, released by Grapevine Video (length 77 minutes). The length of the DVD differs greatly from the length of the German version from 1928 (2,400 m), which again differed from the American original version (which, according to the catalog of the American Film Institute, was 2,514 m long). The existing 77 minutes DVD release is apparently made from a restored 16mm copy from the National Center for Jewish Film (Brandeis University).

The party splits up, but shortly after, when the war breaks out, Konstantin's regiment occupies the town Lea lives in. He wants to see her again and orders a house searched. He eventually finds her hidden in the Torah Ark, where the rabbi has locked her out of concerns for her safety. That very moment, the beginning of the Sabbath is announced, and Konstantin, the uninvited visitor, joins in the Jewish family's celebration. His power and violent intrusion stands in stark contrast to both his ignorance of Jewish rituals and the rabbi's dignity and him being indomitable. The situation gets worse when the Russian guards bring in a young man, Joshua, who wears the habit of an Orthodox Jew. Joshua has already been engaged to Lea for many years, but it is quite obvious that no mutual bond of love exists between the two. Konstantin asks Lea whether she loves Joshua. As she hesitates to answer, her father replies that it is her duty to do so. Joshua agrees. Coldly, Konstantin puts the party to a test: He gives orders that the guards shall execute Joshua on the spot. He would only change his mind if Lea were willing to ask him for mercy on Joshua's behalf and give him, Konstantin, a kiss. She refuses. Konstantin, now enraged, issues an ultimatum saying that the whole town with all inhabitants will be burnt down to the ground if Lea does not visit him in his hotel room on the very evening. Quickly, the whole community gathers in front of the rabbi's house and begs Lea to fulfil Konstantin's demand, thus following the example of the biblical Esther who sacrificed herself for the sake of her people. However, the rabbi answers to the crowd that according to the law of Moses one is not allowed to commit a sin even if this saves you from dying. Thus, it becomes a question is what is more important: ethical values or one's life.

The Russian soldiers nail up the houses and wait with burning torches in their hands for Konstantin's order. Only then Lea walks down the street to see Konstantin who—as if he were another person—now welcomes her in a sweet and gentle way. He tries his best to make her forget the previous night's atmosphere of fear and threat. Finally, the two kiss each other, confessing their mutual affection and exchanging a ring as a token of their love. As at the beginning of the film, the couple is interrupted. This time, Konstantin receives the message that the Austrian are attacking, and his regiment has to retreat immediately, but he remains with Lea until the town is taken by the Austrians. They are surprised by Joshua. When Joshua shoots at Konstantin, Lea takes his gun away and thus allows Konstantin to flee.

The town is liberated but the Jewish community—agitated by Joshua—gathers in a crowd and accuses Lea of treachery. Even her father abandons her. He only changes his mind when people start to throw stones at Lea. As the rabbi tries to save his daughter, he himself is killed by a stone. Years later, Konstantin, in the costume of a simple peasant, returns to the small town where Lea is taking care of her father's grave. The couple meets on a bridge, finally reunited.

As in "*Hotel Imperial*", the film's heroine is a young woman who arouses the desire of an enemy officer. Again, a strong social imbalance accompanies this relationship between a simple Jewish girl and the Russian prince. From this relationship there results a conflict within the Jewish family that resembles the one in "*Light Cavalry*": From the first moment on, the rabbi's daughter is enthralled by Konstantin, the foreigner, a feeling her father clearly objects to. In "*Surrender*", as in the earlier films, the young heroine is responsible for saving a community threatened by enemies.

Made by the Hollywood studio Universal Pictures, "*Surrender*" was shot under the presidency of Carl Laemmle, himself a German immigrant; Austro-Hungarian-born Paul Kohner led the production. The film's story, based on the play *Lea Lyon* (ca. 1915) by Hungarian writer Sándor Bródy, had already been adapted into a film by Hungarian director Sándor (Alexander) Korda in 1915. As with "*Hotel Imperial*", the important figures in the film's production, Laemmle, Kohner, and Bródy, were Jewish, which also applies to the director, the Englishman Edward Sloman. He casted inhabitants of Los Angeles's Jewish quarter as extras and took great care to stage Jewish rituals in his film in an accurate way.[56] By 1927, Sloman had already directed several films set in Jewish milieus, among them "*Vengeance of the Oppressed*" (USA 1916), a drama about a Jewish student who emigrated from Russia to the United States to avenge the murder of his family in a pogrom by a Cossack regiment.

In German cinemas, "*Surrender*" screened beginning in January of 1928. Most of the reviewers disliked the film and criticized the amount of incredible events, weak directing, and poor casting, particularly with regards to the female hero played by Mary Philbin.[57] At the same time, they assumed that the film had a certain box office appeal because of the popularity of Ivan Mosjukin in Germany. They also lauded the accuracy of the images of the Jewish milieu.[58]

Several critics found flaws in the depiction of the film's conflicts which, in their view, appear too trivial, overtly romanticized, and thereby too easily consumable (which should be understood as a blow against the usual Hollywood patterns). The review from *Film-Kurier* notes: "It is an old fairy tale: the blond-haired knight falls in love with the beautiful Jewish mademoiselle. Esther saves the

---

56 Cf. Kevin Brownlow, *Behind the Mask of Innocence* (London: Vintage, 1991), 407–408.

57 Cf. the reviews by M.K. [Michael Kurd], "Hingabe oder Opfer," *Welt am Abend*, no. 15 (Jan. 18, 1928); he says "Der Film verdient den Nobelpreis für Edelkitsch. […] Es trieft von Banalität, Verlogenheit und Unwahrscheinlichkeit"; bon. [Werner Bonwitt], "Opfer," *B.Z. am Mittag*, no. 20 (Jan. 20, 1928); Bonwitt admits that the film's intention to reconcile various peoples and religions may be praised but appears to be very exaggerated; Dr. F.K. [Fedor Kaul]: "Opfer," *Der Film (Kritiken der Woche)* (Jan. 21, 1928); H.P. [Heinz Pol], "Opfer," *Vossische Zeitung*, no. 37 (Jan. 22, 1928); "Hingabe," *Berliner Volks-Zeitung*, no. 41 (Jan. 25, 1928).

58 R., "Opfer," *Vorwärts*, no. 37 (Jan. 22, 1928).

Jews by dispossessing Haman. Judith was an even more hysterical heroine. And Lea Lyon from Alexander Brody's play, on which this film was modeled, belongs into the same line of heroic Jewish women. However, here she acts in the film's spirit like a child of her Americanized time: She saves her Russian Holofernes instead of killing him, and she marries him after the war. Circa 1924."[59]

Surrender Becomes Sacrifice

Prior to the release of "*Surrender*" in Germany, the board of censorship (*Film-Prüfstelle*) decided that the original German release title, *Hingabe*, had to be changed, because it was understood as a sexual surrender and the board imputed to it a corrupting influence.[60]

This change of title raises a few questions. While the original title "*Surrender*" can be understood both as religious devotion and in military sense as capitulation, the new title, *Opfer*, which in German means both victim, victims, and sacrifice, leaves everything open to interpretation. Who or what is meant to be understood as a "victim" or a "sacrifice"? Is the viewer asked to regard Lea's involuntary extradition to the enemy as a "sacrifice"? Or shall we see the civilians, that is, the Jews in occupied Galicia, as "victims" of war and violence? The question is further complicated by the fact that in the course of events "victims" turn into

59 Ernst Jäger, "'Opfer' ('Hingabe')," *Film-Kurier*, no. 16 (Jan. 10, 1928). Mordaunt Hall hints to another literary source next to the bible with Esther and Judith, namely Guy de Maupassant's story "Boule de Suif" (1880), which is set to the backdrop of the Franco-German War of 1870; cf. Guy de Maupassant, "The Ingrates," *New York Times*, Oct. 11, 1927.

60 Cf. decision of the Board of Censorship (Film-Prüfstelle), no. 17911, Jan. 16, 1928 (Deutsches Filminstitut, Schriftgutarchiv), available here: http://www.difarchiv.deutsches-filminstitut.de/zengut/df2tb503zb.pdf.

perpetrators: Not only does Lea sacrifice herself for her community, but in the end Lea is made a victim of this very community when she is expulsed and stoned by a fanatic crowd. Indeed, Sloman depicts the upheaval in the end like a pogrom. The erotic relationship between a Jewish woman and a Russian man that is suggested from their first accidental encounter at the river appears as a deadly sin from the Jewish community's perspective—a sin for which the woman has to pay with her life. In this logic, there is no space between the woman as the savior and the woman as a sinner. The film clearly criticizes this rigor in that it ends with the image of the new couple, with the reconciliation of seemingly opposing attitudes.

Compared with the other films about the occupation of Galicia discussed so far, "*Surrender*" stands out for one reason in particular: No other film is so clear and unmistakable about the depiction of rape, of taking hostages, and the extermination of the Jewish population as a deadly threat. Neither do other movies dealing with the First World War in the mid- and late-1920s (that is, after the period of hate propaganda) show so drastically that the regime of occupation goes hand in hand with rape. In other words, war movies hardly ever speak of the violence committed by enemy soldiers against women. In "*Surrender*" Konstantin's actual raping of Lea does not happen, but the threat and its effects equal those of rape: the social pressure on Lea to act against her will, the shutting away of the people in their houses, and the burning torches ready to set the town on fire.

The Lieutenant and the Beautiful Jewess

The violence against Jewish civilians is also of great importance in the last film set in Galicia shown in German cinemas before the National Socialist Party came into power in January of 1933. The British-German co-production *Zwei Welten* ("*Two Worlds*") is also the only sound film in the corpus of films discussed in this essay. It was directed by E. A. Dupont and shot in three different language versions (English, German, French) with different casts at the Elstree Studios in England.[61] The German version premiered on the 16th of September, 1930 in Berlin, only two days after the Nazi party won the national elections and became the second largest faction in parliament. The political earthquake that followed had its roots not least in the politicization of war experiences, in the contradicting ideas of making sense of the war and its effects, and the attitudes towards Jews and anti-Semitism, that is, issues that are also very much present in "*Two Worlds*" and its contemporary reception.

It is hardly surprising that in this case, too, critics pointed to the close relation between "*Two Worlds*" and the 1927 film "*Hotel Imperial*".[62] The story of "*Two Worlds*" takes place in 1917 in a

61 In 1923 Dupont had already directed another film, *Das alte Gesetz* (*The Ancient Law*), that set into dialogue the orthodox Jewish world of the Galician shtetl and the secular metropolis of Vienna. *Das alte Gesetz*, too, was a story of border crossing and transformation, in this case in the mid-19th century. In "*Two Worlds*", Dupont collaborated with the same set-designer with whom he had worked on *Das alte Gesetz*, Alfred Junge. For an analysis of "*Two Worlds*", cf. Siegbert Salomon Prawer, *Between Two Worlds: The Jewish Presence in German and Austrian Film, 1910–1933* (New York: Berghahn Books, 2005), 140–142.

62 A "remarkable resemblance" between the story of "*Two Worlds*" on the one hand and "*Hotel Imperial*" and *Lea Lyon* was mentioned, e.g. by Eugen Szatmari, "Zwei Welten," *Berliner Tageblatt*, no. 439 (Sept. 17, 1930). *Two Worlds* was even regarded as a—rather bad—rip-off of the "unforgotten film by Mauritz Stiller" by Oly. [Fritz Olimsky], "Zwei Welten," *Berliner Börsen-Zeitung*, no. 434 (Sept. 17, 1930).

Galician town occupied by the Austro-Hungarian Army.[63] After the end of the Easter service in church, a pogrom occurs in the Jewish quarter. There is shooting on the streets, and attackers break into houses. However, the film leaves it open who the attackers really are. The Austrian commander Oberst von Kaminsky (Friedrich Kayßler) orders his son, Leutnant Stanislaus von Kaminsky (Peter Voß), to take his soldiers, go into the Jewish quarter, and end the upheaval. During the street fights that follow, the completely uninvolved young man, Nathan, who is the son of the elderly watchmaker Simon Goldscheider (Hermann Vallentin), is killed. When one of the attackers tries to rape Esther (Helene Sieburg), Goldscheider's daughter, the Austrian Leutnant shows up in time and saves her. Nevertheless, Goldscheider, when learning of Nathan's death, accuses the officer of not having protected the Jews any better and grabs Kaminsky's collar in anger. For this assault against military personnel, the old man is, humiliatingly,

63 My analysis is based on a severely cut, 73-minutes version of "*Two Worlds*" from the Cineteca Nazionale (Rome); the German release version had a length of 119 minutes (3,260 m). The existing version is again based on the German version with German actors; that is, even when the title of the English version is cited in what follows, I am referring to the German version. However, most of the scenes with dialogue are missing (or dialogue has been replaced with music). Instead of the German dialogue, this version has Italian intertitles. Several songs sung in German are still included. Since a number of scenes important for the understanding of the film are missing, my summary is also referring to the information given by Prawer, *Between Two Worlds*, 140ff. Another German version of "*Two Worlds*" is held by the British Film Institute (BFI) in London (length: 1,512 m); at the BFI, there also exists an English version (length: 2,459 m). Given this miserable situation, all of my descriptions and deductions are obviously flawed as they relate to a copy that is far from being complete.

jailed for five days, which makes it impossible for him to say the Kaddish for his son.[64]

Charmed by a Viennese Soubrette who performs for the soldiers in a front theater, Leutnant Kaminsky leaves his post and spends the night with the woman. He thus doesn't notice the Austro-Hungarian army's retreat and wakes up the next morning just as the Russians occupy the town. When he attempts to flee, he is injured and collapses in front of Goldscheider's house. Now it is Esther's turn to save him: She carries him in and, when the Russians conduct a search of the house, she makes her father lie and tell them that Kaminsky is in fact his son. Weeks pass. Esther has nursed the lieutenant back to health. The two of them fall in love, knowing that Esther's father opposes their relationship very strictly. In order to end his love affair, Goldscheider writes a letter in his despair to the Russian commander denouncing Kaminsky. But his letter doesn't find the proper addressee. The town is recaptured by the Austrians, and Kaminsky's father, the new (and old) commander, gets hold of the letter. When his son confronts him with his intention to marry Esther and, if necessary, quit the army, the father leaves him an impossible choice: Either the lieutenant end his relationship with Esther immediately, or Goldscheider will be shot for denunciation. At the end, as the lieutenant leaves Goldscheider's house without saying goodbye, Esther suffers a breakdown.

"Two Worlds" presents us with several confrontations and contrasts, as Siegbert Prawer has shown in his analysis of the film. There is the confrontation of Christian and Jewish religion and rites, of power and powerlessness, of the generation of the sons and daughters and their fathers who are unwilling to accept the

64 The scene in which Goldscheider has to appear at the Austrian headquarters and is imprisoned is missing in the existing Roman copy.

new ways of their children.[65] The confrontations and contrasts can be found on various levels of the film: in the narrative construction, in camerawork and lighting, in casting, clothing, make-up, in the use of parallel editing and songs.[66]

Like "*Hotel Imperial*", "*Two Worlds*", too, is a film of an overwhelming and telling mise-en-scène. Again and again, the protagonist's movements and the viewer's gaze are blocked and framed through doors, window frames, and furniture, which make obvious the people's feeling of entrapment and inability to move about. With its low ceilings, its big staircase, narrowness and meaningful shadows, the watchmaker's house that serves as the lieutenant's hide-out resembles an ancient castle and a prison at the same time. The proximity of "*Hotel Imperial*" and "*Two Worlds*" in terms of aesthetic choices are particularly apparent where events are shown in an almost identical fashion. This goes especially for the scene in which the Austro-Hungarian officer wakes up in a bed which is not his own, in a room whose windows are covered with blinds, suddenly realizing that the Russian troops are invading the town to the air of marching music.

"An Air of Austro-Schnitzlerian Flirtation"

Some of the early sound films are full of experimentation with the mixture of dialogue, music, sound, and noise. One of the boldest films in this regard was Georg Wilhelm Pabst's *Westfront 1918*, the first big German World War I movie in sound, which premiered in May 1930. Together with the American production of "*All Quiet*

65 Cf. Prawer, *Between Two Worlds*, 140–142.

66 For instance, the popular song "Rosa, wir fahr'n nach Lodz" (1915) by Fritz Löhner-Beda (lyrics) and Artur M. Werau (music) is juxtaposed later in the film with a Yiddish song.

on the Western Front" (1930), Pabst's film opened up a completely new chapter in the cinematic depiction and analysis of war.[67]

Compared with these two masterpieces, "*Two Worlds*" rather marks the end of an earlier chapter. Here, the experience of war is still narrated in the form of a heavy melodrama, complete with individual suffering, tragic mistakes, hide-and-seek, and allusions to a spy thriller. In no way does this film come close to the history of the anonymous mass killing of a whole generation as it is portrayed in *Westfront 1918*. Quite aptly, Ernst Jäger in his review notes a "philo-Semitic essence of the story" and mentions the great distance between the two films, *Ostfront 1917* and *Westfront 1918*. In Jaeger's view, the script of "*Two Worlds*" follows on the tracks of Lajos Biro and Ladislaus Vajda (who wrote the script for *Westfront 1918*), but it is mainly characterized by an appeal to the broad audience and its taste for novels; thus, the viewer will detect "an air of Austro-Schnitzlerian flirtation," "Hungarian sensations," and "the strong tradition of Jewish theater." However, what the script completely ignores is the world of today: "The curtain has fallen over these fairy tale worlds. We are standing in front of an entirely different set of still smoking ruins. Six million Hitler voters—we cannot ignore them (and with epic adventure movies this German labyrinth will not be pacified)." Finally, the weakness of "*Two Worlds*" is, according to Jaeger, that it enters the battle of public opinions without a charge, without a certain tendency, without the courage to fight: "Whoever fights for two worlds must step in in favor of *one* world. From the bird-eye's view of a neutral bystander it is impossible to give shape to confessions and passions in a film."[68]

Not surprisingly the Nazis attacked "*Two Worlds*" as soon as the film entered the cinemas. Two weeks after the premiere,

67 In 1933, Pabst's film was banned in Germany.

68 E.J. [Ernst Jäger], "Zwei Welten," *Film-Kurier*, no. 220 (Sept. 17, 1930).

the Ministry of the Interior of the state of Thüringen (in the Southeast of Germany), then headed by the National Socialist Wilhelm Frick, demanded that the film's approval by the Board of Censorship should be annulled. The film, it was argued, was a "hate propaganda film" ("*Hetzfilm*"), which gave the impression that, compared with the officers, the Jews were the better humans. By depicting the Austrian officers as undutiful and lacking discipline, the film, so it was said, might be understood "in Germany and abroad as hateful propaganda against the officer corps of a former German ally, the Austrian army, and thus an immediate threat to the German army and the German reputation in general."[69] This attack was accompanied by a campaign in the Nazi press claiming that "*Two Worlds*" presented "the most evil hate propaganda against the old German army"; it was also said that "the Jews" would spread their "poison" in a new fashion.[70] In this case, the Board of Censorship did not annul the film's approval. However, only several weeks later, the Nazi's succeeded when the approval of "*All Quiet on the Western Front*" was withdrawn due to a massive Nazi campaign.

While for the Nazis, "*Two Worlds*" the depiction of Jews allegedly was too positive and the depiction of the Austrian officers was too unsympathetic, the very same film was criticized by reviewers in the liberal and left press for different reasons. For them, the story was too convoluted and full of cheap showmanship; the direction was poor, the acting weak. The *Berliner Tageblatt* lamented a

---

69 Cf. decision of the High Board of Censorship, no. 952, Oct. 16, 1930, 3 (Bundesarchiv-Filmarchiv, Schriftgutarchiv), available here: http://www.difarchiv.deutsches-filminstitut.de/zengut/df2tb702z.pdf.

70 M.W., "Zwei Welten," *Der Angriff*, no. 79 (Oct. 2, 1930).

"pogrom story set in an operetta world war."[71] The Eastern Jewish milieu at least found some praise, as did the actors who played the Jews and the "atmospheric Ghetto images."[72]

What is Galicia, and Which?

Trying to sum up a few of the observations and suggestions made in this essay might be puzzling. Obviously, none of the five films presented here could be properly described as a war movie. Very little is present of the motifs, themes, and elements that characterize so many films of the war film genre: the display of weapons and military machinery, the hierarchies and oft-depicted friction between simple soldiers and higher ranks, the miserable food supply, the sleeplessness, the lice, the mud, the noise, and, of course, the combat scenes on the battlefield, the killing and dying.

Instead, the films set in Galicia are melodramas or, to an extent, spy films that are located in Galicia during World War I. However, Galicia is not depicted as a space that is recognizable because of its geographical features, its landscape or urban topography. In fact, the Galicia that is presented on screen could be anywhere because it is largely studio-made. (And when, in one of the few exceptions, a natural setting is used in "*Surrender*", the squirrel that catches the protagonist's attention is for any squirrel expert

71 Eugen Szatmari, "Zwei Welten," *Berliner Tageblatt*, no. 439 (Sept. 17, 1930). Mostly negative reviews can also be found in, for example, Kn. [Kurt Kersten], "Zwei Welten," *Welt am Abend*, no. 218 (Sept. 18, 1930); Armin Kessler, "Zwei Welten," *Berliner Börsen-Courier*, no. 459 (Sept. 20, 1930); F.S., "Zwei Welten," *Berliner Volks-Zeitung*, no. 450 (Sept. 24, 1930).

72 Kurt Mühsam, "Zwei Welten," *B.Z. am Mittag*, no. 254 (Sept. 17, 1930). Cf. also Kn. [Kurt Kersten], "Zwei Welten," *Welt am Abend*, no. 218 (Sept. 18, 1930); Oly. [Fritz Olimsky], "Zwei Welten," *Berliner Börsen-Zeitung*, no. 434 (Sept. 17, 1930).

quite clearly not of Eastern European but Californian origin.) This studio-made space offers a few street scenes from a small country town and otherwise mainly consists of indoor scenes, of old, dark, narrow houses, almost fortresses very much stressing the difference between inside and outside world.

Of course, a main characteristic of Galicia is—according to "*Light Cavalry*", "*Surrender*", and "*Two Worlds*"—its Jewish population, which is divided again into the generation of the old fathers and the young daughters. The fathers—religious, bearded, strong in their beliefs and judgements, troubled and shaken by the new situation—appear as embodiments of an altogether orthodox lifestyle and, as such, as embodiments of a long gone past presented as both ethnic and exotic. (It is also a past that is marked by the experience of suppression and violence against Jews, as indicated in "*Surrender*".) In contrast, the daughter embodies an open-minded generation that doesn't carry the burden of trauma. She is active, courageous, and reaches out. Eventually, it is she who heroically saves the Jewish community and the non-Jewish Austro-Hungarian soldiers, too. A new generation, raised in ancient beliefs, overcomes prejudice as well as authoritarian and patriarchal rule. In a sense, the daughter represents a generation of post-religious citizens of Austria-Hungary, or, in other, more historically embedded terminology: The Jewish daughter seeks assimilation (a concept and ideology that, within and outside the Jewish discourse, was hotly debated when the films were made). Adding to that, one might also find that these films, with the possible exception of "*Two Worlds*", paint an affirmative, at times nostalgic, picture of the lost Habsburg empire in a rather astonishing way. And despite the heroine's attempt to withdraw from the old, male, religiously-shaped order, she nevertheless plays the mythical role of the savior who makes a sacrifice and is a victim.

Of course, this whole scenario is riddled with stereotypes and utopian longings: "*Light Cavalry*", "*Surrender*", and "*Two Worlds*" all focus on the love between a noble Christian officer and the legendary Jewish beauty. The films suggest that there is a mutual attraction, and that it is not only the man who saves the woman in distress but in fact it is much more the woman who saves and cures the man. In this concern, the films present a counter-image to those war films that stress that the male, soldierly war experience is incompatible with the experiences of (female) civilians. Here, on the contrary, the war doesn't separate but unites the couple.

Galicia appears as a multidimensional space of erotic and religious encounters, of gender and age conflicts, contrasts and confrontations, movements and attempted reconciliations. Compared with more conventional narratives, the five films discussed in this essay lie on the margins of films from the Weimar Republic that touch on the First World War in some form. Because they give space and voice to the perspective of a civilian population confronted with a military occupation, and because they pay special attention to the trials of the Jewish population in the eastern Habsburg Empire, they place a strong emphasis on, and tell of a chapter of, the First World War that was otherwise ignored by other films from the era.

WORLD WAR I IN HUNGARIAN MOTION PICTURE HISTORY, 1914–1945

Márton Kurutz

Film During the Great War

World wars always leave a considerable mark on a nation's motion picture history. The characteristics of this phenomenon are relatively easily traceable with respect to changes in both quantity and quality. Specifically, among many other aspects, the number and caliber of films about war are the two most important factors by which the shaping of history, the alternation of military victories and defeats, are accurately traceable on the homogeneous body of cinematographic art. Besides the statistical data of economic trends, art can be one of the most authentic gauges of the eras of wartime economic upturns and declines. While those who are interested can get a relatively complete image of the European film industry during World War II through surviving movie productions, the film production conditions of the years of World War I are significantly more difficult to judge because of the substantial lack of material. Approximately ninety-three percent of Hungarian films made in that period were lost, and little survived of the documentation related to movie filmings. We can still undertake an authentic exploration based on the filmography collected and enriched for decades by motion picture historian, Gyöngyi Balogh,[1] which describes, by means of the surviving sources, the data of the roughly 600 Hungarian fiction films produced in the period between 1901 and 1930 with systematic accuracy.

The Hungarian feature film industry was born during the few years preceding the breakout of the war. Therefore it was a relatively new profession and art that immediately came face to face with history. There was not much time for hesitation. Because of the increasingly slow commercial routes, then the gradually closing borders, and eventually the boycott of international markets, the film industry was forced to produce by itself the program quantity that its audience had become used to during the times of peace. The statement "the muses are silent during war" is not true for cinematographic art, since there were never as many filmings in the studios of various nations as during the years of the two world wars.

Hungarian film producers reacted with great enthusiasm to the news of the breakout of the war and the first military operations. Zsigmond Gere, who fought on the front himself, wrote one of the very first wartime dramas, entitled Őrház *a Kárpátokban*[2] (*Guardhouse of the Carpathians*), in 1914. Its hero is a patriotic railway-man, who himself becomes the victim of Russian incursions along with his family. However, before he dies, he conveys crucial information to the Hungarian camp. In a manner characteristic of the optimism in the first years of the war, satires and parodies quickly appeared, the main target of which was the enemy. Imre Pintér, the famous seasonal actor, wrote and directed

1 Gyöngyi Balogh, *Hungarian Filmography / Feature Films (1901–1929) / Hungarian Silent Feature Films* (manuscript).

2 *Guardhouse in the Carpathians*/Őrház *a Kárpátokban*, directed by Gyula Zilahy (1914).

the three-act comedy entitled Ágyú és *harang*[3] (*Cannon and bell*), in which the people of the ”dwarf king,” meaning Italy, waged war against Mihály Magyar (Michael Hungarian) and his compatriots. Among the characters of the story—which relies on the instruments of chauvinism—was the famous Italian author, Gabriele D'Annunzio, who was celebrated as a hero on the other side of the front, and the “Piccolo King” on the other; for the role, the director used a circus dwarf.

The 1914 comedy *Szerbia hadat* üzen![4] (*Serbia declares war!*) is an even more ignoble film: In the spiteful story, the screenplay writer distorts the events preceding the breakout of the war. The main character of the film is the king of Serbia himself, the alcoholic Peter I, who is so indecisive that all those who surround him abuse his weakness. In an empire built on corruption, even the Serbian telephone network is sold to the royal court's supplier Khonovits, a junk trader. The royal palace is depicted as a dilapidated shack, the front gate adorned by a pig-head trade sign; in the course of the story, even the royal crown is pawned, so the monarch can acquire money for waging war. When the war breaks out, the king secretly flees to the “*Poloskavác*” (Bedbug-Ville) spa and watches his country's increasingly hopeless situation from there. The scenes, sinking into burlesque, are eventually ended by Hungarian soldiers arriving in boats on the bank of the Danube in Belgrade, swiftly routing the Serbian army.

It is already quite evident from these few films that the motion pictures produced in the era, dealing with the new war as the fundamental experience, were made along the lines of diverse genre concepts. Based on the surviving sources, roughly four

3 *Cannon and Bell*/Ágyú és *harang*, directed by Imre Pintér (1915).

4 *Serbia Declares War!*/*Szerbia hadat* üzen!, directed by Aladár Fodor (1914).

basic genres can be differentiated: pathetic propaganda, chauvinist propaganda, romantic drama, and comedy. The plots can also be called rather stereotypical. In the stories about heroic military virtues and self-sacrifice, women play important roles, and the path-seeking of single or lonely women is a recurring motif; this is one of the earliest forms of the appearance of melodrama in Hungarian films. The bored wife or girl flees toward a more exciting, richer, and more exotic world. And this world is to be searched for somewhere in eastern Europe, and specifically in the Orpheum or musical theater of a Russian or Polish city. Our heroines become dancers in every case, and instead of shine and splendor, they are victimized by the enemy's army officers and blackmailing civilians. In every case, absolution for them is represented by returning to the family home, forgiveness, or death. During the war, three such films were produced, and of these, two have survived. Both were made in 1917, one of them in Budapest, the other in Kolozsvár, in today's Romania. The latter, entitled *Az utolsó* éjszaka[5] (*The last night*), is a surprisingly captivating drama, in which the World War seemingly does not even play a significant role. However, the breakout of the war is still the event that reverses the plot in the middle of the story and rearranges the characters' relationships with one another. Its heroine is the wife of a landowner who escapes to the Russian theaters. She is unable to control oppression by the people surrounding her and is dragged into such danger that she does not survive. Another film, *A föld rabjai*[6] (*Prisoners of the land*), also shows little of the events of the war, although they are still emphasized in the story. The Hungarian peasant girl who escapes to Russia, and whose fate takes her from the theater to a castle in Tashkent, is confronted

5 *The Last Night/Az utolsó* éjszaka, directed by Jenő Janovics (1917).

6 *Prisoners of the Land/A föld rabjai*, directed by László Békeffy (1917).

with her duty and the patriotism of Hungarian prisoners of war, a group that includes her own father. The third film is lost. It was entitled (*Attack*),[7] and it was produced three years earlier, in 1914. The heroine of this film is also a *vengerka* gone astray, meaning a Hungarian dancer who moved to the east, whose career is derailed by the breakout of the war. She is also rescued by a compatriot, her former suitor who takes her home, back to her village. This time, the plot is set in a castle in Galicia, where the majority of the scenes of the not excessively complex story take place. The selection of this location provides a good opportunity for the director, Alfréd Deésy, not to produce a feature film of the story in its traditional interpretation, but rather make a so-called sketch film, a genre that was becoming increasingly popular at the time. This film, which was the first of this genre[8] according to its director, differed from traditional films insofar as its writer was allowed to insert a multitude of musical and dancing scenes into it, which were performed by actors live in the interior spaces of the castle, that is, on a stage below the screen.

The movie sketch genre was born, and flourished, during World War I. One of the reasons for this was that it somewhat replaced the theater experience, which was increasingly rare at the time. The other reason was that the performing actors could hope to escape the draft by citing their appearances. However, they often did not succeed, and before long the movie copies were taken to various appearances with actors who only looked similar to them. Besides the sketch genre, comedies and operettas were also living their heydays on the screen. The reason for this is that audiences turned away from sorrowful dramas and desired ecstatic

7 *Attack/Attak*, directed by Alfréd Deésy (1914).

8 Alfréd Deésy, *In the Circus Ring, on the Stage, on Movie Screen. Recollections* (Budapest: Magyar Filmintézet, 1992), 116.

entertainment. They were not particularly curious about what was happening on the front, since they could see reality in the motion picture reports played before feature films; up-to-date news was shown in cinemas increasingly often. However, original front footage shot by Austrian and German cameramen was not only shown in the side programs. Sometimes documentary sequences were also integrated into fictional films, creating an impression of authenticity. The sole surviving example of this kind of directorial concept is the anti-war propaganda short feature film entitled *Jön az* öcsém (*My Brother Is Coming*),[9] which was directed by Mihály Kertész[10] in 1919. Kertész was peculiarly attracted to this directorial method; at least, this is evidenced by the surviving documentation of his two films produced in 1917. Moreover, he elevated the captivating nature of his war drama entitled *A magyar föld ereje*[11] (*The Strength of the Fatherland*) to such a level that, beyond the combat scenes edited from the news, he also took his actors to locations suffering from original war damage. Thus, despite the difficult wartime transportation conditions, his crew reached Sofia and Constantinople, as well as besieged cities that resembled the destroyed Russian village of the story. The story of the feature film, the production of which was commissioned by the Hungarian Red Cross, is rather bizarre and completely contrary to the fates and motivations of the characters in other Hungarian films. The hero of Kertész's film is a Russian man who fled the despotism of the Czar and found a new homeland in Hungary. He becomes a Hungarian citizen. The magic of Hungarian land gives him strength to start anew. His son, who was already born on this

9 *My Brother Is Coming/Jön az* öcsém, directed by Mihály Kertész (1919).

10 Michael Curtiz.

11 *The Power of Hungarian Land/A magyar föld ereje*, directed by Mihály Kertész (1917).

land, volunteers to go to the battlefield and fights in the Hungarian army against the Russians, among whom he even encounters his own grandfather. Perhaps Kertész did not consider this film to be among the main achievements of his life, but rather similar to his other wartime work entitled *A béke* útja (*Peace's Road*).[12] The latter was a 300-meter propaganda film that served the success of war-bonds, and of which very few sources survived. Kertész could not pay much attention to the plot, because most of his film consisted of edited documentaries of battlefield events. His attention was rather focused on his romantic adventure films produced in the same year, which he made mimicking American movies that were boycotted at the time. Such is the surviving *Az utolsó hajnal* (*The Last Dawn*);[13] both the content and environment clearly relates to America.

Hotel Imperial,[14] which debuted in the autumn of 1918, was undoubtedly one of the most significant pieces of Hungarian film production during World War I. It was made in Jenő Janovics's motion picture factory in Kolozsvár and was based on Lajos Bíró's theater play, which appeared in the same year. He directed the six-act drama himself, involving many actors and a large number of extras in numerous Transylvanian cities. Even the 51st infantry battalion of the Imperial and Royal Army, still shared with Austria, provided assistance in the course of the filming, during which Russian soldiers were played by Russian prisoners of war working at the farmstead in Gyalu. The lead role was played by Mihály Várkonyi,[15] later of worldwide renown, who was serving as a soldier in the army himself in those months. Critics reviewed

12 *The Path of Peace/A béke* útja, directed by Mihály Kertész (1917).

13 *The Last Dawn/Az utolsó hajnal*, directed by Mihály Kertész (1917).

14 *Hotel Imperial*, directed by Jenő Janovics (1917).

15 Victor Varconi.

the play with these words: "Bíró wrote the play with the spirit of a wide-eyed war correspondent and a brave pacifist journalist."[16] In the following decades, *Hotel Imperial* was adapted for the movie screen several times all over the world. It is a great loss to Hungarian motion picture history that a mere few photos survived of this work. *Lyon Lea*,[17] adapted from Sándor Bródy's 1915 theater play, an important production in the list of Jewish-themed films in Hungary, was also lost. The producers of the film, which was also shot at the beginning of the war, included Sándor Korda,[18] who participated in directing as well as the writing of the screenplay beside Miklós M. Pásztory. The achievement of their work is that they succeeded in producing a film that was more substantial and spectacular than the theater version. They even diverged from the original drama on several points, and they inserted scenes into the screenplay that would've been unimaginable displayed on a stage. In the film, all those events that were only recounted in the play became visible, and the scenery is enriched by bustling crowd scenes and decorative open air shots. The surviving photos prove that it must indeed have been a spectacular movie, in which significant attention was devoted to presenting contemporary everyday Jewish culture and religious liturgy. The story follows the tribulations of Jews squeezed between the Russians invading Galicia and the Hungarian army returning, through the relationship between the beautiful daughter of a miracle-rabbi and the Russian grand duke who is courting her. The Russian commander conquering the village wants to possess Lea, who, if she resists him, may risk the lives of the village's inhabitants. However, she

16 *Nyugat/West* (1918/5 edition); Aladár Schöpflin: Hotel Imperial.

17 *Lyon Lea*, directed and written by Miklós M. Pásztory and probably Sándor Korda (1915).

18 Sir Alexander Korda.

is afraid of death; thus, despite the fact that her father disowns her, she chooses the shame. The Duke, witnessing the girl's heroic stance and pride, falls in love with her, and Lea also is not without feelings for him. However, their love cannot be fulfilled, because the Hungarian counterattack drives the Russians out of the village. At this point Lea is unable to choose. The Duke lifts her on his horse and flees with her. While galloping away, Lea is killed by a stray bullet fired by her former love, and the Duke voluntarily follows her into death. The film was played in cinemas throughout the duration of the World War, but in 1919, in the period of the Hungarian Soviet Republic, it was banned by censors. However, it was shown in Berlin and Vienna; in the latter city, it was introduced as an Austrian film.[19]

That the war was increasingly prolonged and sank into hopelessness also had a disheartening effect on the Hungarian motion picture industry and cinematographic art. The producers no longer believed in victory, and during the last two years of the war, even audiences did not know what to make of the optimistic films that they had been watching enthusiastically in 1914. Even *Károly bakák* (*Károly soldiers*),[20] produced in the last year of the war, did not have any freshness, anything encouraging. The pattern of the film's simple story is found in the motion picture history of almost every warring nation, and in Hungary several times.[21] The village story begins with false news of a fatality at the front. Receiving the news, the bride of the alleged

19 *Mozgófénykép híradó* (Motion picture News), 1916/22.

20 *Károly Soldiers/Károly bakák*, directed by Miklós M. Pásztory and Zoltán Korda (1918).

21 For example, *The Swapped Man/Az elcserélt ember*, directed by Viktor Gertler (1938); *Brothers in Arms/Bajtársak*, directed by Ágoston Pacséry (1942); and *Under Barrage/Pergőtűzben*, directed by Lajos Ágotai (1937).

fallen warrior mourns her love and marries someone else. The soldier believed to be dead unexpectedly returns right before the wedding, and upon seeing the happiness of his former love, returns to the front in his sorrow. Before long, the young husband is also drafted, and the abandoned groom eventually overcomes his hatred toward him at the edge of a bomb-crater, as a brother in arms, when he saves his rival's life by sacrificing his own. The author of the story was Nándor Korcsmáros, the editor of a patriotic-spirited newspaper, whose most well-known work is perhaps this writing. It is a pity that the film did not survive; it is possible that its principal value would have been the realistic view it painted of military life, the everyday experiences of soldiers at the time, since the author was also a devoted explorer of army slang.[22]

The feature film entitled *A métely* (*Infection*)[23] was produced in Kolozsvár during the last weeks of the war, at the initiative of the government and with considerable state subsidy. It was the counter-propaganda of syphilitic diseases that were rampant at the time. The screenplay was based on the drama by Eugène Brieux, entitled *Les Avariés*, which the author wrote in 1901. The drama was banned by French censors at the time, because it was forbidden to discuss syphilitic diseases, especially in the presence of women. In 1905, a permit was still granted for the debut and the play proved to be a huge success. Its first film version[24] was produced in America in 1914; the movie shot in Kolozsvár was the second. The Hungarian film version shot in 1918 based on the powerful dramatic fundamental work was undoubtedly very

22 Nándor Korcsmáros, "Data for Hungarian Military Language," *Magyar Nyelvőr (Hungarian Language Guard)* 54 (1925): 94–96.

23 *Damaged Goods/A métely*, directed by Mihály Fekete (1918).

24 *Damaged Goods*, directed by Tom Ricketts (1914).

convincing, since the director, Mihály Fekete, who also played one of the leading roles, produced the hospital scenes at the Kolozsvár dermatology clinic. During the years of the war, besides Spanish flu, syphilis claimed the most lives; thus it affected a great number of already weakened people, as well as their families. The shocking story presents the disintegration of a marriage, in which medical assistance represents the sole escape.

This film was the symbolic conclusion of Hungarian motion picture production in the lost World War I, of the immense stream, which started with burlesques and satires pointing beyond irony, and of which the valuable Hungarian film drama evolved in the span of a few years. In its entirety, the whole situation ended with a demoralized, lethargic, financially bankrupt motion picture industry in 1918. Despite all of this, after the conclusion of the war, the history of Hungarian motion picture was allowed another short-lived period of enthusiasm. The obvious reason for this was the suddenly commenced peace, the civic-democratic transformation, and the declaration of the Hungarian Soviet Republic. This was the place where film production was nationalized for the first time in the world; thus, numerous productions could be completed by the end of the decade. However, none of the newly produced films emphasized the war, even though the few short films, striving to do away with the destructive cataclysm permanently, were significant. One of these is the single-act propaganda film entitled *Őfelsége a király nevében* (*In the name of his highness the king*),[25] the creators and actors of which are unknown. The sole surviving copy of the film was later placed in the police archive, as criminal evidence, along with the news films shown in the weeks of the communist regime. A roll of film also survived here, which was presumably the last work of Mihály Kertész produced in Hungary.

25 *In the Name of His Highness the King*/Őfelsége *a király nevében* (1919).

This was the previously mentioned *My Brother Is Coming*,[26] which was originally a version of the story of a poem published in newspapers. It debuted in Budapest, on April 3, 1919. Kertész and his wife, who also played a role in this film, were already in Vienna the following month. Oszkár Beregi, who played the lead male character, because of the attacks against him, followed them a few months later. The euphoria of the Hungarian Soviet Republic was followed by the shock of the Versailles peace treaty, in the course of which Hungary lost two thirds of its territory and along with it, one of the bastions of its culture, the Kolozsvár motion picture factory.

The Great War on Film

Starting in the beginning of the 1920s, the number of Hungarian films slowly declined. From 1925 until the end of the decade, the number of great Hungarian feature films produced annually did not reach ten; in the last three years, only two to three feature films were produced. The reason for this was the increasingly intensifying economic crisis and the reopening of borders, across which American and Western European movies practically flooded the Hungarian market. The absence of Hungarian film professionals, many of whom had emigrated abroad, primarily to Austria and the United States, was a significant factor in Magyar motion picture factories. Not only their most talented directors, but also a great portion of their actors, received much more favorable offers in foreign Eldorado locations of international silent film production than they did in Hungary. The actors who stayed home, besides the little work they had, were experimenting with "sketch versions" of previously successful films, which meant the

26 *My Brother Is Coming/Jön az* öcsém, directed by Mihály Kertész (1919).

re-editing of movies produced during the golden age. The newly produced films made at this time, in their genre, show the extreme difference between life in the cities and in villages: They shot folk theater plays, or adventure stories with scenes overseas, mimicking American movies.

The "film-novel" entitled *A kis hős* (*The little hero*),[27] which debuted in the spring of 1927, stands out from this set of productions. The screenplay was written by a ministerial advisor, Henrik Kőrösy, based on a book[28] that was published around that time. The end result of the filming, which started under the working title "Accusatory Graves" (*Vádoló sírok*) is a rather didactic student story, in the center of which is a young Subcarpathian Hungarian student called Pista. During his school years, he chooses Petőfi, the poet symbolic for the Hungarian nation, as his role model, and he escapes to the war after his father and grandfather, where he avenges their deaths on a Russian army officer. Finally, a Russian bayonet is stabbed into Pista's heart, and he dies just as his role model. His teacher holds a eulogy at his grave; the effect of which is his students again dream of Hungary growing to be great. The screenings of the eight-act film were preceded by a live actor prologue, which was performed by students. The production was supposed to be a preparation for the commemorations of the tenth anniversary of the war, however culture politics did not wish to remember it in this way, because of the dramatic losses still alive in everybody's hearts.

Two exhausted prisoners of war are trudging home along the dusty highway; the drama known as the first Hungarian sound film, which was in reality one of the last Hungarian silent films, opens with this symbolic picture sequence. *Csak egy kislány van*

---

27 *The Little Hero/A kis hős*, directed by József Letzter (1926).

28 Gyula Pekár, *The Little Hero* (Budapest: Singer, 1927).

a világon (*There is only one girl in the world*),[29] produced in 1929, and at the time still soundtracked with music, is actually about love, not about the spiritual destruction that the four-years-long war caused in the lives of its characters. On the twentieth anniversary of the breakout of the war, the making of a truly good film commemoration was not successful either. The productions[30] of the time primarily reminisced about the happy years of peace, a tranquility from which the heroes of the stories were awakened by the mobilization. This motif appeared in numerous other sound films that were in some way connected to the war. The world had changed a great deal in the meantime: A new generation grew up, and the war seemed so distant that its previous significance began to fade. In the story adapted from an operetta to the movie screens and entitled *Az iglói diákok* (*The students of Igló*),[31] the war only appears in an incidental way, when at the end of the story the lazy high school student hero is hardened into a real man by the war. The first serious drama that deserves mentioning, and which takes place during the world war in its entirety, debuted in cinemas in the beginning of 1936, under the title *Café Moszkva* (*Café Moscow*),[32] and was directed by István Székely,[33] who later became popular in Hollywood. This story also takes place in Galicia, in Limburg and is reminiscent of the story of *Hotel Imperial* on several points, as well as Mihály Kertész's *Casablanca*.[34] This film is also set in an entertainment spot of a small town located on the

29 *There Is Only One Girl in the World/Csak egy kislány van a világon*, directed by Béla Gaál (1929).

30 E.g. *Purple Locust Tree/Lila akác*, directed by István Székely (1934).

31 *The Students of Igló/Az iglói diákok*, directed by István György (1935).

32 *Café Moscow/Café Moszkva*, directed by István Székely (1936).

33 Steve Sekely, S. K. Seeley.

34 *Casablanca*, directed by Michael Curtiz (1942).

frontline, where the heroes meet each other as citizens of nations at war. Love is the central theme here as well, and the heroes save each other's lives because of it. This melodrama was a great success in its own time, even though it did not manage to cross Hungary's borders, thus unfortunately it did not become an internationally known production.

One year later, three films about the World War were produced[35] at the same time. However, only one deserves emphasis, which by itself also stood out from the Hungarian movies of the era. *Két fogoly* (*Two captives*)[36] was produced based on the work of a world war veteran, Lajos Zilahy. It was directed by István Székely, and the setting is again the Russian front. Its heroes are separated lovers, who slowly give up on each other due to the long duration of imprisonment and war. After news of the husband's death is received home in the hinterland, his wife finds happiness beside her gallant suitor, and—the other way round—the husband beside a Russian village girl during war captivity. The happy ending of the film is unusual: the former lovers' new life is the positive note of the movie.

One year later, in 1938, another masterpiece was born, inspired by a novel written immediately after the war.[37] The author also adapted it to the stage in 1930; in his work, he was the first to address the mental trauma[38] caused by war injury. The heroes of *Az elcserélt ember* (*The swapped man*)[39] are Hungarian army officers who resemble each

35 *Sound of the Heart/A szív szava*, directed by Alajos Bihari (1937); *Under Barrage!/Pergőtűzben!*, directed by Lajos Ágotai (1937).

36 *Two Captives/Két fogoly*, directed by István Székely (1937).

37 Adorján Bónyi, *Swapped Life* (1920).

38 The second one was produced in 1940, entitled *Belated Letter/Az elkésett levél*, directed by Endre Rodriguez (1941).

39 The Swapped Man/Az elcserélt ember, directed by Viktor Gertler (1938).

perfectly in every way, one of whom dies on the front, while the other survives but loses his memories. When he wakes up, he accidentally begins to continue the personal life of the other, and as he slowly realizes this, he is also faced with the thought that he must not conceal himself in front of his friend's wife and son.

In the period of Hungarian sound film that lasted until the end of World War II, there are practically no further significant, remarkable productions. Most of the stories that touch on the war are either only connected to history by a weak thread, or only use the living conditions created by the war.[40] Films aiming to insult other nations appear again; in this case, their targets are the countries that were the winners of the Versailles treaty.[41] Endre Tóth,[42] who became famous in Hollywood, was also shooting an adventurous spy story based on the novel entitled *Toprini nász* (*Wedding in Toprin*),[43] rather than a film about the world war. Beside his multitude of Hungarian masterpieces, Arzén Cserépy,[44] who is mostly known in German speaking countries, produced an expressly poor film under the title *Gorodi fogoly* (*The captive of Gorod*),[45] about the escape of Hungarian prisoners of war from Russia.

The last significant film about World War I, *Sarajevo*,[46] was produced in 1940; the title reveals its fundamental theme. The

---

40 For example: *Belated Letter/Az elkésett levél*, directed by Endre Rodriguez (1941); *Magdolna*, directed by Kálmán Nádasdy (1942).

41 *Hungarian Resurrection/Magyar feltámadás*, directed by Ferenc Kiss and Jenő Csepreghy (1938-39).

42 André de Toth.

43 *Toprin Wedding/Toprini nász*, directed by Tóth Endre (1939).

44 Arzén von Cserépy; Konrad Wieder.

45 *The Captive of Gorod/Gorodi fogoly*, directed by Arzén Cserépy (1940).

46 *Sarajevo*, directed by Ákos Ráthonyi (1940).

love story commencing at the moment of the breakout of the war leads all the way to Russia, where the Hungarian girl arrives as a bride. However, she is not welcome in the castle of the Czar's army officer, and while her fiancé is fighting on the front, she realizes herself that she is attracted to her former love, a Hungarian soldier who is injured on the nearby front. Seeing this, the Russian army officer gives up on the girl with a noble heart; he secretly leads them across the border and surrenders himself. The final outcome of the excellently directed film is also reminiscent of the story of *Casablanca*, and in its other motifs also those of earlier silent films. It is evident from this that the world war theme was not infinitely variable in the film language medium of the era.

For a long time, no further films were produced about the Great War at all, since one year later Hungary entered another world war, which soon made the memory and significance of the first one fade. People needed new films, new stories, and while they received them, the exact same processes occurred in the motion picture industry as a few decades earlier. The upswing of Hungarian films was again followed by failure and collapse, but in a much more severe way than before. Not only film production, but also everyday life, had to be reborn from the ruins, and before long, this is what served as the fundamental theme of new films.

FILMS ABOUT WORLD WAR I IN HUNGARY AFTER 1945[1]

László Deák-Sárosi

Few films about The Great War were produced after 1945, and those that were finished were released for audiences with delay. Some of these films did not deal with the real causes and complexities of the war, while some, disregarding or falsifying the facts, wrote a fake history about the period between 1914 and 1918, about the events that led up to it, and the aftermath, which all appeared to be true. Of course, there are some exceptions to that.

The main reason for not talking about and misrepresenting certain things is the fact that, since the beginning of the twentieth century, possessing and withholding information has been either explicitly or implicitly an important part of warfare. History is written by the victors, who exert their ideological influence on the countries and nations vanquished in the two world wars through historiography and the arts (literature, film), among other means. After 1945, in Hungary it was communist and post-communist influence that was strongest, while in Western Europe primarily the consciousness of guilt—or, for that matter, a self-justifying strategy—of the victorious or of the losing parties was predominant. Neither side promoted the birth and spreading of works of

1 Translated by Dóra Pődör.

art that intended to present facts and unveil the truth; thus, it was mostly the genre of pacifist novels and films, which presented the point of view of an outsider in relation to the causes of the war, that related valid, though only partial, truths.

The following text includes analyses of the banned pacifist film *Ének a búzamezőkről* (*Song of the Cornfields,* 1947, directed by István Szőts), of the pseudo-self-critical communist thesis film *Fábián Bálint találkozása Istennel (Bálint Fábián Meets God,* 1980, directed by Zoltán Fábri), and of the film drama on history prior to The Great War, *Redl ezredes I–II. ("Colonel Redl,"* 1984, directed by István Szabó). The latter is also important in terms of the subject, because the title character, Colonel Redl, sold important military secrets to the Russian state, which—according to some historical interpretations—significantly influenced the outcome of the war.[2] The film, an international co-production, shows the monarchy's decay, a portrayal basically not in line with historical facts. Two documentaries have also been included: *Én is jártam Isonzónál* (*"I was at the Isonzo battle too,"* 1986, directed by Gyula Gulyás and János Gulyás) is one part of a series of films completed ten years later, and practically the only one that still focuses on living veterans of World War I; it raises important and delicate questions with regard to the causes and circumstances of

2 It is right to wonder why *"Colonel Redl"* is a First World War movie when his plot ends in 1913. Apart from debates about Redl's influence on military operations from 1914 onwards, Szabó's film also depicts the lives of high ranking officers who took part in the First World War a year later. The presentation of the "Redl case" is far from historical reality, but it is also important how the communist party state and its film industry has interpreted and rewritten these facts. Besides, it is also important to analyze *"Colonel Redl"* because, after 1945, only six to eight films about the First World War were made.

war relationships. *Trianon* (2004, directed by G. Gábor Koltay) collects the effects and reflections of the Trianon Peace Treaty in a unique way.

A Banned Pacifist Film: Ének a búzamezőkről *(Song of the* Cornfields, *1947)*

The first film made after 1945 that can be connected to World War I is based on the novel of the same title by Ferenc Móra, written in 1927. The story takes place in the hinterland and can be summarized as follows: Ferenc, a widower who has returned from Russia where he had been a prisoner of war, has to start a new life. He marries the widow of one of his fellow soldiers, Rókus, who allegedly died during their escape from captivity. However, Ferenc has a secret: Rókus probably died because Ferenc refused to share his last piece of bread with him. In the meantime, Ferenc's son, Péterke, is brought up by Rókus's widow, Etel, along with her own child. Additionally, after being married, Ferenc and Etel have their own baby. One day, Péterke drowns in the bog as a result of a fight he was having with his half-sister for a piece of bread. As a result of the tragedy, Ferenc confesses his sin to his wife; Etel becomes deranged and starts to follow a religious sect. In the meantime, the news arrives that Rókus is alive, but he has no intention of returning home. Etel, who loses her self-control as the result of her involvement with the sect, drowns herself. Ferenc has no other choice but to bring up the (surviving) children on his own.

The pacifist leanings of the film are obvious and authentic. The film is not closely connected to World War I, only to a war situation in general, but it takes place in the Hungarian reality of the era. By the time the film had been completed in 1947, it had also incorporated the experiences of restarting life after World War II. It does not contain specific military or political references, so it expands into a universal human drama through concrete family tragedies. The story suggests that war disrupts peace in all walks of life: in the individual, in the family, in religious practices, etc. The novel contained only one sensitive thread, according to which a Russian prisoner of war was the lover of Ferenc's wife, Piros, while she was on her own, and that he also fathered Piros's child. Neither the pre-1945 nor the post-1945 censorship liked this idea.[3] Director István Szőts would have liked to shoot the film in 1942, but at that time he persisted on strictly following the details of the novel. In 1947, "the body consisting of the intellectual leaders of the Communist Ministry of the Interior and of the Communist Party" also objected to the role of the Russian captive, because "the memories of the violent deeds of the victorious army are yet too fresh."[4] This criticism is valid, as according to conservative estimates, in 1944–1945 between 50,000 and 200,000 Hungarian women must have fallen victim to the sexual aggression of Soviet soldiers.[5]

Although, according to the director, the intervention in the dramaturgy disrupted the balance of the film,[6] viewed from the present, it does not appear as a shortcoming. The pacifist, humanist, and lyrical character of the story and the film do remain, and in spite of the tragic storyline, the vigor of the Hungarian peasantry and their attachment to the land comes across with great force.[7] The film, which was shot as an independent production, was

3 István Szőts, *Szilánkok és gyaluforgácsok* [Splinters and Shavings] (Budapest: Osiris Kiadó, 1999), 60–61.

4 Ibid.

5 Others put this number at 400,000–800,000; "Hány magyar nőt erőszakoltak meg a szovjetek?" [How Many Hungarian Women Were Raped by the Soviets?], *Múlt Kor historical portal*, Oct. 3, 2013.

6 Szőts, *Szilánkok és gyaluforgácsok*, 61.

7 Ibid., 60.

banned despite it previously having been approved; the reason for this was that it began with a Catholic procession of rogation. The general audience could only watch it after several decades.

"There Is a Mistake in the Creation": Fábián Bálint találkozása Istennel (Bálint Fábián Meets God, *1980)*

The public could not watch any films about World War I in 1947, nor could this happen for a long time afterwards. When the period and the topic were cursorily dealt with at all, the approach taken was ironical and unsympathetic. In the film from 1957, entitled *Bakaruhában*" (*In Soldier's Uniform*, 1957, directed by Imre Fehér), the lies uttered by the protagonist journalist in his romantic relationship are paralleled by the assumed lies in the enthusiastic recruitment for the war. This assumption can be found both in the film and in the short story by Sándor Hunyadi, on which the film is based.

The first film in which World War I plays an important role from the point of view of the dramaturgy is *Fábián Bálint találkozása Istennel* ("*Bálint Fábián Meets God*," 1980, directed by Zoltán Fábri). A full series of scenes are connected to the fights on the Italian front, and the rest of the plot takes place after The Great War is finished, but there are several references in the film to the earlier scenes. The eponymous character is a Hungarian man who had fought at the Isonzo front and is not able to get rid of the bloody memory of the Italian soldier he killed. Bálint Fábián is an honest Hungarian peasant who is righteous and prudent. He does not understand the complexities of life but is instinctively against violence and change. He does not betray his employee, the Baron, during the Hungarian Soviet Republic of 1919, but he, on the other hand, also defends the Communists when the anti-communists want to attack them. Bálint Fábián's wife is a pale, sickly woman who dies after a while. He does not know that his wife had an affair with the local Catholic priest while he has been at the front. The priest was secretly drowned by his sons, and he only has suspicions, "certain signs and hints," but he never learns the truth. A lot of bad things happen to him and around him, so he believes that "there is a mistake in the Creation" and wants to meet God in order to enquire of him about the causes. His solution is to hang himself on the rope of the church bell during the Christmas service.

The pacifism of this film is not as innocent and neutral as that present in the work of István Szőts. The Zoltán Fábri's film, just like the short novel on which the film is loosely based, explores the collective responsibility of Hungarians and the role of God. The series of scenes about the Italian front poses the question of why the war was happening more clearly. Bálint Fábián does not understand it, as he is not among the decision makers capable of causing or stopping the war. As a soldier, however, he should have understood whether the fighting in World War I was going on in the interest of his country or not. If he does not understand this, then he cannot be taken seriously when—according to the message of the film—he is the one to pose the philosophical question: Why does the Creator afflict mankind with so much evil? Even his statement, "there is a mistake in the Creation," has no meaning. His downfall, however, is caused not only by the trauma of war, but by a family tragedy as well.

Bálint Fábián is an antihero. Although this is not stated in the reviews which appeared in Hungary, this word appears in the title of an article from a Swiss magazine: "*Ein Anti-Held im bürgerlichen Ungarn.*"[8] The Hungarian reviews, however, note that the character of the protagonist is not consistent, and the problems presented in

8 "Ein Anti-Held im bürgerlichen Ungarn," *Tele TV Radio Zeitung*, May 8, 1982.

the film are not coherent with each other.[9] A historical drama—if it is one—mingles with a psychological one.[10] The suicide of Bálint Fábián can be attributed at least as much to the events of the war and of the revolution/counter-revolution as to his never fully proven suspicion concerning the infidelity of his wife. The wife could have remained loyal to her husband even while he was away fighting on the front, as news of his death never reached her. Bálint Fábián admits having always felt that his wife did not really love him.

If war is to blame, as well as the infidelity of the woman, and the Church, too, because the lover was a priest, then the root cause of all these events has to be looked for at some higher, more general level. Bálint Fábián does find the cause, namely that their village had been built on a cemetery. However, this is no explanation and no cause, no fault and no myth, only a superstition, which is not valid reasoning for the whole of Hungary or the world. If the spectator accepts this as a valid cause, then the cemetery becomes a symbol, and if the cemetery as a cause should be taken representatively, then Hungary from the very first is a loser, a dead country, God having created it to be so. Those critics who did not feel that the negative representation of Hungary in the film as a dead or suicidal country was authentic stated that the film became stuck at the level of realistic and anecdotic representation, although the novel on which it is based did manage to get to the level of mystical authenticity.[11]

9 László Fábián, "Elmaradt találkozás" [Missed Encounter], *Film Színház Muzsika,* March 22, 1980, 11–12.

10 Béla Mátrai-Betegh, "Temetőre épült falu: Fábri Zoltán: Fábián Bálint találkozása Istennel" [A Village Built on a Cemetery: Zoltán Fábri. Bálint Fábián Meets God], *Filmkultúra,* no. 3 (1980): 20–26, here: 25.

11 Interview with György Báron in Kossuth Rádió (*Láttuk, hallottuk,* March 20, 1980).

However, the same basic problem can already be found in the novel. As a critic writes about the book of József Balázs: At "the bottom of Christian hierarchy," there can be found a "*person who commits suicide,*"[12] and man "is not forsaken by culture even at the moment of his death."[13] Thus Bálint Fábián is an antihero, and his character and fate indicate that he is part of a suicidal culture.

Obviously, not all critics in 1980 thought that this representation of the Hungary of 1918-1920, or of the country, or of the given region, or of Bálint Fábián's village on the shore of the river Kraszna was valid. In an article that appeared in the periodical *Filmkultúra* (*Film Culture*), one can find the following: "He keeps repeating up to his death that no well can be dug in this place as all kinds of bones keep being unearthed, and everywhere there are only cemeteries, cemeteries, as it is stated in the Bible.' This simple man does not realize that in this Nyírség soil, in Hungarian soil, not only bones can be found, not only cemeteries bring malediction on the living ones. In the deep, like rumbling lava ore, there is life and sweat as well."[14]

A Traitor Made a Victim and Hero: István Szabó's Redl ezredes I-II. *("*Colonel Redl,*" 1984)*

István Szabó's film takes place before 1914, however, it is still strongly a World War I film. As the title indicates, it treats the life

12 Emphasis in the original; Károly Varga, "Mikor lehet egyenlő a három a végtelennel? Balázs József kérdéseiről, úgy ahogy itthonról látjuk" [When Can Three Equal to the Infinite? Concerning the Questions of József Balázs, As We See It from Home], *Szabolcs-Szatmári Szemle*, no. 2 (1980): 87–97, here: 95.

13 Varga, "Mikor lehet egyenlő a három a végtelennel? Balázs József kérdéseiről, úgy ahogy itthonról látjuk," 95.

14 Mátrai-Betegh, "Temetőre épült falu: Fábri Zoltán. Fábián Bálint találkozása Istennel," 26.

of Colonel Alfred Redl, who held a high position in the Austro-Hungarian army, and before his death in 1913 he served as the deputy head of the secret service. After his exposure, it turned out that for a long time he had been selling important military secrets for money to the Russians and the Italians. The military leadership of the time, being afraid of public exposure, forced the Colonel to commit suicide. However, the details were discovered and made public by a journalist.[15]

The summary of the plot of the film is the following: Alfred Redl, offspring of a Ruthenian (Transcarpathian Ukrainian) family of railway men, advances to become a colonel and later the deputy chief of the intelligence service of the Austro-Hungarian Monarchy. Already as a little boy, Redl composes a praise poem about his emperor, and he even misses his father's funeral in order to celebrate Emperor Franz Joseph's name day in the military school. All through his life, a special bond attaches him to his aristocratic schoolmate, the Hungarian Kristóf Kubinyi and to his sister, Katalin. He wants to be like them; he wants to efface his past and his family from his memory. He is driven by the ambition to advance and by the loyalty to the Emperor. Based on his investigations as the leader of the secret service, he recommends a purge of the military leadership of the monarchy. However, Redl has a weak point: He is trying to hide his homosexuality. A young Italian man is sent to him on purpose and starts an affair with him. So Redl gives away some important, but not memorizable, military secrets to him. However, Redl realizes from the start that

15 Egon Erwin Kisch, *A Redl-ügy* [The Redl Affair] (Bucharest: Téka, Kriterion Könyvkiadó, 1974). Original: *Der Fall des Generalstabschefs Redl* (1924). In Hungarian on the internet: https://sites.google.com/site/azido-harcokatujraz/home/2-szemelyes-haboruk/redl-ezredes-miatt-veszett-el-a-haboru-uegye

the young Italian is a spy, thus he may as well have withheld the information or may have just shot him. Although the Colonel is the deputy head of the secret service, he is still being watched, and because of his treason the military chiefs of staff give him the order to commit suicide, which he does.

The story of the treason and exposure of Colonel Redl was amply discussed by the press of the day, and several literary representations are also well known. István Szabó and the co-writer of the script, Péter Dobai, discuss their sources in the insert at the beginning of the film: "Our film is not based on authentic historical documents. All the actions of the characters are the result of the imagination. Our work was inspired by John Osborne's drama, *A Patriot for Me*, and by the historical events of our century." One can find a contradiction already in this introduction, as the makers of the film make a claim to interpret history authentically in spite of the fact that they disregard authentic documents.

The weekly periodical Élet és irodalom, (*Life and Literature*), which focuses on literature and public life, published an interview with a military historian, Dr. Márton Farkas, on the 15th February, 1985. He confirmed that the contemporary documents of the investigation and material published by journalists can be regarded authentic: "Nothing new has come to light since then. Thus we have to reconcile ourselves to the fact that there is no Redl-secret or Redl-legend; everything happened the way it happened, and only that happened which we had already known about."[16] Thus the film is based on the falsification of facts, and this was well known already in 1985, both by the makers of the film and the

16 László Szále, "Kém vagy bűnbak: Beszélgetés Redl ezredesről" ["Spy or Scapegoat: A Conversation about *Colonel Redl*"], Élet és irodalom, Feb. 15, 1985.

audience.[17] In spite of this, the film has been accepted as authentic with only a very few exceptions, mostly because of artistic and aesthetic reasons. Even the military historian cited above took the side of this fictional story, which is very far from the truth: "In the end I have to say—even if I cause disappointment—that the story of Redl as conceptualized by István Szabó and Péter Dobai is more interesting than the original one had been."[18]

The author of another article stresses that the fall of Redl is not historically authentic, and that there is no twentieth century history "in general"; moreover, that "the real Redl was not the victim of a set-up plan, and his alter-ego in the film is a thoroughly corrupt careerist, whose fall cannot be compared in any way to the tragedy of revolutionaries who were the victims of the unlawful acts of state in the 1950s; the problem lies in the psychological representation."[19] However, the psychological representation—no matter how the author of the article defends the film—should not vindicate inconsistent characterizations of the protagonist either as a traitor or a victim. The makers of the film should have either stuck to the facts, or should have changed the names, the location, and the time of the events happening.

17 Discussions on historical facts and truths of the Szabo's film are not limited to conservative or right-wing commentators. In the communist press of 1985, the renowned left-wing film critic Ervin Gyertyán also analyzed Szabo's rewriting of the story. In his conclusion, Gyertyán claimed that Szabo should at least have changed the protagonist's name (Ervin Gyertyán, "Stage and Illness: István Szabó's New Film, *Colonel Redl*," in *Népszabadság* 2, no. 16 (1985). Regarding Gyertyán see also the following pages.

18 László Szále, "Kém vagy bűnbak: Beszélgetés Redl ezredesről" [Spy or Scapegoat: A Conversation About *Colonel Redl*], Élet és irodalom, Feb. 15, 1985.

19 Gyertyán 1985.

The makers of the film insist—maybe because of or in spite of the insert—that they are writing authentic history. I quote here the director of the film, István Szabó: "The story of this man takes place in the Austro-Hungarian Monarchy. I want everything accurate and authentic. This is my task, as far as the clothes, the objects, the manners are concerned. I am not thinking symbolically, as in that moment, my desire to make an accurate film would fall into pieces."[20]

If we are seeing an interpretation of history that does not reflect reality, then it is worthwhile to examine the motivation of the makers. These are basically of two categories of motivation, arising from their connection to the ruling power, to the ruling ideology in Hungary between 1945 and 1989. First, it was in their interest to discredit the monarchy and its military chiefs of staff; second, it was also in their interest to acquit the traitor Redl. After the premiere of the film (made as a Hungarian/Austrian/West German/Yugoslavian co-production) in Vienna, a significant section of the Austrian press attacked the film because of its interpretation of history: "The Austrian Colonel Redl was selling the most important military secrets to the Russians for more than a decade. For money. So, for example, he owned two private cars—which was highly unusual before 1914. Now the Hungarians—with Austrian money, with the money of ORF—have made a film about Redl. Although it is emphasized that the actions of the characters are not identical with those of long ago, still, the film is about the old Austria, that is what it is all about, and this history is repulsively misrepresented. Redl is like a champion of peace, who wants to save his country from war, and the Austrian officers are sadists,

---

20 Tamás Skultéty, "Mindig elölről kell kezdeni: Beszélgetés Szabó Istvánnal" [One Always Has to Start from Scratch: An Interview with István Szabó], *Magyar Hírlap*, Feb. 16, 1985.

drunkards, and sons of bitches. It is inconceivable how, after all this, an army with such leaders was capable of fighting for their country for four years at the price of the greatest sacrifices. This film, which is otherwise excellent from the artistic point of view—just like Colonel Redl himself at the time—has again betrayed Austria to foreign countries. In these countries, the film had great success due to a wave of nostalgia. On our part, on the part of Austria, however, we can only state that this is a shame, which is especially aggravated by the fact that the protagonist is played by one of our most prominent actors."[21] One of the journalists of the daily paper *Magyar Hírlap* (*Hungarian Herald*) mentions that Mr. Gerd Bacher, the chief intendant of ORF, gave an interview for the *Kronen-Zeitung* where he stated that he had issued an internal circular several weeks earlier, as—ORF being one of the partners in the co-production of the film—he felt himself responsible for the outcome: "The release to the world of such a falsification of history can not be considered the task of an Austrian state monopoly institution." However, Austrian cinemas seem to have been filled at the premiere of the film in spite of the criticisms. The magazines *Der Spiegel* and *Der Stern* published favorable reviews about the film.[22]

Why the falsification of history provoked resentment in Austria does not need an explanation. Also, it is not by accident that in Hungary this misrepresentation was mostly received favourably. I am going to cite István Szabó, whose views are supported by the journalist: "I have reasoned out, and then, with my colleagues, I have accomplished my own special version, our special version. I am not stating that this is the only possible conception of Redl."

21 Article about the Viennese premiere of *Colonel Redl*. Vienna, April 1985, cited in: *Magyar Hírlap*, April 13, 1985. The journalist was Pál Geszti.

22 Ibid.

And the journalist adds: "But for us—this is the best. This is certain."[23]

Szabó seemingly gave an ambiguous interpretation of the protagonist. He sometimes considers him a traitor, sometimes a victim, and in one sense even a hero. This is the result of the fact that, according to Szabó, Redl was a traitor with respect to himself, his family, the army, and the monarchy; but in selling out the cause of his country and fellow countrymen, he was a hero: "Redl is not simply a compromiser, but a big traitor. He begins with small betrayals: he betrays his parents, his brothers and sisters, his friends, his class, his bosses. He commits a small betrayal every day, which will build up into a huge, unified betrayal—and this is going to

---

23 D. L., "Redl ezredes" [Colonel Redl], *Délmagyarország*, March 14, 1985. "For us"; this expression refers to the leadership of the soft dictatorship of the Communism Regime of Kádár, and to the members of the servile intelligentsia serving the regime—writers, journalist, film directors, film historians, military historians. and experts, who were happy to bury with such a film as well the old Austro-Hungarian Monarchy. The other motive is a much more personal one, and is connected to the director, but is at least as much of public interest as the wish of the leaders of the Communist-Socialist party state and its beneficiaries to discredit the monarchy. Their predecessors were partly responsible for the breaking up of the Austro-Hungarian Monarchy. Compare the facts concerning the effects of the Aster Revolution of 1918 and of the 1919 Dictatorship of the Proletariat (Ernö Raffay, *Szabadkőművesek Trianon előtt* [Free Masons Before Trianon] (Budapest: Kárpátia Stúdió, 2011)). This direct motive was not yet known in 1985, but in 2006 it came to light that István Szabó, the director of the film, had been a very active and very useful III./III. communist secret agent after 1956. Cf. András Gervai, *Fedőneve: "Szocializmus" - Művészek, ügynökök, titkosszolgák* [Cover-Name: "Socialism": Artists, Agents, Spies] (Budapest: Jelenkor Kiadó 2010).

include his self-betrayal as well. He betrays even his own instincts, his own feelings."[24] The reporter (Tamás Sámathy) asks: "After all, is the Colonel a likeable person?" István Szabó replies: "I think he is. His horrible fate makes us see a man struggling in the snare of the contradictions of history and politics. In the case of such a talented man as Redl, there is no judge who could decide whether he is guilty or not."[25] Thus, according to the director, talent stands above truth. Some journalists, agreeing with this view, wrote the following: "The film of István Szabó—in the opinion of one of our historians—is more interesting than historical reality itself, than the documents at our disposal. [...] As a matter of fact, in discussing the film, I believe that it is of minor importance whether Colonel Redl was a victim or a traitor."[26] *Colonel Redl* won awards at several festivals: in Budapest, Cannes, Sopot, Valladoid, Rueil-Malmaison, Rome, Hollywood, London, Warsaw, and Germany. Indeed, it was not necessarily in the interest of the critics, apart from those in Austria and Hungary, to go after the facts.

Hungarians and World War I: I Was at the Isonzo Battle Too *(*Én is jártam Isonzónál, *1986)*

In the 1980s and the 1990s, a documentary about World War I was produced that, despite its small deficiencies, can be considered a landmark, as it deals with the causes of The Great War in full detail. The second film of a series, for which originally three films had been planned by Gyula Gulyás and János Gulyás, was released in 1986. Its title was *Én is jártam Isonzónál* (*I was at the Isonzo battle*

24 István Szabó, quoted in Skultéty, "Mindig elölről kell kezdeni. Beszélgetés Szabó Istvánnal".

25 Sámathy 1985.

26 János Tamási, "Áruló vagy áldozat?" ["Traitor or Victim?"], *Népújság (Tolna)*, March 12, 1985.

too), and the series was named *Magyarok és az I. Világháború* (*Hungarians and World War I*). It is interesting that before the change of regime (the fall of Communism) in 1989–1990, only the second film could be completed and released; maybe because this film was the one that contained the fewest number of facts that were embarrassing for the Communist leadership. The causes and circumstances that led to the war, the events on the Russian and other fronts, the role of the Soviet Republic of Councils of 1919 and of the dictatorship of the proletariat in the military collapse of the monarchy, and the Trianon peace treaty ending the war were all considered taboo.

The above topics were either not dealt with in the second film, or they appeared only indirectly, on the level of references; maybe that is why the film was allowed to be shown in cinemas at all. Én is jártam Isonzónál mostly recalls the events of the Italian front, but it also deals briefly with other locations and aspects as well, such as the general characteristics of the war; the relationship between officers and subalterns; the happenings of the war; the truce at the end of the war and the military collapse of the monarchy; the happenings in the hinterland, among them the Aster Revolution of 1918; demobilization of soldiers and their return home. The filmmakers sought out eighty- to ninety-year-old veterans, who evoked their own memories about World War I with words and pictures in their homes in different parts of the country. In the second part of the film, twenty-three Hungarian veterans took part in a commemorative journey in Italy, in the course of which they visited the fighting locations near Piave and Isonzo; the cemeteries of Doberdo, where their comrades-in-arms rest; and they also met their former Italian antagonists in Fossalta di Piave and Venice at a common reconciliatory commemoration. The tour was organized by General Guiseppe Santoro and the association of veterans called "Ragazzi 99" ("The Lads of 99"), and the Italian deputy minister of defence at the time also took part in the events. A "church of commemoration" was consecrated at a Catholic mass where a child was also baptized, the Hungarian and Italian veterans exchanged the flags of peace, and finally they placed a wreath into the Piave River, where about a hundred thousand Hungarian soldiers, and about the same number of Italian, had lost their lives.

The film had a mixed reception. Some critics enthusiastically welcomed the fact that, after a long time, the subject of World War I was revisited and received publicity,[27] but there were some who were either disturbed by the facts, or considered what can be seen and heard in the film only half-truths.[28] For example, someone in an article vehemently criticized the fact that the veterans dared to mention the role of the hinterland and of the Aster Revolution in the military collapse of the monarchy.[29] However, more recent work by historians justifies the raising of such questions.[30] Moreover, these old veterans also accepted their own responsibility. Dr. Ferenc Sailer, who fought as an officer on the Italian front, admits that it was a mistake to take away the arms from the Hungarian soldiers on their way home and to put all of these into the last wagon of the train; some people uncoupled the

---

27 Article in *Fejér Megyei Hírlap* about the film: *Én is jártam Isonzónál* ("*I Was at the Isonzo Battle Too*"), May 20, 1987.

28 Ágnes Koltai, *Emlék és varázslat: Magyar film. Én is jártam Isonzónál* ("*Memory and Magic: Hungarian Film. I Was at the Isonzo Battle Too*"), Új tükör, May 24, 1987).

29 László Zöldi, *Tőr a hátba* ("*Dagger in the Back*"), Élet és irodalom, May 8, 1987.

30 Ernö Raffay, *Balkáni birodalom: Nagy-Románia megteremtése 1866–1920* [An Empire of the Balkans: The Creation of Greater Romania 1866–1920], (Budapest: Kárpátia Stúdió, 2010). Cf. Raffay, *Szabadkőművesek Trianon előtt.*

wagon, and thus, for example, the soldiers faced grave problems when trying to defend themselves during the troubled times of upheaval. The Hungarian military leadership was also responsible for putting the truce into effect immediately, although the signed agreement allowed twenty-four or thirty-six hours. During this time gap, about 300,000 Austro-Hungarian soldiers were taken captive.

The discussion of the taboos in the film, which did not please the party state, was also criticized by those who basically had a good opinion of the film. Ervin Gyertyán, one of the eminent film critics of the years just before the fall of the Communist Regime in 1989–1990, expresses his belief not only in the responsibility of the Habsburg leadership, but also in that of István Tisza (prime minister of Hungary of the time), and resents the mentioning of the responsibility of Mihály Károlyi (a later prime minister) in any way.[31] The film indeed mentions Károlyi as the one responsible for retreating from the Transylvanian front in 1919, when he was no longer prime minister nor president of the Republic.[32] Some smaller corrections and additions to the recollections of the veterans would have been useful, as they did indeed authentically interpret the events that they themselves had lived through; however, they could have made mistakes concerning far-away events or affecting the whole country (particularly as far as time and location are concerned).

---

31 Gyertyán 1987.

32 However, his Minister of Defense was Béla Linder, who declared on Oct. 31, 1918 that "I never want to see soldiers again!" And the Soviet Republic of Councils of 1919 was a direct result of the Aster Revolution, the leadership of which (including Mihály Károlyi) did not take a stand for Transylvania and the other Hungarian territories when they came under attack.

The other films in the series, which were completed by 1997, partly fill the gaps and correct the historical knowledge that was taught differently before 1989 (when historical knowledge was not always compatible with facts and the truth) and could not be a part of the second film. Even the dissatisfied critics admit that the film (and the films) definitely fill a gap. The Gulyás brothers managed to interview veterans who had been on the front and had immediate experiences about World War I at the very last minute. Several of the most important interviewees above eighty were actually dead by the time the film was released. It also has to be noted that filming started in 1982 and continued well after the premiere of the second film, up to 1991—basically as long as survivors could still be found. The original trilogy became four films, and the episodes released in 1997, as the titles suggest, dealt with both the earlier and the later events of the war from the beginnings to the signing of the Treaty of Trianon, which heavily afflicted Hungary: The first, *Meggondoltan, megfontoltan* (*Prudently, sagely*); The third, *Soha többé katonát nem akarok látni!* (*I do not ever want to see soldiers again!*); The fourth, *Rabló béke* (*Unjust peace*).

The film not only evokes the events of the Great War, but it also shows some of the later life of the veterans, who were living in poverty, often in unworthy circumstances, on a small pension. Some of them were still working though over eighty: for example, Vilmos Steinbach, a former infantryman, or István Hőgyi, a former messenger of the Chiefs of Staff. It is very compelling to see and hear that not only did the state fail to provide a pension that would have ensured a reasonable level of existence for the veterans who had been sent to the front to defend their country by the politicians of the time, but that there were also some whose livelihood was taken away from them in the Rákosi era. József Szücs, one of those soldiers whose legs had to be amputated, related to the filmmakers that, in the 1950s, first his lands, and then his licence for the sale of tobacco, were taken away from him. The party state of the period before 1989 treated the veterans of World War I so unkindly because it tried to distance itself from the Hungary of World War I and the Hungary of the pre-1920 period in general. Some critics stressed the fact that the soldiers did not even know what they were fighting for.[33] There may have been indeed a few such young, uneducated, and ill-informed people, but most of the interviews show that the former soldiers knew very well that they were defending their own country, as it was Italy that attacked the monarchy, even though Italy may have had a reason to do so. Some of the interviewees enlisted in the Transylvanian Szekler Division after returning from the Italian front, as they did not want the Romanians to conquer the territory of Hungary up to the River Tisza. In the other films, there is a veteran who, in spite of his ideological reservations, still joined the Red Army, willing to defend and reconquer some Hungarian territories, later on, for example, a part of Upper Hungary (today Slovakia). Special mention should be made of the Slovak man Jan Kellner from the third film, who supported the Austro-Hungarian Monarchy not only out of emotional, but also ideological and economic, considerations; along with some other Slovaks, he fought on the side of the Hungarians as long as he could after the military collapse of the monarchy.

In the first film, released in 1997, what was not allowed to be stated publicly before 1990 could finally be articulated, namely that prime minister István Tisza and the Hungarian leadership opposed the decision to enter the war. Historians discovered that István Tisza was not among the warmongers—though not for

---

33 György Báron, *Én is jártam Isonzónál* ["*I Was at the Isonzo Battle Too*"], *Képes* (May 7, 1987).

pacifist reasons—even when he had to defend the imperial policy in the Parliament.[34]

The four documentary films of the Gulyás brothers are unparalleled and irreplaceable as far as the memory of World War I and its consequences are concerned. The second film, which was produced in 1986 and released in 1987, *Én is jártam Isonzónál*, was planned to be presented to the public in form of a book edited by the MAFILM Budapest Studio, though the manuscript remained unpublished.[35]

A Lyrical Documentary of the Outcome of World War One: Trianon (2004)

Another film entitled *A vörös grófnő I-II* (*The red countess*, 1984, directed by András Kovács) focused on the era of World War I too and especially on the eve and the aftermath of it. It was produced before the fall of Communism in Hungary and adapts the memoirs of Mrs. Katinka Károlyi (Károlyni Mihályné, née Andrássy, the wife of prime minister Mihály Károlyi), *Együtt a forradalomban* (*Together in the revolution*), published in 1968, for the screen.[36] Her individual point of view cannot, however, be regarded as a reliable historical source. According to experts, the countess idolized her husband to such an extent that she was not able to paint a realistic

34 Participation in the war was voted for by, among others, the representatives of the Romanian minority, who later turned against Hungary because of her participation in the War (Raffay, *Szabadkőművesek Trianon előtt*).

35 *Én is jártam Isonzónál* [*I Was at the Isonzo Battle Too*], MAFILM Budapest Stúdió, manuscript. Budapest, 1987. It is worth reading Dr. József Hary (a former platoon-commander) memoirs of the Italian front (József Hary, *Az utolsó emberig: Isonzói jelentés* ["*To the Last Man: Report From Isonzo*"] (Budapest: Püski Kiadó, 2011).

36 Károlyi Mihályné (Mrs. Katinka Károlyi), *Együtt a forradalomban* ["*Together in the Revolution*"] (1968).

picture of him and of the era.[37] The Andrássy viewpoint is complemented by the work of Cécile Tormay's *Bujdosó könyv* (An outlaw's diary).[38] However, no film adaptation of this book has been yet made.

However, a documentary was made about the aftermath of World War I with the title *Trianon* (2004, directed by Koltay Gábor). This film depicts this era with more accuracy and in a more complex way than any other Hungarian film before. The film, which was released in 2004, deals with the peace of Trianon and also discusses many aspects of the Great War in detail. The 128-minute production reconstructs the era with the help of contemporary photos, documents, and films sources. The reflections of writers, poets, historians, and public figures as well as the shock caused by the partitioning of the Kingdom of Hungary are effectively presented by the interpretation of actors. It is not widely known, for example, that the young Attila József wrote the poem "Nem, nem, soha!" ("No, No, Never!") as a result of the peace treaty. The poem is recited in the film by Gábor Koncz, who had played the antihero Bálint Fábián twenty-four years earlier in Zoltán Fábri's film. Apart from the lyrical reminiscences, writers, historians, and artists recall certain facts and documents that were forbidden or inadvisable to talk about for a long time. The main contributors are the writers István Csurka and Miklós Duray, the historians Ferenc Fejtő and Ferenc Glatz, the literary historian István Nemeskürty, the politician and university professor Imre Pozsgay, the historian Ernő Raffay, the sculptor Tibor Szervátiusz, as well as the politician and Hungarian bishop of the Reformed Church (Romania), László Tőkés.

This film at last presents the causes, facts and circumstances concerning the breakout of the war. The literary historian István

---

37 Tamás Kovács, "*Károlyi Mihályné: a férjét istenítő vörös grófnő*"[Mrs. Katinka Károlyi: The Red Countess Who Idolized Her Husband], *Múlt-Kor*, Sept. 10, 2012). http://mult-kor.hu/cikk.php?id=37365.

38 Cécile Tormay, *Bujdosó könyv* ["*An Outlaw's Diary*"], 1920.

Nemeskürty calls the attention to the fact that—from his own perspective—it was not the monarchy and Hungary that wanted war in the first place, but rather France and Russia; the latter wished to expand its control in the direction of the Balkans. The heir to the Austro-Hungarian throne was shot in Sarajevo by Gavrilo Princip, who had been trained with Russian money, and this event is recognized as the immediate cause of the breakout of the war. It is also Nemeskürty who questions the legitimacy of the Aster Revolution of 1918 and expresses his doubts if it was a revolution at all: For example, Mihály Károlyi was appointed prime minister by the King on the phone during the chaotic days of the truce ending the war.

Gábor Koltay's film is extremely detailed and multi-layered, but it does not deal with important aspects like—among others—the activities and standpoints of left-wing politicians and revolutionaries with regard to the territorial losses of Hungary after the collapse of the Habsburg Empire. Thus, history, literature, and film still have questions to answer.[39]

---

39 Why did the left-wing politicians and the revolutionaries not make a stand for the interests and the territorial integrity of Hungary during and after the military collapse of the Austro-Hungarian Monarchy, in an era when, for example, the Russians defended the last piece of ground of their country even after the socialist/communist revolutions and "coups"? Not even István Nemeskürty, who posed this question in the film, could give an answer to it, although he was interested in World War I not solely from the point of view of literary and film history, but also for family reasons: He describes how his maternal grandfather and his family were chased away by the Czechs from the northern part of the town of Komárom in 1919 to the Hungarian side of the town, where, deprived of everything, they had to start life from the very beginning. Today, the northern part of the town belongs to Slovakia, while the southern part is Hungarian territory.

WITHOUT A NAME AND A FACE:

THE AUSTRIAN ENEMY IN INTERWAR ITALIAN CINEMA

Francesco Bono

Introduction

In the years since the war's end until today, approximately 100 feature films were produced in Italy with references to WWI.[1] However, it must be noted that the number of films in which the *Grande Guerra*, (the "Great War"), as WWI is commonly referred to in Italy, represents the actual focus of attention is relatively rare. As has been widely remarked by scholars, there has been a sort of reticence in Italian cinema about WWI. Discussing the reasons for that would go beyond the scope of this essay, but I shall, in the course of it, provide some explanations for the phenomenon with

---

1 Warmest thanks go to Adriano Aprà, Umberta Brazzini, Alessandro Faccioli, Giuseppe Ghigi, Angela Margaritelli, and Alberto Scandola, as well as Biblioteca di Storia Moderna e Contemporanea (Rome), Centro Studi del Teatro Stabile dell'Umbria (Perugia), La Cineteca del Friuli (Gemona), and Mediateca Toscana for supporting my research. I would like to specially thank Hannes Leidinger for the invitation to contribute to this volume.

A full list is provided by Enrico Gaudenzi. Giorgio Sangiorgi, *La prima guerra mondiale nel cinema italiano: Filmografia 1915–2013*, vol. 1 (Ravenna: Longo 1997), 47–77.

regard to the interwar years and, in particular, the 1930s. Moreover, it should also be noted that it is necessary to make the attempt to assess the body of Italian films that deal with WWI in a comprehensive way. So far, scholars have favored certain periods and films, while others have found only scarce attention. In fact, most of the interest has centered until now on the interwar period, as well as on the films by Mario Monicelli—*La Grande Guerra* (1959)—and Francesco Rosi—*Uomini contro* (1970)[2]—which count among the most important Italian films on WWI. But little consideration has been given so far in the scientific literature on the topic, regardless of the periods or films examined, to the image of the enemy in the Italian films on WWI. This essay will specifically discuss the question, investigating the enemy's depiction in interwar Italian cinema.

2 Here follows a list of works offering an overview of WWI in Italian cinema from the 1920s up to now. They are listed in chronological order: Gian Piero Brunetta, *La guerra lontana: La prima guerra mondiale e il cinema tra i tabù del presente e la creazione del passato* (Rovereto: Zaffoni, 1985); Pier Marco De Santi, *1914–1918: Una guerra sullo schermo* (Roma: Rivista Militare, 1988); Pier Marco De Santi, "La Grande Guerra nel cinema italiano," in *La Grande Guerra degli artisti*, ed. Nadia Marchioni (Firenze: Polistampa, 2005), 133–154; Marco Mondini, *La guerra italiana. Partire, raccontare, tornare. 1914–18* (Bologna: Il Mulino, 2014). Extensively published on the topic is Alessandro Faccioli, "La guerra al cinema," in *Gli Italiani in guerra: Conflitti, identità, memorie dal Risorgimento ai nostri giorni*, ed. Mario Isnenghi, vol. 3 (Torino: Utet, 2008), 942–951; "Pellicole sul fronte: il cinema e la guerra," in *Dizionario storico della prima guerra mondiale*, ed. Nicola Labanca (Bari: Laterza, 2014), 380–387; "Il cinema italiano e la Grande Guerra," in *A fuoco l'obiettivo! Il cinema e la fotografia raccontano la Grande Guerra*, ed. Alessandro Faccioli and Alberto Scandola (Bologna: Persiani, 2014), 14–31.

In the representation of WWI in Italian cinema, *La Grande Guerra* marked a turning point, breaking with the rhetoric that dominated until then. Monicelli's film explicitly distances itself from the films of the interwar period as well as from the wave of other films on WWI made in Italy after the Second World War, as examples: *Il caimano del Piave* (1951, directed by Giorgio Bianchi), *La leggenda del Piave* (1952, directed by Riccardo Freda), *Guai ai vinti* (1954, directed by Raffaello Matarazzo), and *Tradita* (1954, directed by Mario Bonnard). On the whole, a propagandistic and overt patriotic tone characterize the films of the early 1950s on WWI, and they are, in part, productions of mediocre quality. So far, scarce consideration has been paid to them by scholars, but at a closer look, they are not without interest. Ten years after *La Grande Guerra*, the critical reconsideration of WWI in Italian cinema culminates with *Uomini contro*. Rosi's film is an adaptation for the screen of Emilio Lussu's *Un anno sull'altipiano*, one of the most important Italian novels on WWI, first published in 1938 in Paris, where Lussu had found refuge from the fascist regime. Among the Italian films of the 1960s and early 1970s on WWI, of interest are also Alberto Lattuada's *Fraulein Doktor* (1968) and Alfredo Giannetti's *La Sciantosa* (1971). Further, let us mention *Il giorno più corto* (1963, directed by Sergio Corbucci), *La ragazza e il generale* (1967, directed by Pasquale Festa Campanile), and *Armiamoci e partite* (1971, directed by Nando Cicero), which belong to the comic genre, with protagonists who live through picaresque adventures during the war.

Then Italian cinema's interest in WWI decreased. At the beginning of the 1980s, there are *Malamore* (1982, directed by Eriprando Visconti, a nephew of Luchino Visconti, not to be mistaken with one of the masters of Italian cinema), and *Porca vacca* (1982, directed by Festa Campanile). The outbreak of WWI ends Federico Fellini's *E la nave va* (1983), and Paolo and

Vittorio Taviani's *Good Morning Babilonia* (1987) also concludes with WWI, with the protagonists, Andrea and Nicola, who had emigrated to America years before, returning home and dying on the battlefield. Finally, the contribution of Italian cinema to the 100th anniversary of the outbreak of WWI are Paolo Cevoli's *Soldato semplice*, about the comic adventures of a teacher on the front, a "docu-fiction" by Leonardo Tiberi, *Fango e gloria: La Grande Guerra*, and *Torneranno i prati* by Ermanno Olmi, which prosaically describes the hardships of a squad of Italian soldiers crossing snow-covered mountains, where death may strike at any moment. *Torneranno i prati*, by a master of Italian cinema, is an utter condemnation of war, and it stands among the most impressive Italian films on WWI.

An Overview of the 1930s

Our starting point for the following considerations on the representation of WWI in interwar Italian cinema shall be Elter's *Le scarpe al sole* (*Shoes in the Sun*, 1935). Elter's film is commonly regarded as the best Italian production of that time on WWI. It also counts among the major Italian films on WWI in general. Mario Isnenghi, a prominent historian, author of a seminal book in the 1970s on the myth and literary representation of WWI in interwar Italy,[3] considers *Le scarpe al sole* as one of the most significant contributions to the depiction of WWI in Italian cinema, putting Elter's film alongside Monicelli's *La Grande Guerra* and Rosi's *Uomini contro*.[4] The film is about a group of Alpini. The Alpini are a specialized Italian mountain corps who gain great popularity

3 Mario Isnenghi, *Il mito della Grande Guerra* (Bari: Laterza, 1970).

4 Mario Isnenghi, "L'immagine cinematografica della grande guerra," *Rivista di storia contemporanea* VII, no. 3 (July 1978): 345. The essay deals specifically with Elter's, Monicelli's, and Rosi's films.

during WWI. Elter himself served in the Alpini during WWI, and *Le scarpe al sole* is a free adaptation of the homonymous novel by Paolo Monelli from the early 1920s, in which the Italian journalist recalls his memories of WWI. *Le scarpe al sole* was produced on occasion of the twentieth anniversary of Italy's entering the war (the country enters WWI some months after its beginning, in May 1915), and the film, as informs the opening credits, was shot with support of the Italian war ministry.

Le scarpe al sole begins on the eve of WWI. It is summer. A marriage is being celebrated in a village among the Alps. When war breaks out, the camera lingers on the men leaving the village. They say goodbye to wives and children; the younger ones kiss their fiancées, while others leave behind their aged parents, who accompany their sons for a while. We see the men reaching the front, where they fight valiantly for their country. In the scenes showing the Alpini in action, one can detect the influence of the German mountain film genre of the 1920s and especially Luis Trenker's film on WWI *Berge in Flammen* (1931), which may have been a point of reference for *Le scarpe al sole*. Also, Elter seems to have been inspired by Soviet cinema, as remarks a prominent Italian film historian, Gian Piero Brunetta.[5] For example, the opening scene of the marriage and that of the men departing to the front: On their way to the valley, the men grow in number, as more and more join their ranks, coming from other villages. The beginning sets the tone. The accent falls not on individual, exceptional boldness. Elter's film emphasizes rather the collective dimension, and war is represented as a communal experience that equally involves the soldiers and the women waiting at home for them, while fall follows summer, and winter comes, and days pass

5 Gian Piero Brunetta, *Intellettuali, cinema e propaganda tra le due guerre* (Bologna: Patròn, 1973), 111–112.

by. A quiet tone permeates *Le scarpe al sole*. A light melancholy characterizes the scene in which the Alpini leave home. No expressions of enthusiasm accompany the men who join the war. The war's outbreak is not excitedly welcomed. The composed mood of the scene is distinctive for Elter's film. *Le scarpe al sole* does not celebrate war, as has been rightly observed. There are no heroes, and the audience is invited to identify with the film's characters. Simplicity and a strong sense of duty distinguish them. War is represented as a duty, a task that must be fulfilled, and Elter's film appears distant from the shrill rhetoric and propaganda of other Italian films on WWI of that time.

Le scarpe al sole is one of the few Italian films of the 1930s on WWI. The other two are Giovacchino Forzano's *13 uomini e un cannone* ("*13 Men and a Gun*", 1936) and Oreste Biancolis's *Il piccolo alpino* (*The Little Alpino*, 1940). There are some more films in which WWI is more or less important, but in those films, it does not represent the thematic nucleus. That is the case of an earlier film by Forzano, *Camicia nera* (*Blackshirt*, 1933), which will be discussed further on. Another case is Mario Bonnard's comedy *Milizia territorial* (*Territorial Militia*, 1935). This film is about a timid clerk who serves as an officer in WWI. There, he learns to command and finds pleasure in being obeyed. When the war ends, and he comes home, everything is again as before. But one day, he takes courage and rebels. Unfortunately, Bonnard's comedy is lost, making a detailed discussion impossible. Besides these, there are a few more films in the 1930s that make reference to WWI. In particular, let us mention *Passaporto rosso* (*Red Passport*, 1935, directed by Guido Brignone) and *Cavalleria* (*Horsemen/Cavalry*, 1936, directed by Goffredo Alessandrini). *Passaporto rosso* follows an Italian family that emigrates to South America. When war breaks out, the father decides to return and fight for his country, but he falls severely ill, so his son takes his place and dies on the front heroically.

Death is also the destiny of a cavalry officer named Umberto Solaro in *Cavalleria*. The film tells the story of his impossible love for the daughter of an aristocratic family against the background of fin de siècle Italy. When Solaro´s horse gets fatally injured, he joins the aviation service. Then WWI breaks out, and he is killed in a battle. In both films, WWI takes up little space. A few scenes summarize the war. In Alessandrini's film *Luciano Serra, pilota* (*Pilot Luciano Serra*, 1938), the main character again is a pilot who fights in WWI, but he leaves Italy after the war's end. Some years later, he is in Africa, fighting in Ethiopia together with the Italian troops. Among them, there is also his son, who has become a pilot as well. In *Luciano Serra, pilota,* WWI is presented as a crucial experience in the life of the main character that influences him deeply, but the film just refers to it briefly. *Luciano Serra, pilota, Passaporto rosso*, as well as *Cavalleria* shall be left aside in our study on the representation of the Austrian enemy in interwar Italian films; they have been thoroughly discussed elsewhere.[6]

From the Fascist Perspective

The tiny number of Italian films of the 1930s specifically devoted to WWI may surprise at first. In fact, it stands in apparent contrast to the attention paid to WWI by French and German cinema. The striking rareness of WWI being explicitly thematized

---

6 See the chapter dedicated to WWI in Gianfranco Miro Gori, *Patria diva: La storia d'Italia nei film del ventennio* (Firenze: La casa Usher, 1988), 58–73; as well as Pierre Sorlin, "Tre sguardi sulla Grande Guerra: I film di finzione in Francia, Germania e Italia," in *La Grande Guerra: Esperienza, memoria, immagini*, ed. Diego Leoni, and Camillo Zadra (Bologna: Il Mulino, 1986), 827–850. For information on the films, see Gianfranco Casadio's critical filmography: *Il grigio e il nero: Spettacolo e propaganda nel cinema italiano degli anni Trenta* (Ravenna: Longo, 1989).

in the Italian cinema of the 1930s surprises even more, as Mario Isnenghi observes,[7] if one considers the great importance accorded to WWI by fascism. For a better understanding of the Italian films on WWI of that time, let us briefly recall fascism's interpretation of the war: WWI was assigned a crucial place in the nation's history, and the war was celebrated by fascism as the glorious continuation of the *Risorgimento*. The term indicates, in Italy's history, the epoch of the genesis of the Italian state through the gradual unification of the entire peninsula around the middle of the nineteenth century under the Piedmontese king, Vittorio Emanuele II. The liberation of the towns of Trento and Trieste, which were part of the Habsburg empire and annexed by Italy after WWI, represented the fulfillment of the *Risorgimento*, and the war, as Gianfranco Miro Gori remarks in a comprehensive study on the depiction of the nation's history in interwar Italian cinema,[8] was regarded as a decisive turning point, which set in motion the nation's renewal. War became a myth, and victory was celebrated as Italy's triumph, shaping a picture of WWI that was in deep contrast with the historical fact that Italy's entering the war was forced by a minority against most political forces and public opinion. *Passaporto rosso*, *Cavalleria*, and *Luciano Serra, pilota* stand exemplary for such an interpretation of WWI and represent an important transition from an older Italy to a new epoch that finds in fascism its privileged interpreter.

That is also the representation widely given to WWI in the Italian films of the 1920s. Several films of that time present WWI as a decisive chapter in the recent history of Italy that eventually leads to the establishment of the fascist regime. Prime examples are some films by Luca Comerio, *Sulle Alpi riconsacrate* (*On the*

7 Isnenghi, "L'immagine cinematografica della grande guerra," 342.

8 Gori, *Patria diva*, 58.

reconsecrated Alps, 1922) and *Giovinezza, giovinezza, primavera di bellezza* (*Youth, Youth, Spring of Beauty*, 1923), as well as the later *Al rombo del cannon* (*At the Roar of the Cannon*, 1928), or Umberto Paradisi's *A noi!* (*To us!*, 1923); all four films are feature-length montage films.[9] Also focusing on the transition from WWI to fascism are *Il grido dell'aquila* (*The Eagle's Cry*, 1923, directed by Mario Volpe) and *I martiri d'Italia* (*The Martyrs of Italy*, 1928, directed by Domenico Gaido). *I martiri d'Italia* recalls Italy's history from the far Middle Ages to WWI, paying homage to its heroes; the film ends with fascism's seizure of power. Among the films that celebrate the ideal continuity between WWI and the fascist movement, there also may be counted *La leggenda del Piave* (*The Legend of the Piave*, 1924, directed by Mario Negri), *L'Italia s'è desta* (*Italy has risen*, 1927, directed by Elvira Notari), *Redenzione d'anime* (1928, directed by Silvio Laurenti Rosa) and *Brigata Firenze* (1928, directed by Gian Orlando Vassallo). But the large number of films in which reference is made to WWI should mislead no one; WWI seldom occupies a central place. As Gian Piero Brunetta aptly writes, "There is never the intention of fully making a film in which WWI becomes the specific object of the narration."[10] A major part of the films can be assigned to the genre of melodrama, and WWI represents simply a component of the story. For example, *Fenesta ca lucive…* (1925, directed by Mario Volpe) and *Nun è Carmela mia* (1928 Ubaldo Maria Del Colle), films in which WWI causes the sorrowful separation of loving couples. In *Fenesta ca lucive…*, Emma dies from sadness when she and Mario

---

9 For a description of the films, see Vittorio Martinelli's critical filmography "Documentari degli anni Venti," *Immagine: Note di storia del cinema*, Nuova Serie, no. 27 (Summer 1994): 1–12.

10 Gian Piero Brunetta, "L'immagine della prima guerra mondiale attraverso il cinema," in *Operai e contadini nella Grande Guerra*, ed. Mario Isnenghi (Bologna: Cappelli, 1982), 274.

get separated by the war's outbreak. When Mario comes home and hears of her death, he commits suicide on her grave. War seems to be a fateful moment in the life of many main characters. That is, as well, the representation of WWI in *Napoli è sempre Napoli* (1925, directed by Mario Negri), *Fantasia 'e surdate* (1927, directed by Elvira Notari), and *L'Italia s'è desta*, in which a Neapolitan scalawag is given the chance of rehabilitating himself in war. War becomes on the screen the "symbolic place of purification and penance," as has been remarked,[11] where past crimes can be redeemed.

Let us consider in particular Comerio's *Sulle Alpi riconsacrate* and *Giovinezza, giovinezza, primavera di bellezza*, as well as *Il grido dell'aquila*, which look back at WWI against the background of fascist seizure of power. At the end of the nineteenth century, Comerio worked initially as photographer before moving to film, and he belonged to the most important figures of prewar Italian cinema. In WWI, Comerio was active as a cameraman at the front on behalf of the Italian ministry of war. *Sulle Alpi riconsacrate* and *Giovinezza, giovinezza, primavera di bellezza* are montage films in which footage from the war is combined with scenes of fascist gatherings in the early postwar years. As remarks the press of the day, *Sulle Alpi riconsacrate* intends to celebrate Italy's renewal after WWI, and Comerio's film ends with pictures of the *Camicie nere*, the fascist militias, through whom the spirit of the soldiers fallen in WWI lives on. *Giovinezza, giovinezza, primavera di bellezza* also demonstrates the ideal connection between fascism and WWI. The film is divided in three sections. The first part, *Epopea nazionale*, is devoted to the war. The second section, *Riscossa civile*, depicts the beginnings of the fascist movement, while the third part, *Il trionfo dell'idea*, shows its growing diffusion. The film's title also refers to the continuity between fascism and WWI. It is

11 Ibid., 280.

a strophe from a popular song of the early 1910s, sung in WWI by the Alpini, which then becomes the fascist hymn.

The fascist revolution as a continuation of WWI is also the topic of *Il grido dell'aquila*. Work on the film started after fascism's seizure of power, and *Il grido dell'aquila* came out in fall 1923, on the occasion of its first anniversary.[12] WWI is regarded in the film as a prologue of fascism's fight for a new Italy. The story takes place in a little town in Northern Italy. The first part, which will be examined in detail later, briefly evokes the war. Here, let us focus on the second part. It illustrates the immediate postwar period and constitutes the film's nucleus. Chaos is reigning, workers strike, and when they destroy a tavern and hit an old, blind man, a former officer who initially supports the strike, a protagonist realizes the mistake. He defends the man, but is killed. Now the "Camicie nere" intervene, and *Il grido dell'aquila* ends with pictures of fascists marching on Italy's capital. The scene evokes the actual march on Rome of thousands of "Camicie nere" on October 22, 1922, which symbolically marked the beginning of the fascist regime.

Il grido dell'aquila clearly suggests a parallel between WWI and the fascist revolution. An ideal line connects the fight against the foreign enemy with the one against the leftist forces conducted by the fascists after the war's ending. At the same time, WWI is celebrated as a continuation of the *Risorgimento*, and fascism represents its glorious fulfillment. The connection is expressed in *Il grido dell'aquila* through the characters of the tavern's owner and his nephew, Peppino. The

---

12 For an in-depth analysis of the film, see Battista Copello, "Un film fascista degli anni '20: Il grido dell'aquila di Mario Volpe," *Cinema e cinema* VII, no. 22-23 (January–June 1980): 118–130. In the essay little attention, however, is paid specifically to the film's section on WWI. In part dedicated to "Il grido dell'aquila" is also Vittorio Martinelli, "Primi approcci tra cinema e fascismo," *Immagine: Note di storia del cinema* IV, no. 2 (April–June 1985): 7–12.

boy is an enthusiastic fascist. Pasquale, the owner of the tavern who is attacked by the strikers, once had fought on the side of Giuseppe Garibaldi, the legendary hero of the *Risorgimento*, who in summer 1860 landed in Sicily with a thousand volunteers to free Southern Italy from the Bourbons, who then reigned over it. The characters of Peppino and his grandfather emblematically embody the intimate link between the *Risorgimento*, WWI, and fascism.

Depictions of the Enemy

The little attention in Italian cinema of the 1930s for WWI is a marked contrast to the various films about WWI in the previous decade. Scholars generally explain the decreasing presence of WWI in Italian cinema during the 1930s by the overall evolution of the fascist regime. At the beginning of the 1930s, the regime "changed skin," so to speak. The time of the "Camicie nere" was over; the black shirt that originally identified fascist adherents was exchanged for the double-breasted suit. Hereby, I recur to the metaphor that Italian scholars commonly submit to in order to summarize the ideological metamorphosis of the fascist regime at the decade's turn. The established fascist dictatorship, which then enjoyed a broad-based support in Italy, increasingly assumed bourgeois-conservative features and strove to remove the memory of the revolutionary and violent character of its earlier days.[13] In the

13 As Christopher Duggan, *A Concise History of Italy* (Cambridge: Cambridge University Press, 2014), 224, puts it, "by the 1930s 'fascist man' was no longer a young barbarian. He was a patriotic, hard-working, church-going father." "In the early 1930s, the fascist regime changed its tactics," observes Gian Piero Brunetta: "Any reference to fascist intimidation tactics was expunged as policymakers attempted to create the image of a pacified, harmonious Italy that was dominated by a petit-bourgeois ideology." Gian Piero Brunetta, *The History of Italian Cinema: A Guide to Italian Film from its Origins to the Twenty-First Century* (Princeton: Princeton University Press, 2009), 91.

1930s, the regime reluctantly looked at its past, and WWI was too problematically and tightly connected to the origins of the fascist movement to fit into the new self-image that the regime wished to spread.

Elter's *Le scarpe al sole* stands exemplary for the depiction of WWI in the Italian cinema of the 1930s. War is celebrated and at the same time its memory is distorted, mystified, and somehow repressed. The film's opening sets the tone: The credit sequence rolls on the background of a pathetically presented mountain landscape. High peaks stand out against a crystal-clear sky, and ascetic cliffs and snow-covered plateaus dominate the imagery. It is an awe inspiring scenery, on which the camera lingers for a while, and it recurs at the end, closing the film. The mountains and the snow and the blue sky form a frame for the narrative that follows, a majestic backdrop for the deeds of the Italian soldiers. The opening credits are unsatisfactory. It is striking that no chronological and geographical information are provided throughout the film. Where exactly the story is set, or when a given episode takes place, remains unsaid. Almost no specific dates or places are mentioned. We do not know where the village is, for instance, where the narrative starts, or where the fights take place, or the year in which war breaks out and when it ends. An exception is the reference to the city of Trient in the course of a scene in a coffeehouse that we enter together with an Alpino who returns home wounded. As has been briefly mentioned earlier, the present capital of the Italian region Trentino Alto Adige still belongs to the Habsburg empire at the beginning of the last century. The city is annexed by Italy as a result of WWI. In fact, the liberation of Trient and Triest is one of Italy's goals when the country enters WWI in spring 1915 on the side of Paris and London and against Austria-Hungary and the German Reich. In the coffeehouse, we overhear a discussion about the necessity to reach Trient as quickly as possible. At the beginning of *Le scarpe al sole*, there is a reference to Russia, too. Some peasants sit in the village's tavern drinking. They talk about the war, and a reference is made to Russia's offensive against Austria. But these aspects are only brief hints. In Elter's film, WWI is explicitly idealized. As Gianfranco Miro Gori remarks, the war depicted in *Le scarpe al sole* is barely characterized as WWI.[14] What is shown on the screen evokes WWI, but does not intend to depict it graphically.

The process of abstraction that WWI undergoes in *Le scarpe al sole*, the vagueness with which WWI is depicted, are all the more apparent if we take into consideration the enemy's representation. It is an anonymous entity. Almost never is the adversary called by name. Most of the time, he simply is referred as "the enemy," without clarifying his nationality. He is nameless, and his identity remains undetermined. Only one reference is made to Austria-Hungary during the film. It happens near the ending: We see the Alpini reconquer their village after it has been occupied by the enemy for some time. There is a board hanging on a wall containing the lettering *K.u.k. Orts-Kommandantur* ("Imperial-Royal Command Unit"). Then an Alpino removes the sign with a stroke of his rifle. The scene is observed from some distance, and it remains a detail. It must be noted, too, that the inscription is in Gothic-style letters, so it is hard to read for a non-German-speaking audience. Apart from that, there is only one point in *Le scarpe al sole* where a clear reference to Austria is made. In the cellar of a deserted house, the Alpini hit upon some barrels of wine, but their officer warns them that the Austrians might have poisoned it. For a moment, they appear troubled, then they seem to not take the danger seriously, as if

14 Gori, *Patria diva*, 64.

it were inconceivable that Austrians could commit such an act of meanness. An Alpino dares a sip; a second sip follows, and it tastes good, and now all drink the wine and merrily empty the barrels. It is worth noting that the scene in which reference is made to the Austrians does not depict a military action; rather, it is all a joke.

Such an image of the enemy stands in marked contrast to its representation in the films of the 1920s. The difference between *Le scarpe al sole* and films from ten years earlier, such as *Il grido dell'aquila* is evident and significant. *Il grido dell'aquila* opens with Italian soldiers marching through a jubilant crowd, on their way to the front. War is still a distant affair, and in the little town in Northern Italy, life goes on serenely and pleasantly. An officer, Manlio Acerri, courts a pretty girl. Her name, not by chance, is Italia. Then, suddenly, enemy airplanes cross the sky. Fear takes possession of the population. Everybody seeks shelter. Bombs fall and buildings collapse. Also, the house where Italia lives with her little brother is destroyed by the enemy attack. Beneath the debris also lies Italia's brother. Some days later, a new play is staged at the local theater, but the show is abruptly interrupted by the news that the front has been broken; the enemy is rapidly advancing. Panic breaks out. The scenes that follow show enemy troops on the march. A cavalry squadron rushes through the landscape. The Italian population flees in fear. The Austrians rage and destroy; they know no mercy. Women and children are prey to the enemy's violence. Then the Austrians attack the town, and a bloody fight ensues. Unfortunately, the only preserved print of *Il grido dell'aquila* has a gap of about ten minutes minutes at this point. In its present version, the film goes on after the enemy's attack, depicting life in town after war's end. That part has already been discussed.

Also noteworthy are the films *Sufficit animus* (*Courage suffices*, 1921, directed Giuseppe Sterni) and *La leggenda del Piave* (1924, directed by Mario Negri), which shall be taken under consideration here as further examples of the negative image of the Austrian enemy in the Italian cinema of the 1920s. The protagonist of *Sufficit animus* is a young officer. When he returns home from the front on a short leave, he finds his village completely destroyed. All inhabitants have fled before the enemy. Over the ruins flutters an Italian flag in shreds. *La leggenda del piave*, instead, revolves around an Austrian spy, and that makes it of special interest for our investigation. The spy worms his way into the confidence of an Italian family, but when the man tries to seduce the young Elena (played by an Italian diva of the 1920s, Diomira Jacobini), he is removed from the house. WWI breaks out, and Elena helps out as a nurse. Then the villa where Elena lives with her family is occupied by the enemy, and the spy appears again and rapes her. The scene, as can be gathered from an old review (the film must be considered lost),[15] is rendered by the metaphor of a white lily crushed by a man's hand and trampled under a pair of boots. Finally comes the day of Italian victory. The enemy retreats. Elena's fiancé, Corrado, dies heroically, while Italian troops are advancing.

The shift in the representation of WWI in Italian cinema at the beginning of the 1930s mirrors the contemporary mutation of the fascist dictatorship and the new character that the regime assumes, as has been previously mentioned. But a further element apparently plays a major role, and attention must be directed at this point to the development of Italian foreign policy in the interwar period. In particular, the different depictions

---

15 See Vittorio Martinelli, *Il cinema muto italiano: I film degli anni Venti. 1924–1931* (Roma: Centro Sperimentale di Cinematografia, 1996), 38.

of the enemy in the early post-war years and in the later films of the 1930s must be put in connection with the evolution of the Austrian-Italian relations during that period.[16] Since the late 1920s, the fascist regime showed an increasing interest in making Austria a closer partner. The strengthening of the Italian-Austrian relations became a primary goal of Italy's foreign policy. Italy engaged itself in favor of Austria's independence, opposing Nazi Germany's ambition to expand its influence along the Danube, and Vienna found in its southern neighbor a supporter against Berlin's aspirations to incorporate the country into the Third Reich. When, in July 1934, a Nazi-supported coup attempt shook Austria, Italian troops were ordered immediately to the Italian-Austrian border, a gesture that exemplarily marks Italy's role at that time as a protector of Austria and its sovereignty. The political friendship also encouraged more intense economic relations, and in spring 1934 a comprehensive agreement of cooperation was signed; it is known as the Rome Protocols. A further agreement with the aim of promoting cultural relations followed in February 1935. Together with the Rome Protocols, it marked the high point of Austrian-Italian collaboration during the 1930s.

The undetermined identity of the enemy in Elter's film, the apparent vagueness as to its nationality, its name, may find an

16 For an overview of the Italian-Austrian relations in the interwar period, see, in Italian, Ennio Di Nolfo, "I rapport italo-austriaci dall'avvento del fascism all'Anschluss," *Storia e politica* XIII, no. 1-2 (January–June 1974): 33–81; and, in German, Angelo Ara, "Die italienische Österreichpolitik 1936–1938," in Österreich, *Deutschland und die Mächte: Internationale und* österreichische *Aspekte des Anschlusses vom März 1938*, ed. Gerald Stourzh and Birgitta Zaar (Vienna: Österreichische Akademie der Wissenschaften, 1990) 111–129.

explication in the political alliance between fascist Italy and Austria. In the depiction of the enemy in *Le scarpe al sole*, in its anonymity, one finds mirrored, I would argue, the special relationship binding Rome and Vienna at that time. That explains the carefulness with which *Le scarpe al sole*, as well the other Italian films of the 1930s about WWI, avoid an explicit identification of the enemy with Austria. In fact, the Italian-Austrian friendship may represent a further reason (so far gone unnoticed) why WWI is so scarcely present in the Italian cinema of the 1930s.

From Enemy to Friend

Interesting cases are also presented by Forzano's films *Camicia nera* and *13 uomini e 1 cannone*. Forzano was a peculiar and remarkable figure in the Italian cinema of the 1930s. In the 1910s, he made his name as author of opera librettos for Roberto Leoncavallo, Pietro Mascagni, and Giacomo Puccini. He was also a successful playwright. Among his most important plays are the historical dramas *Danton*, *Campo di Maggio*, and *Villafranca*, written in the early 1930s. Apparently, *Campo di Maggio* and *Villafranca* were conceived together with the head of Italian fascism Benito Mussolini, with whom Forzano was in good relations. In the course of the 1930s and early 1940s, Forzano directed ten films in total; *Camicia nera* was his first one, and the film is exemplarily for the process of indetermination of the enemy's image in the 1930s Italian films on WWI. It is one of the few Italian films from the 1930s that explicitly celebrates the fascist movement; the film was produced by Istituto Luce, a state organization for the production of didactic, documentary, and propaganda films, established by the fascist regime in the early 1920s. Since 1927, Istituto Luce also produced a weekly newsreel, *Giornale Luce*. *Camicia nera* was produced by Istituto Luce as a contribution to the tenth anniversary of the fascist seizure of power, and the film was released at the beginning of 1933.[17]

Camicia nera displays strong ideological affinity with the films of the 1920s about WWI, which celebrate the beginnings of Italian fascism.[18] Forzano's film presents "a filmic synthesis of Italy's history from 1914 to 1932," as the message at the end of the opening credits submits. The story begins on the eve of WWI, in summer 1914, and the main character is a blacksmith who lives in poorest conditions in the "Paludi Pontine," then a swampland region, south of Rome, with his wife and a little son. When Italy enters the war, the blacksmith volunteers for the front. The neutrality position initially assumed by Italy after WWI breaks out is severely criticized by Forzano's film, where merit for Italy's entering the war is solemnly attributed to the future head of the fascist movement. As a matter of fact, the young Mussolini, who in the

17 On the film's production, see Patrizia Minghetti, "Lo 'scandalo' di Camicia Nera," *Immagine: Note di storia del cinema* III, no. 2 (April–June 1984): 20–27. Further, on Forzano can be seen, in English, Clive Edward John Griffiths, *The Theatrical Works of Giovacchino Forzano: Drama for Mussolini's Italy* (New York: Edwin Mellen Press, 2000); in Italian, Stefano De Rosa, *Giovacchino Forzano: Un protagonista del Novecento* (Firenze: Borgo San Lorenzo, 1996); and Marco Sterpos, *Scrivere teatro nel regime: Giovacchino Forzano e la collaborazione con Mussolini* (Modena: Stem Mucchi, 2015).

18 For analysis of the film's ideology, see, besides Gianfranco Miro Gori, *Patria diva: La storia d'Italia nei film del ventennio* (Firenze: La casa Usher, 1988); Mino Argentieri, *L'occhio del regime* (Roma: Bulzoni, 2003); and Lorenzo Cuccu, "Il cinema di propaganda: Il 'caso Forzano,'" in *Storia del cinema italiano*, vol. 4, *1924–1933*, ed. Leonardo Quaresima (Venezia: Marsilio, 2014), 463–472. In the above analysis, however, little account is taken of the film's representation of WWI.

early 1910s was one of the prominent figures of Italian socialism and directed its newspaper *Avanti!*, played a major role in the political debate that accompanied Italy's entering the war, and the newspaper, *Il Popolo d'Italia*, which he founded after leaving the Socialist party, becomes an important voice for the interventionist party. In *Camicia nera*, we see the blacksmith solemnly reading an article by Mussolini, and the film shows workers and bourgeoisie, peasants and students moved alike by Mussolini's words, while jubilant crowds salute Italy's entering the war. Like the montage films by Comerio and Paradisi, or *Il grido dell'aquila* one decade earlier, Forzano's film underlines the intimate connection between WWI and Italian fascism. After a first part devoted to the immediate pre-war time and WWI, there follows a description of the dramatic situation in which the country finds itself after war's end, and the film recalls the beginnings of the fascist movement. When the blacksmith returns home, chaos dominates. There is no work, and the communists paralyze the nation. The blacksmith thus joins the fascists who fight "the reds," reestablishing order. Until the day of the fascist seizure of power comes; then *Camicia nera* celebrates Italy's economic and social progress under the fascist regime. Under Mussolini's lead, there is social peace, and Italy experiences economic growth. Here lies the nucleus of *Camicia nera*: Like *Il grido dell'aquila*, Forzano's film also puts the accent on the time after WWI, celebrating the fascist movement. The film's title is emblematic. Through the cloth, the "Camicia nera" that becomes the symbol of Italian fascism, the days of its origins and seizure of power are evoked on the screen.

Camicia nera thus contrasts with the evolution of Italian fascism at the beginning of the 1930s. As scholars generally remark, the film seems unaware of the metamorphosis of the fascist regime at the turn of the decade. In its ideology, in the way it depicts the fascist movement and its origins, *Camicia nera* rather mirrors the 1920s. In this sense, Forzano's film seems out of time, and it marks the end of a period in Italian cinema, in its representation of the fascist movement. At the same time, *Camicia nera* clearly differs from the films of the previous decade about WWI as regards the enemy's image. The film recalls with meticulousness the outbreak of WWI: As a starting point, the assassination of the heir to the Austrian-Hungarian throne, Franz Ferdinand, in Sarajevo on 28 July 1914. Then the film reports in detail the chronology of every nation entering the war. By superimposed text, we are informed that Austria declares war against Serbia on July 28. On the 2nd of August, Germany declares war on Russia. On 3 August, there follows the declaration of war against France and Belgium. On 4 August, England declares war on Germany. On 5 August, there follows Austria's declaration of war against Russia. France declares war against Austria on 11 August, and England follows on 15 August. In the background are images of the various armies, with soldiers marching toward the camera. The national hymns accompany the sequence. But in *Camicia nera*, when it comes to Italy's entering the war, there is no explanation of the countries Italy fought against. Throughout the film, it is never told that Italy's enemy is Austria. Against the background of footage from WWI, there appears a list of towns and mountains where the Italians successfully fought the enemy. It is a long and symbolically leaden list that rolls on the screen: Pogdora, Oslavia, Monfalcone, Sacile, Doberdo, Sabotino, Vodice, etc. But the enemy's name is never pronounced. Its identity appears implicit, but the enemy remains nameless throughout Forzano's film, as if it were not to be recalled that the present friend once had been Italy's enemy.

Little attention has been paid so far in the literature on the representation of WWI in Italian cinema to Forzano's *13 uomini e 1 cannone*. On the contrary, the film appears of great interest. It came out in fall 1936, and there is also a German and an English version of Forzano's film, titled *Dreizehn Mann und eine Kanone* and "*Thirteen Men and a Gun*", directed respectively by Johannes Meyer and Mario Zampi and co-produced by the Italian company Pisorno with the German Bavaria and the London-based Two Cities. The film tells of a gigantic cannon and the patrol of thirteen men referred to in the title. The story starts with the cannon having already been in use on the front for some time. It has become a legend amongst the troops. The cannon almost never misses a shot, and all efforts by the enemy to make out its position are unsuccessful. The gun is hidden deeply in the woods and ingeniously masked. Worth noting is the narrative's location, for *13 uomini e 1 cannone* plays in the east, along the frontier between the Habsburg empire and czarist Russia. It makes Forzano's film a remarkable exception among the Italian films about WWI. In fact, it is one of very few films that is not set in Italy or whose protagonists are not Italians. Further examples are Lattuada's *Fraulein Doktor*, which takes place on the western front and features a female German spy, and Sergio Grieco's *Il sergente Klems* (1971), which begins on the western front and then goes on in North Africa after war's end; the protagonist is a German sergeant. Captured by the French, the man manages to escape. Also worth mentioning is a film from the 1920s, *Non è resurrezione senza morte*, by Edoardo Bencivenga, that is set in the Balkans, with two brothers, separated by destiny, who fight in WWI on opposing sides.

In Forzano's film, the soldiers plus a captain in charge of the astounding cannon are Austrians, and that makes *13 uomini e 1 cannone* quite unique among the Italian films on WWI. They are the film's heroes, while the Russians represent the enemy; *13 uomini e 1 cannone* clearly stands on the side of the Austrians. The men come from different backgrounds, and the patrol stands symbolically for all and everyone. Among them, we meet a teacher and a peasant, a pharmacist and a student, a musician and a librarian. There is also an acrobat and a painter, while one of the men openly admits that he does not work: "My father is very rich," he explains. They are presented as capable, courageous, and cheery. When fights temporarily stop, they sing some song, and the musician plays his violin. Meanwhile, the teacher teaches a comrade to read and write, and when a high-ranked general announces inspection, the men take a bath in a nearby brook, and all are merry. In spite of the social differences, they are sincere comrades, and happy to share at table what delicates they may privately own. The audience is explicitly invited by the film to identify with the Austrians. They stay at the center of the narrative and from the very beginning gain our sympathy.

Our investigation concludes with *Il piccolo alpino*. It was the last Italian film on WWI produced during the *Ventennio,* a term that commonly refers to the twenty years of fascist regime, from the end of 1922 to July 1943, when the Italian king after the Anglo-American landing on Sicily removed Mussolini and had him arrested, and a new government was formed under Marshal Pietro Badoglio. Biancoli's film is an adaptation of the homonymous novel of 1926 by Salvator Gotta. One of the most popular Italian novelists of the interwar period, Gotta sympathized with fascism from early on. He was the author of numerous novels and theatrical pieces, many of which were brought to screen; he also contributed to various films. Among others, he conceived, together with Biancoli, the idea for Alessandrini's *Cavalleria*. *Il piccolo alpino* enjoyed huge success, being one of the most read books for children in Italy in the 1930s. It was also the most successful Italian novel on WWI of the interwar period. In second place ranks Monelli's *Le scarpe al sole.*[19]

19 For a chart of the most popular Italian novels on WWI, see Marco Mondini, *La guerra italiana: Partire, raccontare, tornare. 1914–18* (Bologna: Il Mulino, 2014), 172.

The protagonist of *Il piccolo alpino* is a boy named Giacomino. He is the little Alpino referred to in the title. Giacomino lives with his father and a grandmother in a town in Northern Italy. In the film, in contrast to the novel, his mother has long been dead. While hiking in the mountains, Giacomino and his father are surprised by a storm. The boy is saved by some mountaineers. His father is believed to be dead. When the war breaks out, the boy joins a group of Alpini. Biancoli's film is released at the end of 1940; a new war was ravaging great parts of Europe. In June 1940 Italy, too, entered the war at the side of Nazi-Germany, believing that war would last just a few weeks and be easily won. While the country joins in WWII, Biancoli's film clearly aims at reassuring the Italian audience. A harmless picture is given of the war. Giacomino experiences a thrilling adventure, and everything ends well, with the boy also finding his father again. It is noteworthy that death has almost no place in the film. With one exception, it does not exist. A boy joining Giacomino on his adventure is wounded near the film's end by an enemy's shot. He dies on the day of Italy's victory, with Giacomino and his father at his side, to the sound of a military fanfare playing in the background.

At the same time, the new world war that fascist Italy enters in summer 1940 influenced the whole way in which WWI is depicted in Biancoli's *Il piccolo alpino*. In particular, let us consider again the enemy's image. In *Il piccolo alpino*, the enemy practically disappears from the screen. While it could occasionally be seen in *Le scarpe al sole*—although it is mostly shown briefly and from some distance—in Biancoli's film, the enemy disappears fully. Throughout the film, we get to see the enemy only a couple of times. References to the enemy are made in the dialogues, but without ever mentioning the enemy by name. The occasional roaring of cannons in the distance reminds of its presence, but we hardly catch a glimpse of the enemy. The first time that we see the enemy is the moment when two spies kidnap Giacomino. They wear Italian uniforms, and they make no comment; their nationality remains concealed. They are rather clumsy and do not really seem dangerous, and Giacomino easily frees himself and warns the Alpini, who promptly capture the spies. Later, we briefly glimpse the enemy while Giacomino and the other boy attempt to deliver an important message that they are trusted with to the Italian headquarters. It is just one shot, quite short, and what we get to see of the enemy are barely a couple of legs. It is a meaningful shot. In *Il piccolo alpino*, the enemy has no name and no face, and that is meant literally. The last time that we get a sight of the enemy is while Giacomino and his companion cross the river to reach the Italian positions. Two enemy soldiers notice the boys and fire. Again, they do not speak any words. Their muteness further contributes to their anonymity; it makes an identification impossible.

Giacomino gets in direct contact with the enemy after losing his way during a snowstorm. The year is 1917, and it is Christmas, as informs a superimposed text, and the building that we are entering is an Austrian orphanage. Here we find again Giacomino. As we learn in the ensuing scene, the boy was found in the mountains by Austrian soldiers and accepted into the orphanage. He is fine; the statement that sometimes can be found in the literature on WWI and Italian cinema that Giacomino is captured and held prisoner by the Austrians,[20] is wrong and misleading. On the contrary, the enemy actually saves Giacomino's life. In the orphanage, they are celebrating Christmas. There is a joyous atmosphere. Under the guidance of the institute's director, the boys sing a Christmas song. Then the director urges Giacomino to sing a song, too, and

20 Thus write for instance Gori, *Patria diva*, 63; and Gianfranco Casadio, *Il grigio e il nero: Spettacolo e propaganda nel cinema italiano degli anni Trenta* (Ravenna: Longo, 1989), 79.

suggests "O sole mio." Instead, Giacomino sings a patriotic song, and everybody seems outraged, and the boy is brought back in his room. The reason for the outrage is purposely left unclear. Is it the song's tone, which contrasts with the Christmas atmosphere? Is it because it is an Italian song? The director himself had expressed the wish of hearing one. In fact, nothing suggests in this scene that Giacomino is standing in front of the enemy. That the Austrians among whom the boy finds himself are actually the enemy remains untold, and when an Italian prelate later visits the orphanage asking about the boy, the director is ready to entrust Giacomino to the clergyman. But Giacomino in the meantime escaped from his room through the window.

At two points in *Il piccolo alpino*, the enemy is actually mentioned by name, but the film is careful not to identify that image with the Austrians. The film opens by a superimposed text that reads: "March 1915. On the eve of the war against the Habsburgs." It is a peculiar and meaningful phrasing. It is just a detail, but quite significant. The film evidently takes care to avoid any explicit reference to Austria. Instead, it evokes a historical entity, the Habsburg Empire, that already belongs to history. At the film's end, the enemy gets called by name again. At the hospital, Giacomino reads to his friend the communiqué by the Italian general-in-chief Armando Diaz announcing the victory against Austria-Hungary. Once more the enemy is referred to by the name of an old historical entity lying back in the past. The effort is evident to present WWI as a conflict led by Italy against an old dynasty and a state that do not exist anymore. Manifestly, any parallelism between the enemy and the later Austria, which in the 1930s became a close partner of fascist Italy, was to be avoided. In the meantime, Austria, too, ceases to exist. The country was now part of Nazi-Germany. Its annexation by force to the Third Reich takes place in March 1938. That might be a further reason why, in *Il piccolo alpino,* there are hardly any references to Austria. As if the film wanted to remove the fact that an Austria had actually ever existed. Once again, the history of WWI is being reshaped on the screen to adapt to the present.

Gavre Princip - Himmel unter Steinen (*Gavre Princip - Sky among Stones*, A/FRG/GB/YU 1990)

Das Attentat - Sarajewo 1914 (*The Assassination - Sarajevo 1914*, A/CZ/GER 2014)

Dobrý voják Svejk (*Good Soldier Svejk*, CZ 1956)

Zwei Welten ("*Two Worlds*," GER/GB 1930)

Hotel Imperial (HU 1917)

Ének a búzamezökröl (*Song of the Cornfield*, HU 1947)

Camicia nera (*Black Shirt*, I 1933)

Pukovnikovica (*Colonel's Wife*, YU 1972)

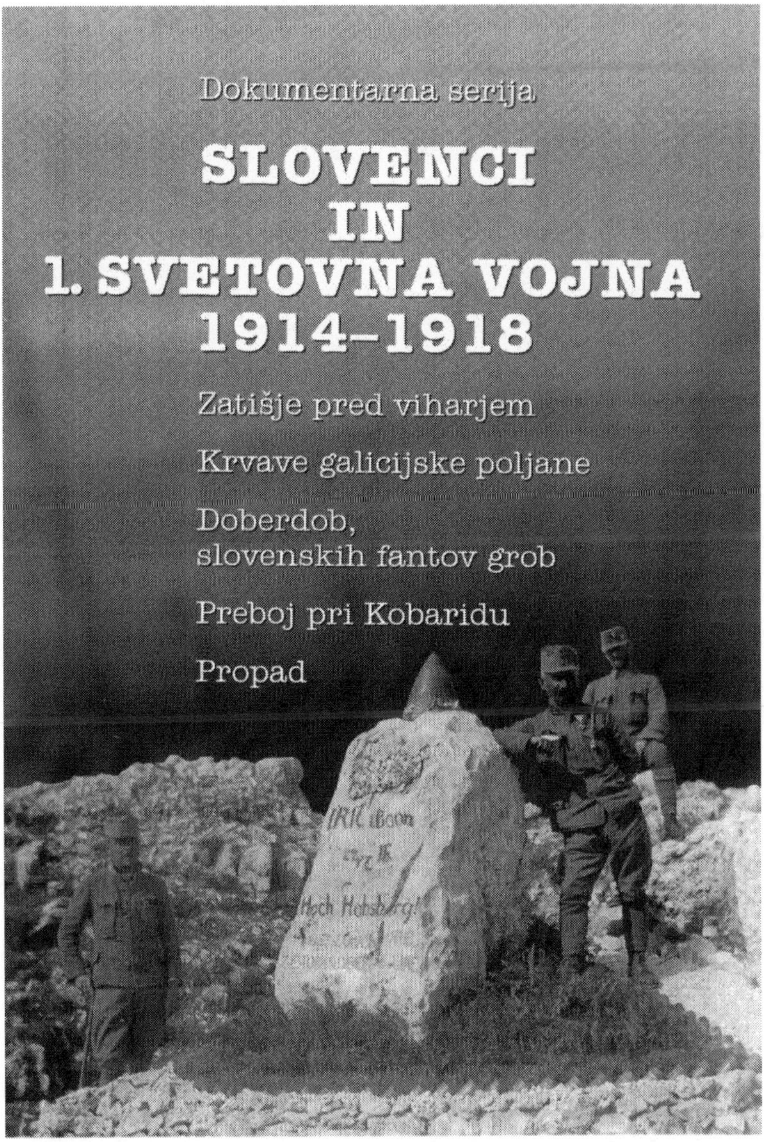

Slovenci in Prva svetovna vojna ("*Slovenes and the Great War of 1914-1918*," SLO 2013/4)

THE DECAYING EMPIRE AND THE HUMAN DILEMMAS:

THE LAST WAR OF AUSTRIA-HUNGARY IN POLISH CINEMATOGRAPHY FROM 1918 ONWARDS

Piotr Szlanta

Introduction

As a result of the First World War, after 123 years, Poland reappeared on the political map of Europe. It was the fulfillment of the dream of generations who, in the long nineteenth century, fought for the rebuilding of a sovereign, independent Polish state.[1] During the dramatic years of the Great War, deep structural changes irreversibly transformed Polish society in Galicia and Silesia. Costly military defeats of the Austro-Hungarian troops resulted in a months-long occupation of the largest part of Galicia by Russian troops. Subsequently, many circumstances and political developments undermined the emotional ties of Poland and the Danube Monarchy, weakening the Polish loyalty to this empire: Political repression after the liberation practically abolished the autonomy status of Galicia by proclaiming direct

1 Cf., for example, Piotr Szlanta, "Poland," in *1914–1918-online: International Encyclopedia of the First World War*, ed. Ute Daniel et al (Berlin: Freie Universität, 2014), DOI: http://dx.doi.org/10.15463/ie1418.10255.

military rule in 1915. The dependency on the powerful German Empire prevailed. Provision problems and failures of the state organs increased. Unfavorable agreements regarding Poland made by Ukrainians and the Central Powers against the backdrop of the Brest-Litovsk peace negotiations exacerbated the situation, together with the loss of prestige of the Habsburg dynasty. The Poles started to orientate themselves more toward the building of their own national state and the uniting of all Polish territories, rather than identifying with the Austro-Hungarian imperial interests.[2]

Interwar Legion Films

It is obvious that, after 1918, dramatic events aroused the interest of Polish cinematography, which was strongly supported by government circles. During the interwar period, films concentrated on the war experience of Polish Legions, who fought at the side of the Central Power against Russian armies from 1914 to 1917. The fighting route of this army, small in comparison to the "millions-strong" armies of belligerents, was intensively used by the political elite of a newborn Polish state as a grounding myth of the so-called Second Republic (1918–1939), especially after the coup d'état staged by Józef Piłsudski and his followers in May 1926. Another key issue was the Polish/Soviet War of 1920–21. More movies on the war were shot in the 1970s and

2 Cf. Jerzy Z. Pająk, *Od autonomii do niepodległości: Kształtowanie się postaw politycznych i narodowych społeczeństwa Galicji w warunkach Wielkiej Wojny 1914–1918* (Kielce: Wydawn, 2012); Piotr Szlanta, "'Najgorsze bestie to są Honwedy': Ewolucja stosunku polskich mieszkańców Galicji do monarchii habsburskiej podczas I wojny światowej," in *Galicyjskie Spotkania*, ed. Urszula Jakubowska (Zabrze: inforteditions, 2011); Ludwik Mroczka, *Galicji rozstanie z Austrią: Zarys monograficzny* (Krakow: Wydawn, 1990).

1980s. Nevertheless, there was a very narrow margin within the production of Polish war movies.

The First World War's stories were present in the Polish cinematography in the interwar period. Many movies were shot in Poland, set in the reality of the Piłsudski's legionnaires, for example: *Maraton Polski* (1927, directed by Wiktor Biegański), *Dzikie Pola* (1932, directed by Józef Lejtes), and *Rok 1914* (1932, directed by Henryk Szaro); or the Polish-Soviet war, for example: *Dla Ciebie Polsko* (1920, directed by Antoni Bednarczyk), *Cud nad Wisłą* (1921, directed by Ryszard Bolesławski), *Tajemnice medalionu* (1922, directed by Edward Puchalski), *Mogiła Nieznanego Żołnierza* (1927, directed by Ryszard Ordyński), and *Z dnia na dzień* (1929, directed by Józef Lejtes). Their screenplays presented predominantly typical, banal, pseudo-romantic stories, full of pathos, with a readiness for self-sacrifice for the sake of the fatherland and love, promoting the legion's myth. The movies mentioned above did not reach a high artistic level. Partly these productions were co-financed by the state.[3]

The most successful of them, in all probability, turned out to be a comedy *Dodek na froncie* (*Dodek at the front line*, 1936, directed by Michał Waszyński), which tells the story of a Polish soldier from Cracow, a smart aleck former footballer Dodek Wędzonka

---

3 Ewa Mazierska, "Between Parochialism and Universalism: World War One in Polish Cinematography," in *The First World War and Popular Cinema 1914 to the Present*, ed. Michael Paris (New Brunswick: Rutgers University Press, 2000), 194–204; Łukasz A. Plessnar, *100 filmów wojennych* (Krakow: Rabid, 2002), 123; Władysław Banaszkiewicz and Witold Witczak, *Historia filmu polskiego*, vol.1, 1895–1929 (Warsaw: Wydawnictwa Artystyczne i Filmowe, 1966), 126, 159–160, and 196–197; Barbara Artymys, Leszek Artymys, and Wiesław Stradomski, *Historia filmu polskiego*, vol. 2, 1930–1939 (Warsaw: Wydawnictwa Artystyczne i Filmowe, 1988), 257–261.

serving in the Austro-Hungarian army, who during a patrol service accidentally finds himself in a Russian uniform and is regarded by Russians as one of their own officers, freed from Austro-Hungarian captivity. The action of the movie is mostly played out in the headquarters of the Russian staff, where Dodek is taken, located in the Polish manor house in the village of Majewo. Beyond a love affair, the action of the movie is focused on the Russian officers, presented as stupid (for a long time they did not recognize that Dodek belonged to the enemy), cowardly, unprofessional (they could not even properly read a military map), arrogant, servile toward their superiors, and having thieving instincts. Concerning Austro-Hungary, at the beginning of the movie, Dodek, played by Adolf Dymsza, one of the most popular Polish actors in the interwar period, bluntly declares in the trenches that he is not highly motivated to fight in the ranks of the imperial forces and that he is waiting for transfer to the Polish Legion. His direct superior shares the same dream. In the final scene, a group of Polish legionnaires attacks and takes over the manor house holding the entire Russian staff. Among the successful conquerors is the superior of Dodek, who, in the meantime, has managed to join the Legions. As the audience could guess, Dodek finally leaves the Austro-Hungarian army and joins the Polish Legions, where he will be successful fighting for the re-establishment of the Polish state.[4]

Embodiments of the Empire's Downfall

After the Second World War, for many decades, the First World War experience almost disappeared from the scene. The unprecedented scale of the tragedies of the Second World War eclipsed

4 On the Polish Legions, cf.: Jarosław Centek, "Polish Legions," in *1914–1918-online: International Encyclopedia of the First World War*, ed. Ute Daniel et al (Berlin: Freie Universität, 2014), DOI: http://dx.doi.org/10.15463/ie1418.10337.

the commemoration of the First World War. In comparison with the First World War, the Second World War, with its tremendous human and material losses, occupation terror, Holocaust, the Warsaw Uprising of 1944, mass migration, re-shaping of borders, and subjection to the Soviet Union, held a much larger place in the historical consciousness of Poles. After 1945, cinematography found itself under the control and serving almost exclusively to the official communist ideology. Even after the limiting of state control over culture, as a result of the de-Stalinization process which started in Poland in 1956, the events between 1914 and 1918 did not find much interest among Polish filmmakers, producers, and audiences.[5]

In 1979, the movie *Lekcja Martwego Języka* (*Lesson of dead language*) was produced and directed by Janusz Majewski. The main character of this psychological drama, which is set in the last weeks of the Great War, is a young, well-educated, elegant Austrian dragoon officer, Alfred Kiekeritz, terminally ill with tuberculosis, who serves in the small, multinational town of Turka, lying in the Carpathian valley in Eastern Galicia, inhabited by Poles, Jews, Ukrainians, Roma, and Austrian officials. As a commandant of the post in the communication zone, he has not much more to do than to control traffic at the railway station and to supervise a small group of Russian POWs whose main occupation is to clean a former battlefield. Aside from symptoms of intensification of his illness, namely high fever, coughing fits, and the growing weakness of his organs, he suffers from boredom and the primitivism of the people surrounding him. He fills his free time by collecting art pieces, which he sends to his mother in Graz. Knowing that his own end is fast approaching, Kikeritz is unhealthily fascinated by the phenomenon of death—by killing as well as by dying. Especially while sleeping, he is faced with dramatic

5 Ewa Mazierska, "Between Parochialism and Universalism," 204–214.

occurrences during his service on the frontline, when his dragoons took part in fighting with Bolsheviks in Ukraine, also killing Jewish civilians and executing POWs. Despite his fragility and humanity (he treats his subordinates well and even orders a funeral for the rest of the bodies of Russian soldiers found at the former battlefield), Kikeritz looks for an opportunity to kill somebody; nearing the last hours of his life, despite his service on the front, he has not personally shot anybody. Finally, while hunting in the surrounding forest, he accidentally comes across an escaped Russian POW and kills him. Only a few hours later, the capitulation and the end of war coincide with the death of Kikeritz. Thus, Kikeritz's dying is taking place simultaneously with the process of the failing of the state: "Decay of the Austro-Hungarian monarchy is prejudged [...] in Majewski's film, finally, with the Great War of White Men, and the nineteenth century coming to an end. Manhood will never come back to the state of youthful faith in ideals, even if these ideals are incontestable," wrote one of the film critics.[6] In his last words, Kikeritz declares that death is not fascinating but only nonsensical. Far away from heroism and pathos, the message of *Lekcja Martwego Języka* is one of pacifism. War changes human nature even with regard to the good, well-educated, sensitive man; it produces only victims. The movie gives spectators the possibility to interpret on their own the presented occurrences and humane attitudes during the war, which in Majewski's eyes is completely deprived of heroism and pathos.[7]

---

6 Lekcja martwego języka, in *Głos Wielkopolski,* Nov. 8, 1996.

7 See also: Maria Malatyńska, "Piękni i Martwi," Życie Literackie, Oct. 14, 1979); Cezary Wiśniewski, "Śmierć porucznika Kikeritza," *Sztandar Młodych,* Oct. 19, 1979); Anna Tatarkiewicz, "Requiem dla rycerza," *Kultura,* Oct. 28, 1978; Czesław Dondziłło, "Cierpienia dające rozkosz," *Film,* Oct. 14, 1979); Mirosław Winiarczyk, "Studium umierania i kryzys kultury," *Ekran,* Oct. 14, 1979); Aleksander Ledóchowski, "Diana z Efezu," *Kultura,* Oct. 28, 1979.

Without any doubt, the most influential movie presenting the Austro-Hungarian army is still *C.K. Dezerterzy* (*King's and emperors' deserters*), a comedy also directed by Janusz Majewski and released in 1986. The scenario was based on a novel of Kazimierz Sejda of the same title. It tells the story of a multinational sentry company, stationed in a remote garrison, located hundreds of kilometers off the frontline, in Sátoraljaújhely, Hungary. All of its soldiers and officers just want to live a quiet life, far away from the dangers of war, until war's end. This calm atmosphere is suddenly broken by the coming of an ambitious, brutal, nationalistic, careerist Oberleutnant von Nogaj. Soon after his arrival, there erupted a conflict between him and his chief superior, Hauptmann Wagner, an intellectualist indifferent to the fate of the Empire and result of the war, who enjoys reading books and smoking cigarettes. Wagner hates and condemns the brutal methods of training used by Nogay, who endeavors by any means to introduce to the company a new order, strengthening the discipline and morale of its soldiers, and who wants just to maintain the existing status quo convenient for him. Nogay is hated by his subordinates, who try to take revenge and make his life as miserable as possible among others by disgracing him in the eyes of the visiting general. An informal leader of soldiers, a shrewd Polish corporal, Jan Kania Kaniowski, surrounds himself with a group of comrades who try to survive in good physical and mental condition, wanting to enjoy life as much as possible under war conditions. As summarized by one critic: "Everybody pretends […] not to see the degeneration and absurdity of the system, which is still functioning by the power of inertia, though it evokes only contempt and derision, and is not even worth being hated. The fact that they [the soldiers] hang around on their positions proves only the existence of their instinct for self-preservation: the breakdown of the state machinery is still a danger. […] The fall of the Habsburg

Monarchy was preceded by a long period of decay of structures, ideas, mechanisms, by long painful mechanisms that did not fit in the world."[8]

In the second part of this movie, after burning military archives, soldiers of the company escape en-masse from the barracks and travel through the country, pursued by military police. Finally, after many strange and funny adventures, they are caught and put on trial. But during the session of the military court, which without any doubt would sentence the deserters to death, the garrison gets the message that war has ended. The news delights all soldiers (without exception of Nogay). *C.K. Dezerterzy* is rather more about the universal absurdity of war, presenting different human attitudes toward war cruelties and the survival strategy of soldiers, than about showing Austro-Hungary.[9] The film presents the growing tensions between different nationalities in the army (especially Germans and Slavs), conservatism of high officers, and the prevailing longing for peace. It is quite often projected on TV and used even in commercials.[10]

The fall of value systems

Contrary to the message of *Lekcja Martwego Języka* and *C.K. Dezerterzy* is the beginning scene of the 1988 psychological drama Łuk Erosa (*Bow of Eros*), based on a novel Juliusz Kaden-Bandrowski published in 1919, and directed by Jerzy Domaradzki.

8 Maciej Pawlicki, "C.K. Dezerterzy", *Tygodnik Kulturalny*, Oct. 14, 1986.

9 Elżbieta Dolińska, "Kania i maszkarony," *Film* Sept. 21, 1986; Jan Marx, "Koszary i zamatuz," *Kultura*, Nov. 19, 1986; Adam Horoszczak, "Na pół gwizdka," *Ekran*, Aug. 31, 1986); Stefan Jurkiewicz, "C.K. wieża Babel," *Mówią wieki*, no. 3 (1998): 47–48; Stanisław Wyszomirski, "Dalecy krewni Szwejka," *Expres Wieczorny*, Aug. 22–24, 1986.

10 See for example https://www.youtube.com/watch?v=ZkpLZXI45rw.

We see in the first scene a farewell of mobilized soldiers departing from Cracow's main railway station. A crowd in a joyful atmosphere, with patriotic music and alcohol, and cheers for the soldiers, who, when they are leaving for the front, see the war merely as a short-term male adventure. They are not conscious of the real face of modern war, hoping for a quick return to their home after defeating their enemies, a seemingly easy task. One main character, the young and pretty woman Maria Michnowska, mother of a small boy Feluś, says goodbye to her husband Zdzisław, an academic teacher at Jagiellonian University. More common sense and emotional distance toward war is portrayed only by Maria's maid Nastka and a military doctor, an old veteran of the January Uprising of 1863 and its bloody suppression by Russians. Soon the war reveals its real face: A front line is established near Cracow, evoking thoughts of evacuation among the populace. Michnowska engages in patriotic activities (sewing underwear and collecting money for the legions) but feels alone and disoriented in this unexpected situation ("Sometimes one does not know what for to live"). One of the friends of her husband, after paying a bribe for his release from the frontline service, informs her that Zdzisław is missing in action. That shocking information—and courtship of one of her friends—forces Maria to leave Cracow and move to the home of her mother, a retired teacher in a small town. There, in Maria's arms, dies a young, wounded legionnaire, a fiancé of Maria's friend. After returning to Cracow, she surprisingly finds that during her absence her apartment has been seized by her maid Nastka, who has arranged a public house there. Threatened by Nastka with intervention of her influential clients from the military police (gendarmerie), Maria decides to move in with a family she knows. She has lost hope for the return of her husband and suffers from loneliness and growing financial problems. Maria engages in a sexual relationship with one of her husband's friends, a married professor named Ciąglewicz. After being exploited and abandoned by her lover, Maria seduces Adam, a young son of her host, introducing him to love affairs. But when she becomes pregnant by him, Adam abandons her. From that point, alone and despairing, Maria, who aborts her child and loses all illusions, is now unfettered from moral scruples. Sad and tired, she starts intentionally to use her body to manipulate men and earn money. She ends up as a prostitute in the brothel managed by her former maid. There, during a revue performance and striptease, her husband, who surprisingly has survived the war, tries to shoot her. But in the final scene, they reconcile with each other.

The movie depicts the fall of the pre-war morality and value system. The "bankruptcy of ideas, slogans, faith, and fatherland" is presented bluntly, during a sumptuous reception in a casino, by the perverted and egotistical Cięglewicz. People shocked by war atrocities just try, by any means—moral and immoral—to survive and, at least for a while, to forget about the war's brutal reality. "I'm not unhappy, that's already something," declares indecent Janina, one of Maria's friends, who, as a nurse in a military hospital, enjoys contact with many young males and wishes not to remember about her fallen fiancé. For a small group, (high officers, businessmen, madams), the war provides a chance to become, rapidly, very rich and live on a very high material level. The traditional social hierarchy no longer exist. Symbolically, a pledged count's palace is sold for a brothel to a madam, coming from the lower classes. Her new husband, a professor, accepts this way of life as a means for survival. The film Łuk Erosa is also an accusation against the male world. Men trigger the war. "We women suffer, men are cowards! Is it allowed to kill?" quarrels Maria with a doctor who refuses to abort her child. "We have to decide for ourselves, we are able to show off our talents," says

Janina to Maria. Thus, despite its tragic dimensions, the war offers new opportunities to women and broke male domination. In Łuk Erosa, high politics are not present, in contradiction to the novel from which the scenario of the film was written. In the novel, war realities in Galicia are mentioned, and, among other aspects, the anti-Jewish pogroms carried out by Cossacks.[11]

The action of the film *Austeria* (1983, directed by Jerzy Kawalerowicz) takes place in an almost exclusively Jewish milieu. As in all films presented in this article, this one is also based on a novel, published in 1966 and written by Andrzej Stryjkowski. The action of this psychological drama is centered around the first day and night of the First World War. In an inn named "Austeria," close to the Austro-Russian border, lives an old inn owner, the main character named Tag, with his daughter-in-law, a grandchild, and a Ukrainian servant, Jewdocha. After the outbreak of the war, a group of various war refugees look for shelter in Tag's rooms, among them many Jewish Chassids with their Tzadik, as well as conservative Jews. Expecting the coming of the Messiah, the Chassids seem to be completely unaware of the mortal danger nearby, that Cossacks could enter the inn at any moment. This mortal danger is visibly confirmed by a skirmish between Cossacks and Hungarian Hussars that takes place in front of the building, with a rattle of gunshots and the setting fire to a nearby town. Fatalistic, rationalistic, and skeptical, Tag tries to keep

11 Sławomir Wyszomirski, "Eros trafił we wdzięki Maryśki," *Ekspres wieczorny*, Jan. 22–24, 1988; Jerzy Peltz, "Kaden przyprawiony na różowo," *Kultura*, Feb. 17, 1988; Joanna Wawerska, "Pogranicze polskiego filmu," *Stolica*, Apr. 10, 1988; Marek Sadowski, "Wyzwolenie Maryśki", *Rzeczypospolita*, Jan. 9–10, 1988; Krzysztof Kreutzinger, "Maria i Maryśka," *Film*, Mar. 13, 1988); Maria Brzostowiecka, "Pocztówka ze starego Krakowa," *Ekran*, no. 12 (1988).

common sense and calm during these hours full of uncertainty and growing fear. As a humanist and good man, he feels responsible for his unexpected guests and refuses to leave with his family, rejecting an offer of shelter given by his old friend from childhood, a Catholic clergyman ("How can one leave people in one's own home?" Tag asks his friend, rhetorically). In his home, there is also a Hungarian cavalryman who has lost contact with his own unit. Tag also takes care of the funeral of a teenage Jewish girl accidentally killed by a stray bullet. Some Jews hope for the success of the Austro-Hungarian army and praise Emperor Franz Joseph I for his pro-Jewish stance. Together with his close friend, the aforementioned Catholic priest, and despite the mortal danger of this mission, Tag, who has started to lose his faith, voluntarily decides to go to a burning town where Cossacks have taken a young boy, with the aim of begging Russian occupants not to execute him. The characters of the film are torn between different emotions: "It's a time of fear and political arguments, despair and reckless light-heartedness, arguing with God and reconciling with each other, a time of love and death, a time of anticipation and unconsciousness" was written in one of the reviews.[12]

In the last scene of the movie, dancing and worshiping Jews undress and, in religious elation, naked, enter the river, where they meet their death, killed by artillery fire. Bodies of innocent victims resemble a mixture of blood and water. This image is symbolic of the Holocaust, which in the next world war almost completely annihilates Jewish life in this part of Europe. Stryjkowski himself was a Holocaust survivor. In *Austeria,* the old traditional order, rules of social life, and morality are failing rapidly and are

---

12 Małgorzta Dipont, "Przepadła cywilizacja," Życie Warszawy, Apr. 15, 1983.

irreparably damaged.[13] "It's just a first death and you have already grown accustomed to it?" Tag admonishes a group of Jews quarreling over the body of the young Jewish girl.[14]

Recent Developments

The end of the communistic rule failed to bring about substantial change in the Polish perception of Austro-Hungary during the First World War. Of course, one could observe a slight rise in interest in the First World War from the Polish public, but that

---

13 Maria Malatyńska, "Żydowski fresk," Życie Literackie, Apr. 24, 1983; Ewa Staśki, "Austeria-świat, który zaginął," *Film*, Apr. 26, 1991; "Taniec rozstrzelanych chochołów," *Rzeczypospolita*, Dec. 13, 1982; Adam Horoszczak, "'Tonący kontynent Austerii,'" *Ekran*, May 1, 1983; Oskar Sobański, "Karczma na polskich rozstajach," *Film*, May 29, 1983; Tadeusz Solbolewski, "Austeria," *Tygodnik Powszechny*, Jan. 23, 1983, Krzysztof Demidowicz, "Austeria," *Film*, Apr. 21, 1991.

14 For more on the war experience of Galician Jews during the First World War, see for example: Szymon An-ski [Salomon Rappoport], *Tragedia Żydów galicyjskich w czasie I wojny światowej: Wrażenia i refleksje z podróży po kraju* (Przemyśl: Południowo-Wschodni Instytut Naukowy, 2010); Piotr Wróbel, "The Jews of Galicia under Austrian-Polish Rule 1869–1918," *Austrian History Yearbook* 25 (1994): 133–135; Peter Holquist, "The Role of Personality in the First (1914–1915) Russian Occupation of Galicia and Bukovina," in *Anti-Jewish Violence: Rethinking the Pogrom in East European History*, ed. Jonathan Dekel-Chen, D. Gaunt, Natan M. Meir, and Israel Bartal (Bloomington: Indiana University Press, 2010), 52–74; Marsha L. Rozenblit, *Reconstructing a National Identity: The Jews of Habsburg Austria during World War I* (Oxford: Oxford University Press, 2001); Piotr Szlanta, "Doświadczenie wojenne Żydów galicyjskich: Zarys problematyki," in Żydzi i Polacy w okresie walk o niepodległość 1914–1920, ed. H. Węgrzynek (Warsaw: Polin, 2015), 65–76.

interest concentrated on the military activity (*czyn zbrojny*) of the Polish voluntary units (*Legiony Polskie*) that fought on the Austro-Hungarian side against Russia. Historians, journalists, and movie directors were no longer bound to the Marxist interpretation of the past. First of all, 11 November was re-established as a state holiday, with the central form of celebration being the changing of the honor guard at the Tomb of the Unknown Soldier in Warsaw and an accompanying military parade. In 1995–1998, two monuments of Piłsudski were erected in Warsaw, one of them opposite the Tomb. The memory of the Great War period has, in Poland, strong regional components. In the Great Poland region, local authorities and inhabitants are proud of the so-called Great Poland Uprising, which broke out against the Germans in December 1918. In Upper Silesia, the memory of the Silesian Uprisings, from the years 1919–1921, remains dominant, and in South-Eastern Poland especially the memory of Piłsudski's legions and the hostilities with Ukrainians over L′viv (Lwów) and Eastern Galicia is cultivated. Generally, in public opinion, the memory of the War is still overshadowed by the fights for the establishing of the borders of a reborn Poland, which lasted between 1918 and 1921, climaxing in the Polish-Soviet War. That period is well reflected in popular culture. One of the Polish film productions from recent years, *Bitwa Warszawska 1920* (*The battle of Warsaw 1920*, 2011, directed by Jerzy Hoffman), depicts the successful resistance to the Red Army at the outskirts of the Polish capital, the so-called "miracle on the Vistula River."

Some film plots referring to Austro-Hungary in the years 1914–1918 could be found only in a few documentary movies. The authors of *Wymarsz*[15] (*Departure*, 1988, directed by Wincenty Ronisz) admitted that among the powers that at the

15 *Wymarsz*, https://www.youtube.com/watch?v=DyKzikEHmHI.

end of eighteenth century partitioned the Polish-Lithuanian Commonwealth, Austro-Hungary ensured to Poles the best conditions for the development of their national life (giving political autonomy, freedom to establish political parties, permission to use the Polish language in administration, judiciary, and educational systems, and to commemorating the Polish national holidays such as the celebration of the 500th anniversary of the battle of Grunwald/Tannenberg, held in Cracow in 1910). However, at the beginning of the war, despite the fact that emperor Franz Joseph I enjoyed—especially among peasants—sympathy and trust, the Austrian central government offered to Poles only mobilization cards. "Trust and sympathy ended in bitter disappointment," commented a narrator. During the war, Austria seemed to be a minor contributor to the policy of the Central powers toward the Polish question. Thus, it had to yield to the powerful Germany being "hostile to the Poles." The Austro-Hungarian forces are presented in *Wymarsz* as weak and poorly commanded, constantly in need of the support of Germany. During the Brusilov offensive, in June 1916, the stout resistance of the Polish legionaries helped the Habsburg forces to stabilize the frontline after a retreat. The final blow against the pro-Austrian circles was triggered by the treaty between the central Powers and the newly born Ukrainian People's Republic concluded in February 1918. In Polish public opinion, this treaty was regarded as a betrayal to the Polish cause, as the next partition of Poland, due to the incorporation of the "Chełm-land" (Chłemszczyzna) into the Ukrainian state.

The audience of *Straszna Wojna*[16] (*Horrible war*, 2014, directed by Rafał Geremek) learned that from the very beginning of the hostilities the Austro-Hungarian army fought pretty poorly, and, after several costly defeats, had to retreat, in late 1914, almost to

16 *Straszna wojna*, https://www.youtube.com/watch?v=MShw8herqc4.

the city gates of Cracow in the western part of Galicia. In March 1915, after a few months of siege, the biggest and the most modern fortress of the Danube Monarchy, namely Przemyśl, capitulated and was taken by the victorious Russians. During the so-called Brusilov offensive, the Habsburg soldiers, in contrast to the Polish legionaries, gave up their positions en masse and surrendered or escaped in a state of panic. After some frontline changes and after the Russian occupation, many towns and villages lay in ashes at the end of the war. For example, on 2 May 1915, Gorlice, a town in western Galicia closely linked with the memory of a successful counter-offensive of the Central Power´s troops, was almost wiped off the map. Ninety percent of its buildings were destroyed and burned out. The memory of these tragic days is still vivid among contemporary inhabitants of Gorlice and is an important element of its local identity.

Generally, both documentaries and movies stress the fratricidal character of the Great War for Poles and present a history of the Habsburg monarchy strictly from the Polish national point of view, occupying only a marginal place in the Polish consciousness.

Summary

The last war of the Habsburg empire is rarely represented in Polish feature films and TV series. It has never raised a great interest in Polish public opinion. In this small quantity of movies, the depiction of the Habsburg Empire is quite negative, seen as decaying and gradually vanishing from the political map of Europe. Many of the above-mentioned movies are film versions of novels. Most of them were shot in the 1980s. The authors of these novels, however, concentrated more on the psychological analysis of persons involved in war than on presenting the picture of the Danube Monarchy. The films dealing with the war and depicting the last years of the Danube Monarchy examine the psychological impact of war on the human beings and on society as a whole and, regardless of their genre (comedy, drama), they are united in a final conclusion that the phenomenon of war is more a crime against humanity than a method of solving international conflicts. The only outcome of war is physical, material, geographical, and human loss. Plots with a more heroic vision of war, delivered in great numbers by the Polish cinematography, depicted the tragic and dramatic occurrences of the years 1939–1945. The films about this era exceeded, considerably, the quantity of those presenting the first Great War. Only in vain can one can look in the Polish movies for traces of sentiments towards Austro-Hungary, sentiments that actually still exist as part of the regional identity and historical heritage of southeastern Poland.[17]

17 Cf.: Renata Hołda, *"Dobry" władca: Studium antropologiczne o Franciszku Józefie I* (Katowice: Wydawnictwo Uniwersytetu Slaskiego, 2008); Ewa Wiegendt, *Austria Felix, czyli o micie Galicji w polskiej prozie współczesnej* (Poznań: Wydawnictwo Naukowe UAM, 1997); Alois Wodan, *Mit Austrii w literaturze polskiej* (Kraków: MCK, 2002); Adam Kożuchowski, *Pośmiertne dzieje Austro-Węgier: Obraz monarchii habsburskiej w piśmiennictwie międzywojennym* (Warsaw: MCK, 2009).

"THE EMPIRE MEANS ORDER":[1]

IMAGES OF THE AUSTRO-HUNGARIAN MONARCHY IN ROMANIAN FICTIONAL FILMS ABOUT THE FIRST WORLD WAR

Enikö Dácz

This paper focuses on Romanian cinematography about World War I, which Radina Vučetić regards as the richest in feature films in southeastern Europe "in not only the variety of the themes but also the topics they covered."[2]

First, a chronological overview of Romanian films about World War I will be given, guided by the question how they present the 1914–1918 catastrophe, with special emphasis on the role of the Austro-Hungarian Monarchy. Just as in Western Europe,[3] in

1 Quotation from the film *Pădurea Spânzuraților* [*The Forest of The Hanged*] (1964).

2 Radina Vučetić, "Film/Cinema (South East Europe)," in *1914-1918-online: International Encyclopedia of the First World War*, ed. Ute Daniel et al., issued by Freie Universität Berlin, Dec. 18, 2014, accessed July 8, 2015, DOI: http://dx.doi.org/10.15463/ie1418.10520.

3 Geert Buelens, "'They wouldn't end it with any of us alive, now would they?': The First World War in Cold War Era Films," in *The Great War in Post-Memory Literature and Film: Media and Cultural memory/Medien und kulturelle Erinnerung*, ed. Martin Löschnigg et al., vol. 18 (Berlin: De Gruyter, 2014), 365–383, here: 367.

Romania films on this topic came in waves; the productions in the communist period mostly followed the regime's ideological line, where only a few works managed to create their individual filmic language and solutions. The second part of the paper concentrates on a milestone production in Romanian cinema, which shaped collective memory in the long run and was chosen by forty critics as the second best Romanian movie ever.[4] The adaptation of the novel *Pădurea Spânzuraților* (*Forest of the Hanged*) by Liviu Rebreanu is the best-known Romanian World War I film for which, in 1965, Liviu Ciulei won the award in the category "Best Direction" in Cannes.[5] The press reviews in this period mirror a warm reception on the national (including the media of the minorities) and international level.[6] *Pădurea spânzuraților* was presented at several festivals, in Romania, Bulgaria, Germany, France, Canada, the USA, Israel, and even Mexico, among others. The paper analyzes the cultural schemes underlying the film and shows national discourses and their reflections.

4 Marian Țuțui, "Pădurea spânzuraților [Forest of the Hanged]," in *Cele mai bune zece filme românești ale tuturor timpurilor stabilite prin votul a 40 de critici*, ed. Cristina Corciovescu and Magda Mihăilescu (București: Polirom, 2010), 25–42.

5 The film received some further awards: three prizes at the Romanian Film Festival in Mamaia in 1965 and the Prize of Excellence for the quality of the images (Ovidiu Gologan) in Milan in 1964; Virgil Petrovici, *Pădurea spânzuraților: Un film de Liviu Ciulei* [The forest of the Hanged: A Film by Liviu Ciulei] (Bucharest: Editura Tehnică, 2002), 15.

6 The author thanks Helga and Thomas Ciulei for giving her access to the personal archive of Liviu Ciulei (Film Vol. III-IV, F-Padu) that, among other things, contains a collection of the film's press materials (F-Padu Press).

Images of the Austro-Hungarian Monarchy in Romanian Fiction Films

The first Romanian World War I feature film *Datorie și sacrificiu* (*Duty and sacrifice*, 1925) was produced for soldiers by the Photo-Cinematic Service of the Romanian Army. The movie includes earlier newsreels, establishing a long tradition in the Romanian cinema, and presents in a moralizing manner the story of two rivals who love the same girl, but because of the war have to fight together on the front. *Vitejii neamului* (*The heroes of the nation*, 1926) applies the same pseudo-documentary style and plot of two boys loving the same girl. In a media scandal, the movie had become famous before the premiere, as German diplomats protested against its anti-German character. Due to the prohibition, it appeared on the screens in a slightly cut version. In the next production, *Lia* (1927), the war serves only as the background to a romantic plot. These early feature films depict no images of the Austro-Hungarian Monarchy. The enemy is usually identified as German, another characteristic that lived on in the following decades.

The most popular World War I movie in the interwar period was *Ecatarina Teodoroiu* (1931), also because it was the first sung and spoken war film in Romania. Although critics considered it qualitatively inferior to similar Western productions,[7] it owes its fame to its topic and the handling of notions regarding the national identity. The romanticized biography of the Romanian heroine Ecatarina is based on a real story[8] and depicts how, in the face of

7 Manuela Gheorghiu, *Filmul și armele: Tema păcii și a războiului în filmul European* [The Film and the Weapons: The Topic of Peace and War in the European Film] (Bucharest: Editura Meridiane, 1976), 231.

8 That was first applied (among other stories) in the documentary film *Evocațiuni eroice* [*Heroic Evocations*] produced in 1921.

social prejudices, a young girl succeeds in becoming a soldier after her brother dies. The tragedy and the heroism of the protagonist is amplified by her death. Another important part of the plot is the love story between a spy and a Romanian soldier. The use of earlier newsreel montages, as well as the fact that the film was shot in Ecatarina's native village and that her mother acted her own part, strengthen the realistic documentary style. The Austro-Hungarian Monarchy is no central reference point; the Germans again are identified as the enemies. However, the fight for national unification with Transylvania—one of the main topics—implies the presence of an oppressive Habsburg Empire, a motive that was a constant cliché in later productions.

World War I seemed to disappear from Romanian films in the coming decades, a period when the country still did not have any significant cinematic output.[9] In 1957, *Viața nu iartă* (*When the mist is lifting*), a film inspired by Alexandru Sahia's literary sketches, picked up the topic again. Although the movie is set in World War II, it is the first production focusing on the traumatic consequences of World War I. The son of a former teacher tries to clarify the causes for his father's psychic collapse after his return from World War I. In flashbacks that invoke the French New Wave and melt the different temporal dimensions (present, past, and future), the father is portrayed as a man obeying the rules even in extreme situations; so, for example, he shoots a pacifist violinist who tries to desert. Being unable to live with the moral consequences of his deed, he flees into insanity. Just as his father, the son is not able to make a decision. He wants peace and is killed in World War II. Again, the Austro-Hungarian Monarchy is not present as a point of reference:

9 Cf. Dominique Nasta, *Contemporary Romanian Cinema: The History of an Unexpected Miracle* (New York: A Wallflower Press Book published by Columbia University Press, 2013).

In general, the two world wars are the setting for moral conflicts. Finally, the production pleads for peace policy.

In 1964, as already mentioned, the most representative film, *Pădurea spânzuraţilor*, was produced. Beginning with the seventies, a series of movies was produced that—in the words of Radina Vučetić—"use war as the setting in which any atrocity becomes possible in order to emphasize the meaninglessness and absurdity of war."[10] In 1975, the list opens with *Prin cenuşa imperiului* (*Through the Ashes of the Empire*), which already in its title features the Austro-Hungarian Monarchy. The film is based on Zaharia Stancu's novel *Jocul cu moartea* (*A gamble with death*). The fact that the film project began in 1968 is a sign of a gradually growing interest in the topic. Andrei Blaier's production won the Special Jury Prize in the youth section of the 1977 Cannes Film Festival and, in addition to Romanian awards, also the Best Actor Award in the Karlovy Vary International Film Festival in 1976.[11]

The plot of *Prin cenuşa imperiului* is based on the motif of travel and operates with such emblematic figures[12] as the anti-imperialist, the villain, the artist, and the dreamer. The movie presents

10 Vučetić, "Film/Cinema (South East Europe)." The exclusively state-paid cinema of the communist regime reached its peak in the eighties, producing about thirty long feature films annually; in the same period, the number of cinema theaters increased even in rural areas so that a much wider public could be reached; Marian Ţuţui, *O istorie a filmului românesc/A history of Romanian cinema* (Bucharest: Balkanski Proiect, 2004), 24.

11 Bujor Râpeanu, *Filmat în România: Un repertoriu filmografic* [Filmed in Romania: A Filmographic Repertoire], vol. 2 *1970–1979* (Bucharest: Edituar Fundaţiei Pro, 2005), 119.

12 Marilena Ilieşu, *Povestea poveştii în filmul românesc (1912–2012)* [The Story of the Story in the Romanian Film (1912–2012)] (Bucharest: Polirom, 2013), 81.

occupied Bucharest in 1917: Men are accidentally taken hostage in the street by German occupants. They are sent by train to an unknown place, where they are supposed to work as shepherds. The dissolution of Franz Joseph's Empire is predicted at the beginning. The anti-imperialist discourse is only briefly contradicted by a young protagonist who longs to see the world: For him, Serbia, Hungary, and Austria promise adventure at this point. The main figure is not individualized: Darie is unwilling to reveal his second name, remaining a symbolic traveller born as a peasant who cannot influence historical events, while history influences his life. According to the common traveller narrative, he is shaped by the experiences on the road, a continuous balancing between life and death. The film applies several symbols belonging to the same formula, such as the snake or the hedgehog. According to the same traveller scheme, nature shelters and protects the protagonist.

The Austro-Hungarian Monarchy is staged at different levels. The evergreen topos of the empire as a prison appears in variations: Nationalities are literally hunted by authorities, so that they can hardly leave their home. People are imprisoned and killed—often hanged. One of the hostages, who trusts Darie, turns out to be a Romanian Transylvanian and a deserter of the Austrian-Hungarian Army. He wants to join the Romanian Army and to contribute to the liberation of Transylvanian Romanians. However, the former soldier is betrayed by another hostage, the "diplomat"—the emblematic figure of the villain—and is executed in the name of the Emperor. This way, the Monarchy's theoretically debated credo that small nations have to obey without being given rights is proven by an example. Nationalistic stereotypes are also remembered when the officers speaking exclusively German reproduce nationalistic clichés, calling the hostages "dirty *Wallachs*." Having the chance to visit a city, Darie faces the soldiers' cruelty: There are hanged peasants awaiting him, and a Serbian woman has to save him from being shot. According to the prevalent ideology of the seventies, all peasant figures are positive and morally impeccable; they help each other irrespective of their nationality, although German or Hungarian peasants do not appear at all. In the hostages' dialogues about war and killing people on the front, Germans and Austro-Hungarians are hardly differentiated.

As Darie and the "diplomat" can flee, that earlier wanderlust no longer motivates the young man; his only wish is to return home. Their way is marked by symbolic encounters with partisans and peasants. Back in Bucharest, they are accidentally arrested again, but the possibility that the (his)story might repeat itself is obliterated by Darie's act of throwing away the gold coin of the "diplomat" that might have guaranteed freedom. The main topic of the previous discussions between the hostages is a future without empires (and a "Kaiser"), "where people are free." It is repeated by a new comrade who remembers the former Transylvanian deserter.

Adopting the new ideological expectations, in 1978 a new version of *Ecaterina Teodoroiu* was shot in a somewhat similar glorifying style as earlier. Using the well-known motifs of the soldier who is killed while trying to flee the Austro-Hungarian Army or the dream of "Great Romania," the Monarchy is depicted as the Romanians' oppressor. As previously, the enemies are identified with the Germans in general without any further specification, and the "enemy is not human," Ecatarina concludes. Heroic patterns dominate the movie: Transylvanian Romanian soldiers who managed to desert from the Austro-Hungarian Army fight for national unity in the Romanian Army. Pathetic scenes propagate patriotic feelings, quotations from a poem by the famous poet and politician Lucian Blaga are reflected.

Ecatarina Teodoroiu is the only women in Romanian war cinematography about World War I who joined the army and was actively engaged in fights. Women mainly appear in the background and make sacrifices at home. Ecatarina's courage is underlined by the music that emphasises her almost religious devotion to the national cause, overcoming any difficulty (German captivity, injuries, and disease) except death. A romantic thread presents Ecatarina's love for an officer and that of a Transylvanian Romanian for her. The doctor from Blaj (symbol of national unity in the Romanian collective memory) is the voice of the Transylvanian problem, while his death resembles his compatriots' martyrdom. Disease is visualized as a constant threat, as Ecatarina has to learn that her native village was devastated by typhus, and her mother died. In *Prin cenușa imperiului*, the same disease was only a marginal topic.

The movie *Ultima noapte de dragoste, prima noapte de război* (*The Last Night of Love, the First Night of War*, 1930), based on Camil Petrescu's famous novel set in World War I, is in the tradition of French existentialism. The novel, which has two film adaptations and is part of the Romanian curriculum, first inspired the movie Între oglinzi paralele (*Between facing mirrors*, 1978), which focused on the social dimension of war and avoided battle scenes. Even inheriting a great fortune, the main character cannot develop any interest in material goods. Although he is a member of the high society, especially because of the ambitions of his wife, he remains faithful to his philosophy and to his friend Gore, an active socialist. He finally joins the army, as he considers the war an existential experience he does not want to miss. The psychological drama involves the Austro-Hungarian Monarchy only on the level of topics discussed in conversation.

Sergiu Nicolaescu's adaptation of Petrescu's novel, *Ultima noapte* (*The last night*, 1979) concentrates on the individual tragedy of Tudor Gheorghiu, who is destroyed by his jealousy and is eventually executed. The sentimental war movie displays long battle scenes, and reflects the social differences of the time, but avoids any references to the Austro-Hungarian Monarchy.[13]

13 It is noteworthy that all these movies were awarded at least one time by the Romanian Association of Filmmakers, a fact that implies the importance of the topic for the communist regime.

Iulian Mihu's *Lumina palidă a durerii* (*The Pale Light of Sorrow*, 1981) is one of the rare works of the time that managed to develop a complex symbolic language. As the plot takes place in the period of German occupation in a small settlement in Buzău County, the Austro-Hungarian Monarchy does not play any role in the depiction of the rural milieu.[14]

Capcana mercenarilor (*Trap of the hired guns*, 1981) mirrors the intensifying nationalistic tone of the regime. The narrator explicitly claims to reflect reality, emphasizing that the story is inspired by facts and the characters are only partly fictional, which is also underlined by the newsreels integrated. In accordance with the mainstream political discourse, the bourgeoisie is blamed for social conditions in Transylvania. The story of a baron taking revenge on a village for having devastated his castle—which the villagers clearly deny—follows the motto that "the bourgeoisie is responsible for the tragedy." Although the social dimension of the topic is of primary importance, the nationality question cannot be overlooked. It is the Hungarian baron who recruits people to kill peasants and demonstrates pure barbarism. The three Hungarian and five Saxon peasants, unlike the Romanians, need to be explicitly accepted as helpers against the baron, which strengthens the national connotation of the class fight.

The image of the Austro-Hungarian Empire is dominated by the oppressive upper class with solely negative connotations. The plot begins in Vienna, where men are hired for an unclearly defined task; these scenes present a decadent world and society. Arriving in Transylvania, (dominated by the pure white of the snowy landscape), the mercenaries who refuse to execute peasants are shot. Cruelty is increasing continuously. After a Hungarian peasant succeeds in escaping, he informs

14 Ilieşu, *Povestea poveştii* ⊠*n filmul românesc*, 166–170.

a Romanian community about the event. The baron is immediately recognized as a cruel former officer in Galicia, and a Romanian major assumes the task of confronting him. The reminiscences highlight the moral decadence of the upper class, underlined by the fact that the military leadership is reluctant to help. Besides the narrative about the oppressed Romanians in Transylvania, further nationalistic slogans are reproduced and only sporadically refuted in the case of peasants. The heroic fight for the liberation of the village ends with the expected victory of the Major, who loses his corporal integrity, thus paying for his former moral decadence. The Western-style music emphasizes the heroic narrative that intends to be didactic and entertaining at the same time, but falls back on the sheer reproduction of schemes and stereotypes.

Regarding World War I films in Romania, Radina Vučetić concludes that in the communist period these productions "became more anti-war than patriotic, emphasizing the absurdity of war. Romanian cinema of the time," Vučetić continued, "generally avoided spectacular and grandiose battle scenes with the deployment of troops, while emphasizing individual sacrifice on the dramas of those who bore the brunt of battles on their shoulders."[15] Clichés, schematic representations of soldiers, as shown above, served nationalist mobilization and partly contradict Vučetić, who seems to disregard some central aspects of the movies to which *The Handbook of Soviet and East European Films and Filmmakers* also refers. *The Handbook* states that Romanian cinema during the communist period was in general "aesthetically insignificant, adhering rigidly to the somehow formulaic necessities imposed by the film's illustrative and ideological functions in a totalitarian regime. For these reasons Romanian cinema has not gained the

15 Vučetić, "Film/Cinema (South East Europe)."

world stature of other East European cinemas."[16] At the same time, the 1949–1970 period is the phase in Romanian cinematography in which the filmic language and grammar are consolidated.[17] Thus a few significant individual works, such as those of Liviu Ciulei, Andrei Blaier, or Iulian Mihu, should be excluded when speaking about the rigidity and formulaic necessities[18] dictated exclusively "by political prescriptions."[19]

After a longer break following the system change—which can be partly explained by the difficult situation of the Romanian cinema in the nineties, when filmmakers found it hard to adapt to the new economic situation, and partly by the diminishing interest in the topic—the next World War I feature film were produced in two parts in 1999. The already named Sergiu Nicolaescu, who during communism earned his fame for producing a long series of historical films that followed the ideological line, directed *Triunghiul morții* (*The Death Triangle*). This film preserves the nationalistic ideas and discourse of the former regime. As Romania's most famous nationalist politician, Corneliu Vadim Tudor, co-wrote the screenplay, the collection of notions of national identity is imposing. The feature film offers a narrative of World War I, embracing almost all the topics and motives listed: enthusiastic young soldiers fighting for the unification of the nation, the heroine Ecatarina Teodoroiu, Transylvanian deserters,

16 Judith Roof, "Romania," in *Handbook of Soviet and East European Films and Filmmakers*, ed. Thomas Slater J. (New York: Weatport, 1992), 309–342, here: 309.

17 Ilieşu, *Povestea poveştii în filmul românesc*, 37.

18 Lutz Haucke, "Rumänische neue Welle?," in *Nouvelle vague in Osteuropa? Zur ostmittel- und südosteuropäischen Filmgeschichte 1960–1970* (Berlin: Rhombos, 2009), 424–437, here: 424.

19 Roof, "Romania," 313.

and honest peasants. Austria-Hungary is also included at the level of discourse, as the enemy mentioned even in the narrator's closing remarks. Based on his own memoirs, the portrayal of Marshal Alexandru Averescu is one-dimensional: He is a hero. In contrast to earlier movies, the King and the Queen appear as figures active during the war. The narrator, the long battle scenes, and the newsreels all depict a heroic army. This one-dimensional picture is disturbed only by a part of the elite trying to cooperate with the Germans.

Although Sergiu Nicolaescu's historical documentary *Carol I - Un destin pentru România* (*Carol I: A Destiny for Romania*), made in 2009, does not strictly belong to our topic, it is noteworthy because it combines archival newsreels with feature film scenes and operates with some central topoi of earlier works. It also continues the tradition of monumental historic productions meant for mobilizing people rather than critically reflecting the event.

Pădurea spânzuraţilor (The Forest of the Hanged)

Liviu Ciulei's adaptation of Liviu Rebreanu's novel is a "landmark of innovation" in Romanian cinematography.[20] The literary text—part of the national curriculum—served as the starting point for a modern actualization that focuses on the main character's mental torments, and the destruction of certainties and conformities that in his youth Apostol Bologa took for granted. In Ciulei's interpretation,

---

20 Marian Ţuţui, "Pădurea spânzuraţilor" [Forest of the Hanged], in *The Cinema of the Balkans,* ed. Dina Iordanova (London: Wallflower Press, 2006) 33–41, 34. See also: Nasta, *Contemporary Romanian Cinema: The History of an Unexpected Miracle,* 21–23. Screen adaptations of novels were very common in the Romanian cinema of the communist period; the best-known authors in this respect include Liviu Rebreanu, Marin Preda, Mihail Sadoveanu, Ioan Slavici, and Camil Petrescu.

the protagonist is the victim of his wrongly chosen isolated path of individualism.[21] Besides the novel, the short stories *Catastrofa* (*Catastrophe*) and *Iţic Ştrul, dezertor* (*Iţic Ştrul, the deserter*), both by Liviu Rebreanu, also served as sources for the film and led, among other things, to the creation of a new figure, Johann Maria Müller,[22] a Viennese antiquarian and hardcore antimilitarist soldier. At the same time, Bologa's youth, which Rebreanu depicted in great detail, is fully missing. The film has a baroque structure and is a "perfect circular story" beginning and ending with execution scenes that prove the absurdity of war.[23] In the opening scene, soldiers disappear in the fog heading for an unpredictable and unknown place, with mud dominating the image; the topography displays a complexity which is continuously amplified.[24]

To reproduce the atmosphere of the Austro-Hungarian Monarchy, several scenes were shot in Transylvania. The ruins of the baroque Bánffy castle in Bonţida, where the Austrian General von Karg has his headquarters, are a metaphor for the decaying empire, just as the rich breakfast reflects the preference for luxury, building a contrast to the poorly equipped soldiers fighting in the trenches. In the same way, nationalist issues are handled in all their nuances: the actors' accents, including both ethnic Hungarians and Germans (for example., Ilona played by Anna Széles, Karg by György Kovács, Emmerich Schäffer by Johann Maria Müller) suggest the population's and the army's linguistic diversity without making it difficult for viewers to appreciate the plurality of languages.

21 Petrovici, *Pădurea spânzuraţilor: Un film de Liviu Ciulei*, 30.

22 Ibid., 29.

23 Ţuţui, "Pădurea spânzuraţilor" [Forest of the Hanged], 26.

24 Ţuţui, "Pădurea spânzuraţilor" [Forest of the Hanged], 37; Ilieşu, *Povestea poveștii ⊠n filmul românesc*, 62.

In this context, the multi-ethnic Austro-Hungarian Army stands for all repressive systems, but the desperate situation of the troops repeatedly questions nationalist schemes. Despite the national dividing lines, there is a high degree of human solidarity between the officers, which is manifest in their conversations. The Hungarian officer Varga, who claims the perfect internationality of the Austro-Hungarian Army, points at the representatives of the nationalities in the officer corps and voices the popular belief: "The empire is order." He is apparently incapable of understanding his comrades' moral struggles, but remarks in a debate that, if they continue the discussion, he might accept fleeing as a solution. Varga also apologizes to Bologa after cursing the Romanian enemy because of the death of Czerwenko, a pacifist unwilling to hold a weapon. Although Varga does his duty in the end and arrests Bologa for deserting, he cannot resist showing his feelings.

The topos of the national martyr, often connected with the figure of the Transylvanian Romanian soldier in World War I, is missing. Bologa's inner battle begins when he is supervising the execution of a Czech deserter in whose sentencing he previously took part. He later tries to avoid fighting against his kinsmen by destroying an enemy searchlight, thereby risking his life. In spite of Bologa's heroic deed, General von Karg refuses his request to be sent to another front. However, Bologa is wounded and hospitalized while trying to escape. Thus, he is given leave of absence and can visit his mother and fiancé, whom he subsequently leaves without an explanation. Returning to his comrades, Bologa falls in love with the Hungarian peasant girl Ilona, and they get engaged. Now the ethnic dimension of the story gains in complexity. Bologa's happiness comes to a sudden end when he is in a court martial that has to convict Hungarian and Romanian peasants who tried to work in the field next to the frontline. As a last desperate attempt, he wants to desert, but is caught. After harsh inner struggles, Bologa accepts his fate and does not plead madness in order to save himself.

The plot is only of secondary relevance when compared to the symbolic narrative Ciulei develops a second level of the story:[25] that of Bologa's confrontation with himself. Actually, several figures "seem to be in different phases of the same crisis," and therefore already on the verge of deserting.[26] Several other officers or soldiers could find themselves in a similar situation to Bologa or Varga; it is the contingent geographical position of the front that decides one's individual fate. Almost all figures lose their faith and hopes, caught in the middle of a mass of people and faced with events they cannot influence anymore; all they are left with is their fear.

Mass scenes of soldiers, in which mud and fog penetrate everything, and dialogues between Bologa and Müller, for instance, alternate, elaborating two central themes emphasized by the producer himself and several critics: the search for happiness and fear.[27] According to Irina Coroiu, the film gains symphonic dimensions through suddenly changing the narrative style between inner depictions or comic moments.[28] The figures are emblematic: Ilona represents pure innocence and dignity, while others personify frivolity. In the scene of the last meal, Ilona reaches the greatness of classical characters,[29] becoming a widow in mourning who

25 Ilieşu, *Povestea poveştii în filmul românesc,* 65.

26 Ibid., 64.

27 Petrovici, *Pădurea spânzuraţilor: Un film de Liviu Ciulei,* 212.

28 Ibid., 209. Anyway, some critics e.g. George Sadoul reproached Ciulei because of the length and slow development of the film; Ţuţui, "Pădurea spânzuraţilor" [Forest of the Hanged], 34; Richard Roud, "The Knack of the British," in *The Guardian*, May 29, 1965, 6.

29 Petrovici, *Pădurea spânzuraţilor: Un film de Liviu Ciulei,* 29–30.

adapts to reality. Not only Ilona, but peasants in general, appear as embodiments of normality (wanting to plough the field). Morality is shown also through another key figure: the Romanian peasant Petre, who is supposed to eliminate Müller for spreading his anti-militaristic views that threaten to undermine other soldiers' morale. Petre allows Müller to escape and is punished by Bologa, who sends him in the first line to his certain death. Bologa later learns from Petre's son that Müller managed to escape, while Petre died. As an officer and philosopher, the main character tries to justify his behavior in the same way as he always does evoking his duty to the Austro-Hungarian state. In contrast, Petre as an emblematic peasant is led by his feelings and duties to humanity. Finding his real self in the end, Bologa symbolically transforms into a peasant. His metamorphosis is represented in the closing meal, one of the most lyric scenes of the film. The eating ceremony demonstrates an inner harmony reached by accepting fate as the unavoidable order of life. Bologa seems to regard his death as a punishment for the lies in his life: falsely interpreted duty, honor, pride, and hesitations.

The detailed depictions of the unspectacular aspects of life are central in the movie: breathing and swallowing assume an expressive function, and the surroundings reflect Bologa's inner state. The objects characterize the figures: Karg's palace is luxurious but at the same time deserted, suggesting cruelty. Similarly, the soldiers are more often shown in their dirty clothes fighting against the mud rather than the enemy. Frozen faces express the soldiers' fear not only in the opening scene, when the deserter is hanged, but keep returning as leitmotifs during the whole film.

Ovidiu Gologan's black and white camera work operates with contrasts and close-ups that reflect the figures' inner state and visually present their psychological motivations. The expressivity of the looks is remarkable.[30] According to Gologan, the eyes convey a wide range of feelings: sometimes Bologa's harshness, sometimes his goodness, his remorse, his calm, or resignation; sometimes Ilona's innocence or Karg's cruelty.[31] The light metaphor, which Marilena Ilieşiu perceives as a character on its own,[32] also belongs to the repeated elements continuously gaining and lending new meaning, expressing in the end the euphoria of Bologa's love for Ilona. The returning white could be interpreted as a kind of reconciliation with fate, which is suggested also by Theodor Grigoriu's minimalist music, sharing some similarities with Alban Bergs's *Wozzek*.[33]

Conclusion

Marilena Ilieşiu describes the history of the Romanian film as a road from primitivism, in terms of its technical solutions and plot constructions, to postmodern configurations.[34] This development has not occurred in the field of World War I movies, as the topic nearly disappeared from the screens because World War II is more vivid in the collective memory.

Regarding the question of historical representation and national stereotyping, several of the discussed war films helped "implant, strengthen, and nurture stereotypes."[35] German barbarism, imprisoned nationalities, and Transylvanian martyrs belonged to

30 Ibid., 19.

31 Ibid., 87.

32 Ilieşu, *Povestea poveştii ⊠n filmul românesc*, 62.

33 Petrovici, *Pădurea spânzuraţilor: Un film de Liviu Ciulei.*, 79.

34 Ilieşu, *Povestea poveştii ⊠n filmul românesc*, 5.

35 Michael T. Isenberg, "The Friend: The Image of the Ally," in *War on Film: The American Cinema and World War I, 1914–1941* (London: Associated Presses, 1981) 161–175, 161.

the reiterated motives of mostly ideologically underpinned films. However, outstanding individual artistic performances were also created during the communist period. Besides the most significant exception, *Pădurea spânzuraţilor*, or Iulian Mihu`s *Lumina palidă a durerii*, Andrei Blaier's *Prin cenuşa imperiului* succeeded only in part, as although the film displays a high degree of dramatic sensibility and has numerous masterly scenes, it does not exclude national narratives and ideological undertones.

Thanks to its multi-layered nature, *Pădurea spânzuraţilor* could gain international attention both through its peasant figures and its artistic complexity and satisfy the ideological expectations of the time by raising current social problems.[36] Since desertion was a frequent theme of European WWI films at the time, Liviu Ciulei took up a common topic that *pars pro toto* demonstrated "this conflict's quintessential cruelty and injustice."[37] *Pădurea spânzuraţilor* resembles films like Joseph Losey's *The Servant* (1963), but Ciulei has also been compared to Alain Resnais, Lewis Milestone, or Michelangelo Antonioni.[38]

Explicit denunciations of Austria-Hungary as oppressive and imperialistic were ideologically welcomed in the communist period, but mainly remained at the discourse level. Only a few

36 Emphasized in the press of the time, mainly in 1964-1965, among others in: *Contemporanul, Făclia, Scânteia, Saptămâna Culturală a Capitalei, România liberă, Infirmaţia Bucureştiului, Viaţa culturală, Luceafărul, Tribuna, Utunk, Előre, Művelődési Élet, Új Élet, Neuer Weg, Fáklya;* Liviu Ciulei's personal archive: F-Padu Press. An overview through selected quotations of the reception in the media is given by Petrovici; Petrovici, *Pădurea spânzuraţilor: Un film de Liviu Ciulei.* 206–228.

37 Buelens, "`They wouldn't end it with any of us alive, now would they?`: The First World War in Cold War Era Films," 369.

38 Ţuţui, "Pădurea spânzuraţilor [Forest of the Hanged]," 34.

films reflect more accurately the complexity of the topic. *Pădurea Spânzuraţilor* offers many scenes where ethnic Czech, Romanian, Polish, Ruthenian, Hungarian, and Austrian soldiers and civilians deal with one another in respectful, caring, and even loving ways. But even here, the military system, represented by the Austrian General von Karg, shows no mercy."[39] This production was "successful by addressing the difficult issues of Austria-Hungary's dissolution at the end of World War I and in exploring its intricate Transylvanian dimension, while staying away from propagandistic patriotic leanings. Ciulei's stylish adaptation of Rebreanu's novel is a memorable historical fresco that addresses complex Balkan confrontations and reinforces the importance of this early analysis of Balkan history."[40]

The scheme of ethnic vs. imperial nationalism was propagated in several of the films, such as Ecatarina Teodoroiu, Prin cenuşa imperiului, or Capcana mercenarilor. The formula of exceptional heroes with a historical mission was also repeatedly used (Ecatarina Teodoroiu or Capcana mercenarilor). "In the whole period of communism, and also after the fall of communism, the most representative Romanian World War I films violently attacked the institution of arms; they have a tragic outlook, focusing on the despair of individuals caught up in the war-machinery."[41] Even if some specification is needed, as Vučetić does not talk about post-1990 productions—and her description only partly fits the films analyzed above—the horror and brutality of the war can be regarded as a consistent thread, and pacifist ideas were indeed promoted as part of the official ideology. In this sense,

---

39 Buelens, "'They wouldn't end it with any of us alive, now would they?': The First World War in Cold War Era Films," 374.

40 Ţuţui, "Pădurea spânzuraţilor" [Forest of the Hanged], 41.

41 Vučetić, "Film/Cinema (South East Europe)."

bodies hanging at the gallows in Pădurea spânzuraţilor represent the "absurd fruits of the war,"[42] while at the same time the film stresses the fact that everybody's behavior is understandable—though resulting in tragedy and death.[43]

42 Ţuţui, "Pădurea spânzuraţilor" [Forest of the Hanged], 40.

43 Ibid., 37.

TRACES OF AUSTRIA-HUNGARY AND THE FIRST WORLD WAR IN TSARIST/SOVIET/RUSSIAN CINEMATOGRAPHY

Verena Moritz

The "Great War" and its "Comeback"

Against the backdrop of the 100th anniversary, Russia's evident interest in the history of the years from 1914 to 1917/18 was often perceived as a revival of a long suppressed and unwanted commemoration. In 2014, Russia, it seemed, rediscovered World War One. A "war forgotten" was remembered in various exhibitions, scientific and popular publications, illustrated books, TV-documentary films, and even in the cinema. The way the Great War was exhibited, characterized, interpreted, and adapted for the screen in some cases more or less obviously corresponded to Russia's present-day self-portrayal as "home of the brave." Those brave men and women dominated the filmic narratives of WWI in 2014, and the general public must have been convinced that Russian soldiers' overwhelming patriotism and readiness to make sacrifices during WWI would result in a just and well-deserved victory, unless their enemies and allies were more or less satanic combatants (especially the German Empire) and deceitful traitors (France and Great Britain). According to this interpretation, Russia was abused by its allies and had to carry the major burden of the war. Obviously, an analogy between past and present was intended by the architects of a strong patriotism and a new patriotic culture in Vladimir Putin's Russia, which was ostracized by the USA and the European Union since at least its proceeding in the Crimea and in the Ukraine. The message is clear: Russia stood alone during the First World War, cheated by its allies and beaten only because of a revolution that was supported by the Germans, and it stands alone now, misapprehended and wrongly stigmatized by the rest of the world, which, without plausible reason, considers itself morally and ethically superior to Russia.

In 2014, on 1 August, when Putin inaugurated a monument to Russian soldiers of the First World War, he offered a "stab-in-the-back explanation of Tsarist Russia's defeat and collapse," alluding "of course, to the Bolsheviks" who had been sent to Russia by the Germans.[1] In doing this, the Russian President more or less adopted the perception of emigrated Tsarist officers who had interpreted the lost war as a "German-Bolshevik plot to destroy the nation."[2] In

---

1 Many thanks to J. Köstenberger and V. Denisov for their help regarding investigations for this article in Moscow.

Transliteration of Russian follows Library of Congress transliteration table.

Cf. Vladimir Socor, "Putin Re-Interprets Russia´s Participation in the First World War," in *Eurasia Daily Monitor Volume* 11, no. 143 (2008). accessed Jan. 25, 2016, http://www.jamestown.org/single/?tx_ttnews%5Btt_news%5D=42714&no_cache=1.

2 Aaron J. Cohen, "Oh, That! Myth, Memory, and World War I in the Russian Emigration and in the Soviet Union," *Slavic Review* 62, no. 1 (Spring 2003): 69–86, here: 74.

any case, Putin spoke of "'re-establishing the unbroken continuity of our history,' incorporating the First World War's 'sacred memory' into the official accounts of Russia´s history. [...] Amid its ongoing war against Ukraine, the Kremlin is reaching into history to recuperate yet another militarist narrative for popular consumption."[3]

There are many critical and stimulating analyses of Russia's past and current commemorative culture and the official conception of history that was repeatedly modified even in the Soviet era.[4] After 1989 and the following fundamental changes that Eastern Europe, including the USSR, faced, a mere reversal of former interpretations by communist doctrines in regard to the history before and after the Bolsheviks seized power was an evident temptation for those countries. In post-Soviet Russia, historiography ran through various phases of reorientation. Putin's Russia obviously did not abandon communist interpretations of the past as a whole, in order to adapt them for its own purposes. As a result, Stalin, for example, remains the "father of the nation" who led Soviet people to a glorious victory against German barbarism between 1941 and 1945. Historiography and the conception of history in today's Russia are not free from contradictions. Still accepted communist interpretations of history and a reinterpretation of communist history as an antipode of former narratives are in juxtaposition with each other, but they somehow coexist. Moreover, popular interpretations of history introduce additional dimensions. But all of those variations that are initiated or accepted by official Russia, notwithstanding the lack of stringent reflections, share

3 Ibid.

4 See for example: Lars Karl and Igor J. Polianski, eds., *Geschichtspolitik und Erinnerungskultur im neuen Russland (Göttingen:* V&R unipress, 2009); or Catherine Merridale, *Night of Stone: Death and Memory in Twentieth Century Russia* (London: Granta, 2000).

the same intended purpose: the strengthening of patriotism, completed by the advice to distrust the world beyond the borders of Russia.[5]

In regard to the appraisal of the role of the Tsarist army, recent Russian fiction and documentary films have made a distinct turning away from former communist perceptions. Nonetheless, there are some striking continuities to Soviet cinema as, for instance, the near complete absence of Austria-Hungary.

The Tsarist Empire and the War on the Screen

After 1945, the so-called "Habsburg myth" played an important role in the process of identity in the Second Austrian Republic. While World War One itself was largely neglected in cultural

5 It has to be underlined that this text concentrates on the Russian official narratives in films on the First World War. There are, of course a lot of "deviant" interpretations including, for example, differentiated approaches by historians. In this respect, it has to be mentioned that, in 2012, Kees Boterbloem has examined Russian historiography of the First World War in regard of the Russian participation. He saw a lack of Russian-language monographs on Russia in WWI and reasoned that this lack had "much to do with the continued unease felt in Russia about the Great War." Boterbloem´s result obviously differs from recent interpretations of the First World War and Russia's role by official Russia today. Cf. Kees Boterbloem, "'Chto delat'?: World War I in Russian Historiography after Communism," *The Journal of Slavic Military Studies* 25, no. 3 (2012), 393–408, accessed Feb. 1, 2016, DOI: 10.1080/13518046.2012.705655. On historiography of the Russian Revolution with an overview of current Russian interpretations of the Revolution see: S. A. Smith, "The Historiography of the Russian Revolution 100 Years on," in *Kritika* 16, no. 4 (Fall 2015), 733–749.

avenues, completely uncritical depictions of Habsburg history presented the Austro-Hungarian Empire as role model for a peaceful coexistence of different nations and Franz Joseph I as the "the good old Kaiser." The Dual Monarchy was portrayed as an ideal state, and in regard of World War One, this "paradise" was only misled and abused by the Germans seeking world supremacy. After World War II, the Austrian people have become accustomed to such interpretations of the Habsburg past. They could not even imagine that Austria-Hungary was not seen in a similar way in other countries. Austrian feature films of the 1950s introduced soldiers of the "k.u.k." army as clumsy and harmless guys or as smart womanizers. The First World War on the screen, all in all, was either completely absent or presented as if there had been neither misery nor bloodshed, but only "Waltz" and "Schmaltz."[6] It was unthinkable that soldiers of the Habsburg army had committed war crimes.[7] In addition, historiography for decades focused on Germany, claiming that the militant *Kaiserreich* bear the chief responsibility for the war that started in summer 1914. The Danube Monarchy was either exculpated or more or less ignored. Until now, some historians complain, Austria-Hungary is rather perceived as victim of German warmongers than as autonomous player.[8] In fact, there was already a movement to marginalize the Habsburg monarchy during the war, concentrating on its lack of

---

6 Sabine A. Haring, "Between the Topos of a 'Forgotten War' and the Current Memory Boom: Remembering the First World War in Austria," in *Remembering the First World War*, ed. Bart Ziino (London: Routledge, 2015), 207–222, here: 214–216.

7 See for example: Karin Moser, ed., *Besetzte Bilder: Film, Kultur und Propaganda in* Österreich *1945–1955* (Vienna: Verlag Filmarchiv Austria, 2005).

8 Lothar Höbelt, *"Stehen oder Fallen?"* Österreichische *Politik im Ersten Weltkrieg* (Vienna: Böhlau Verlag, 2015), 131.

strength and its dependence on German economic and military support. The longer the war lasted, Entente powers tended to perceive Austria-Hungary as a pure appendix of German authorities, as "junior partner" of the *Kaiserreich*, which made important decisions without asking the young Habsburg Emperor Karl. Nevertheless, for Tsarist Russia, the Danube monarchy was its main adversary. While in 1914 Germany's main effort was concentrated against France, requiring approximately ninety percent of its manpower, Austria deployed the bulk of its forces against Russia.[9]

So, how did Tsarist cinematic propaganda portray the Danube monarchy, whose conflict with Serbia figured at the beginning of a European war that broadened to a world wide struggle? Whom did Russian cinema blame for the outbreak of the conflict that, in the end, swept away the Romanovs and their Empire? Who was deemed to be "worse" or more "condemnable"? The German Empire or the Danube monarchy? And was Russian film production able to comply with the requirements of an effective propaganda?

The war seriously affected Russian cinema: "On the eve of the conflict nearly 90 percent of film productions shown in Russia had come from abroad."[10] Before the war, a large number of films distributed in Russia had been of German origin. After the outbreak of hostilities, French film companies in Russia especially

---

9 Timothy C. Dowling, "Eastern Front," in *1914–1918-online: International Encyclopedia of the First World War*, ed. Ute Daniel et al. (Berlin: Freie Universität Berlin 2014), DOI: http://dx.doi.org/10.15463/ie1418.10316.

10 Alexandre Sumpf, "Film/Cinema (Russian Empire)," in *1914–1918-online: International Encyclopedia of the First World War*, ed. by Ute Daniel et al. (Berlin: Freie Universität Berlin, 2014), DOI: http://dx.doi.org/10.15463/ie1418.10383.

benefited.[11] Besides, the Tsarist Empire saw a growing number of Russian companies and "the strengthening of national champions, as the Khanzhonkov, Drankov and Ermol[′]ev Studios."[12] Native film production increased rapidly. On the other hand, "it would be a mistake to underestimate the profound influence of Western European filmmaking had overall in Russian filmmakers and audiences."[13] German companies, however, were forced to shut down their production, and German theater owners and distributors were exiled. In 1915, all German films were banned.[14]

Tsarist propaganda identified Germany as a responsible aggressor and as the most dangerous enemy, "the one against which the greatest patriotic efforts had to be directed."[15] Germans turned out to be the main target of people's anger in Russian metropoles, and anti-German riots seemed to express the degree of hate toward the enemy, including the German minority in Russia.[16] Spy mania was widespread already before the war and explosively increased during the July Crisis 1914. German speaking people, including Jews, were

---

11 In 1914, ninety percentof the films distributes internationally in the world were French; Michael Wood, *Film: A Very Short Introduction* (Oxford: University Press, 2012), 48

12 Sumpf, "Film/Cinema (Russian Empire)." On the Russian "Movie Moguls" see: Louise McReynolds, *Russia at Play: Leisure Activities at the End of the Tsarist Era* (Ithaca: Cornell University Press, 2003), 269–276.

13 Denise J. Youngblood, *The Magic Mirror: Moviemaking in Russia 1908–1918* (Madison: The University of Wisconsin Press,1999), 13.

14 Hubertus F. Jahn, *Patriotic Culture in Russia During World War I* (Ithaca: Cornell University Press, 1995), 152.

15 Jahn, *Patriotic Culture*,173.

16 On the riots in Moscow of 26–29 May 1915 see: Eric Lohr, "Patriotic Violence and the State: The Moscow Riots of May 1915," in *Kritika* 4, no. 3 (Summer 2003), 607–626.

considered the prime suspects by Tsarist counterintelligence, and "private citizens flooded government agencies with denunciations of suspected spies."[17] Recently, however, Russian historians have questioned if Germanophobia would have emerged that intensely without the massive efforts of propaganda especially in 1914–15.[18]

Russian propaganda had to go all out to shape a convincing concept of the enemy. Finally, "convincing" meant to present a primitive and distorted image. Germany and its "Kaiser" were demonized, and Wilhelm was portrayed as the "Antichrist."[19] In a feature film of the same title (*Antichrist*), the German Emperor acted like a real

---

17 Jonathan W. Daly, "Security Services in Imperial and Soviet Russia," in *Kritika: Explorations in Russian and Eurasian History* 4, no. 4 (Fall 2003), 955–974, here: 969.

18 See respective deliberations in contributions of: Wladimir Fedjuk, "Der Kampf gegen die ′deutsche Überfremdung′ in der russischen Provinz," in *Verführungen der Gewalt: Russen und Deutsche im Ersten und Zweiten Weltkrieg*, ed. Karl Eimermacher and Astrid Volpert (Munich: Wilhelm Fink Verlag, 2005), 95–119; Boris Kolonizkij, "Metamorphosen der Germanophobie: Deutschland in den politischen Konflikten der Februarrevolution," in *Verführungen der Gewalt: Russen und Deutsche im Ersten und Zweiten Weltkrieg*, ed. Karl Eimermacher and Astrid Volpert (Munich: Wilhelm Fink Verlag, 2005), 121–144; Dimitrij Olejnikow, "Von Ritterlichkeit zu Verachtung: Auswirkungen des Ersten Weltkriegs auf das Verhältnis zu den Deutschen," in *Verführungen der Gewalt: Russen und Deutsche im Ersten und Zweiten Weltkrieg*, ed. Karl Eimermacher and Astrid Volpert (Munich: Wilhelm Fink Verlag, 2005), 179–204.

19 Jekaterina Chochlowa, "Vom Dialog zu Konfrontation: Russischer und deutscher Film zwischen den Weltkriegen," in *Stürmische Aufbrüche und enttäuschte Hoffnungen: Russen und Deutsche in der Zwischenkriegszeit*, ed. Karl Eimermacher and Astrid Volpert (Munich: Wilhelm Fink Verlag, 2006), 927–952, 930.

monster, brutal and completely immoral.[20] According to the belief of some Russian peasants, he was even drinking human blood.[21] The film was very popular and became a tremendous box office hit, as an exhibitor from Moscow wrote in the *Kine-zhurnal*.[22] Wilhelm was a "negative hero," a character that united all what was considered to be evil. He was blamed to be responsible for the shocking attacks on Belgian civilians committed by his soldiers. In *Liliia Bel´gii* (*The Lily of Belgium*, 1915, directed by Ladislas Starevich), an animated film that is perceived as a masterpiece of early Russian cinematography, German soldiers figured as "barbaric Huns" who "raped" Belgium.[23] The film journal *Ėkran Rossii* called the film an "allegory" of Belgium´s "suffering."[24] Far from "allegory," however, was the plot of *Dykhanie antikhristov* (*The breath of the antichrists*), which was released in 1915 by the company G.I. Libken. In this film, German soldiers are not only killing Russian prisoners of war, but also raping women, beating children, and burning down peaceful villages. The journal *Sine-fono* predicted a huge success of *Dychanie antichristov*.[25]

"War terror films played extensively on the audience's fascination with the unknown and therefore dangerous aspects of the

---

20 Jahn, *Patriotic Culture*, 166.

21 *Sine-fono*, no. 13 (April 25, 1915), 90.

22 *Sine-fono*, no. 14-15 (May 23, 1915), 78–79.

23 Sumpf, "Film/Cinema (Russian Empire)."

24 *Ekran Rossii*, no. 1 (1916), 20.

25 *Sine-fono*, no. 19-20 (Aug. 22, 1915), 66. See also pictures from the film in: *Vestnik Kinematografii*, no. 114 (1915), 15–16, 32, 51, 53. There was a Russian film—perhaps—*Dychanie antichristov* that showed German nurses, searching through the battlefields and stabbing Russian wounded soldiers; Arthur Ponsonby, *Absichtliche Lügen in Kriegszeiten: Eine Auswahl von Lügen, die während des Ersten Weltkrieges in allen Völkern verbreitet wurden* (Seeheim: Buchkreis, 1967), 135.

war. The psychological function was clearly more important than the historical authenticity of the episodes. In this respect, it should be noted that 'German horrors' were already being advertised in a film produced at the very outbreak of the war, before any atrocities had been reported."[26] It has to be noted that the Russian audience, seemingly already before the war, preferred more dramatic and morbid films than the Western moviegoers: Russia's movie studios had "manufactured dreams that audiences in other cultures would have considered nightmares."[27] Obviously, people found "unhappy endings" more consolatory than "happy endings" that were far from real life.[28] This, perhaps, helps to understand why in 1916 a film with the depressing title *The Poor Chap Died in an Army Hospital* was one of the most viewed picture in wartime Russia.[29]

---

26 Jahn, *Patriotic Culture,* 166. "All the belligerents in World War One employed atrocity propaganda associated with the enemy and, as a result, stereotypes emerged that had been largely developed in the period leading up to the outbreak of war. The recognition of stereotypes is an important part of understanding the use of anti-symbols and the portrayal of the enemy in propaganda"; David Welch, "Depicting the enemy," British Library, accessed Feb. 2, 2016, http://www.bl.uk/world-war-one/articles/depicting-the-enemy. See also: David Welch and Jo Fox, eds., *Justifying War: Propaganda, Politics and the Modern Age* (Basingstoke: Palgrave Macmillan, 2012).

27 McReynolds, *Russia at Play,* 290. See also: 276.

28 See also: Richard Stites, *Russian Popular Culture: Entertainment and Society Since* 1900 (Cambridge: University Press, 1992), 33–34. With explanations for the Russian type of "melodrama": Schamma Schahadat, "Leidenschaft und Ökonomie: Das russische Stummfilm-Melodrama zwischen Fin de Siècle und Moderne," *arcadia: International Journal of Literary Culture* 44, no. 1 (Jan. 2009): 137–186, here: 160 and 140–142.

29 Sumpf, "Film/Cinema (Russian Empire)."

"Fear and horror" attracted an audience that wanted to learn what the enemy was like. German war crimes flourished in all Russian arts. Some popular Russian feature films interestingly mainly focused on violence committed on the French front rather than on the situation in Galicia, East-Prussia, or Armenia.[30] But, by only skimming over the pages of Russian film journals,[31] one will realize that there are some feature films, like the above mentioned *Dykhanie antikhristov* and various documentary films, that dealt with atrocities on the Russian Western Front. The latter were shown in various newsreels (*kinokhronika*), produced, for example, by the Skobelev Committee, which, in 1914, "had obtained exclusive rights from the emperor to film on the front lines, to raise funds for soldiers wounded in combat with the sale of the footage."[32] The Skobelev Committee, however, was ill-equipped and underfunded. Less than a dozen cameramen tried to get pictures of military operations and life at the front lines. Hence, historians claim, the Skobelev Committee was not able to provide a visual record of the war on the Russian Western Front and that, consequently, Russian moviegoers learned more about what was

30 Ibid. and Alexandre Sumpf, "In Szene gesetzt: Der Erste Weltkrieg im russischen und sowjetischen Kino," *Osteuropa* 64, no. 2–4 (Februar–April 2014): 339–350, here: 340; *Kine-zhurnal*, no. 19-20 (Oct. 18, 1914).

31 On Russian film journals see for example: Natascha Drubek, *Russisches Licht: Von der Ikone zum frühen sowjetischen Film* (Vienna: Böhlau, 2012), 117.

32 Sumpf, "Film/Cinema (Russian Empire)." On the history of the film department of the Skobelev-Committee see also: G. E. Malysheva, "K istorii kinematograficheskoi dejatel´nosti Sokobelevskogo komiteta 1913-1914 gg. Opyt i metodiki issledovatel´skoi raboty spetsialistov Rossiiskogo gosaudarstevennogo archiva kinodokumentov (RGAKFD)," in *Vestnik archivista*, no. 1 (2012): 3–17.

going on at the theaters of War of their allies.[33] Undoubtedly, footages delivered by France or Great Britain outnumbered Russian newsreels to give an impression of the war. But, obviously, at least in 1914–15, Russian feature as well as documentary films on war crimes committed by the enemies did not completely omit the Western Front. After all, to show enemy barbarity on the screen was a matching part to press propaganda, where news about cruelties of the adversary had become ubiquitous.[34]

Violence against Tsarist prisoners of war in Austria-Hungary was picked up by Russian propaganda, which published various pamphlets or reports of soldiers who succeeded in escaping. It is not amazing, that atrocities committed by Austrian-Hungarian soldiers did also reach the screen.[35] Only few weeks after the outbreak of war the *Kine-zhurnal* announced the release of the feature film *Tsivilizovannye varvary* (*Civilized barbarians*), where Austrian soldiers arrested a defenseless young woman and only at the last moment were restrained from shooting an old man who was suspected to be a spy. Interestingly, at the end of the description of the film in the *Kine-zhurnal,* the old man is dooming the

33 Peter Kenez, *Cinema and Soviet Society, 1917–1953* (New York: Cambridge University Press,1992), 22.

34 Cf. Laurent Véray, "Cinema," in *The Cambridge History of the First World War,* vol. 3, *Civil Society*, ed. Jay Winter (Cambridge: Cambridge University Press, 2014), 475–503, here: 492. See also: *World War I and Propaganda*, ed. Troy R.E. Paddock (Leiden: Brill, 2014), 1.

35 On atrocities committed by Austro-Hungarian soldiers and the "image" of them among Russians see: Elena S. Senjavskaja, "Die Völker Österreich-Ungarns im Ersten Weltkrieg aus der Sicht des russischen Gegners," in *Jenseits des Schützengrabens: Der Erste Weltkrieg im Osten. Erfahrung – Wahrnehmung – Kontext,* ed. Bernhard Bachinger and Wolfram Dornik (Innsbruck: Studienverlag, 2013), 325–340.

"German hangmen" ("*palacham-nemtsam*") and not the Austrian ones.[36] Another movie, which was also produced by the company of A. O. Drankov, is described in the same issue of the mentioned *zhurnal* and deals with the very first period of the war, too: *Za tsar-ja i otechestvo ili liudi-brat΄ia* (*For Tsar and fatherland*). It shows the situation at the frontier to Austria-Hungary shortly after the hostilities had started. The Austrians are brutal, but they act cowardly, unsuccessfully trying to incite the different nations against the Russians: "Russians, Jews, Georgians, Ingush: all are fighting to save the home country."[37] Generally, the Austrian brutes are of German or Polish origin. Concentrating on those nations, the propaganda corresponded with existent animosity and distrust. It was plausible that the scene of anti-Austrian feature films was mainly situated in the neighboring Austrian crownland Galicia, with its multifaceted ethnic conflicts.

Due to Germany's part as the aggressor to blame the most for the outbreak of war it makes sense that Russian wartime feature films mostly focused on Germany and the Germans, who were transgressing "all moral and religious bounds."[38] On the other hand, there are no studies on Russian film production in wartime that are trying to find out if there were significant differences in presenting either the German or the Austrian or the German-Austrian (German speaking Austrians/*Deutschösterreicher*) enemies on the screen. A first and rough analysis of Russian wartime feature films, based on Russian film journals published between 1914 and 1917 and filmographies for this period, supports the assumption that patriotic feature films dealing with "anti-German plots" predominate. But is has to be stated that the

36 *Kine-zhurnal*, no. 15-16 (Aug. 23, 1914): 33.

37 Ibid.

38 Jahn, *Patriotic Culture*, 165.

"German preponderance" in comparison with Austria-Hungary's presence is less striking than supposed—at least at the beginning of war.[39]

Tsarist filmic propaganda used traditional stereotypes of the enemy states and intensified and even exaggerated them to the point of a burlesque: "As in other warring nations, enemy leaders became convenient personifications and focal points of broader sets of clichés. [...] Images of a weak and crumbling empire, expressing imperial rivalry with Austria, were projected onto the figure of the old and frail Franz Joseph."[40] But did the Habsburg monarchy, which was considered to be weak and damned to crumble, appear to be less dangerous than the "German huns"? And did Russian cinema portray Franz Joseph in a similar way as it did German Kaiser Wilhelm?

In 1916, when the *Kine-zhurnal* indicated that there were about 4,000 motion picture theaters in Russia, with two million moviegoers a day,[41] a film about the tragedy of the Austrian crown prince Rudolf and his concubine Mary Vetsera was advertised.[42] *Mariia Vechera*, produced by the company Drankov, was obviously released already in the year before and announced as film

39 See for instance: *Velikii kinemo: Katalog sokhranivshikhsia igrovykh fil´mov Rossii 1908–1919* (Moscow: Novoe literaturnoe obozrenie, 2002); V. Vishnevskii, *Dokumental´nye fil´my dorevoliutsionnoi Rossii 1907–1916 gg.* (Moscow, 1996); Ven. Vishnevskii, *Khudozhestvennye fil´my dorevoliutsionnoi Rossii (Filmograficheskoe opisanie)* (Moscow: Goskinoizdat, 1945); S. S. Ginzburg, *Kinematografiia dorevoliutsionnoi Rossii* (Moscow, 1963); *Sovetskie khudozhestvennye fil´my: Annotirovannyi katalog* (Moscow: Iskusstvo, 1961).

40 Jahn, *Patriotic Culture*, 173.

41 *Kine-zhurnal*, no.15-18 (1916): 82.

42 *Kine-zhurnal*, no. 19-20 (1916): 104.

about a "secret affair in the live of a foreign court."[43] In this picture, retelling the history of the unhappy son of Emperor Franz Joseph who killed his concubine and then committed suicide, the audience is confronted with an abstruse version of the tragedy: the pregnant Mary Vetsera and her blue-blooded lover Rudolf are shot by officers who were instructed by Franz Joseph to arrest Rudolf's concubine. The death of the old monarch's only son buries the hopes of a whole Empire. Franz Joseph and Empress Elisabeth figure as broken parents. One can suppose that there is some sort of compassion toward the aged "Kaiser," who had lost his son under such tragic circumstances.[44]

In 1932, the magazine *Proletarskoe kino* analyzed Russian wartime propaganda and asserted that the Germans had been portrayed as barbarians, whereas the Austrians had been described as cowards and scoundrels.[45] As I have already shown in connection with Russian film productions shortly after the outbreak of war, there are some examples that illustrate that Austrians were considered to be cruel and merciless as well, notwithstanding portraying Franz Joseph as an old and broken-hearted man. In fact, there was no need for Russian propaganda to present the Austrian enemies as less damnable than the German ones. Above all, the oppression of Russia's "Slavonic brothers" by Habsburg authorities served as a drastic example of the wickedness of the neighbor. This, for example, correlated with a film that was released in 1916 and advertised by the company Gomon as "vigorous drama." *V okovakh Avstrii* (*In Austria's chains*) follows the experience of young Anton, living in Galicia. An Austrian named Prokop wants to get rid of him because he desires

43 *Kine-zhurnal*, no. 13-14 (1915): 116.

44 *Kine-zhurnal*, no. 19-20 (1916): 112–113.

45 V. Sorokin, "Kino in vojna," in *Proletarskoe kino*, no. 9 (1931): 48–53, here: 50.

Anton´s girlfriend, Praskeda. Because of Prokop's influence, Anton is enlisted by the Austrian army. Now Anton is full of hatred against Austria-Hungary. He decides to desert and fight against the Habsburg monarchy.[46] Finally, he is arrested by Austrian authorities and sentenced to death. His lady lover Prakseda goes mad and is killed by Anton's uncle to "save" her from Austrian cruelties. The advertising pictures in *Kine-zhurnal* show a Russian soldier (probably Anton) who is executed by Austro-Hungarian soldiers.[47]

Austrian brutality is also the main subject in a feature film on Czechs who had acquired Russian citizenship and united in a "legion of victory or death." The film, titled *Druzhina pobedy ili smerti,* showed the tragic fate of "Czech heroes" who fought against Austrian oppressors and had to face the death penalty when being caught by the Austrians. In fact, "some 10 per cent of Czech prisoners volunteered" for the Czechoslovak Legion in Russia.[48] The film *Druzhina pobedy ili smerti* was announced as an impressive example for the struggle between Slavs and Germans.[49] Furthermore, *Slava nam – smert´ vragam* (*Glory to us, death to the enemy*), a film directed by Evgenjj Bauer and produced by A. Khanzhonkov, showed that heroism could overcome apparently invincible enemies: Disguised as an Austrian nurse, the heroine of this film stabs a love-crazed Austro-Hungarian officer to get an important secret message. In the end, she is decorated with military honors, after having handed over the secret documents to Russian troops.[50] However, *Slava nam – smert´ vragam* did not

46 Sine-Fono, no. 6-7 (Jan. 10, 1915): 67.

47 *Kine-zurnal*, no. 21-22 (Nov. 1916): 76 and 131.

48 Aviel Roshwald, *Ethnic Nationalism and the Fall of Empires: Central Europe, Russia and the Middle East, 1914–1923* (London: Routledge, 2001), 148.

49 *Sine-fono*. no. 1-2 (Oct. 18, 1914): 38.

50 Stites, *Russian popular culture,* 35.

reveal "before the audience ... 'scandalous and blatant horrors,'" with the exception of "almost colorless, grey episodes in which the nightmare of reality appears so clearly."[51]

Whereas the treason of former Austrian citizens was interpreted as a heroic act, espionage was either damned or appreciated, depending on the question who was spying and for whom: "Espionage and treason fitted nicely into a wave of detective novels and films that swept over the Western world and Russia alike." [52] Many of these films merely adapted the war to an established taste, but some contained more or less elaborate patriotic messages. In fact, there were a lot of spy films that focused on German espionage in particular.[53] The writer and son of Ekaterina Breshko-Breshkovskaia, Konstantin Breshko-Breshkovskii, succeeded as the author of some of those spy films, where male and female spies were trying to obtain secrets about Russian warfare. Breshko-Breshkovskii appeared as a screenplay writer for a film, titled *Grafinia-shpionka (avstrijskaia avantiura)*. The film was released only few days before the war broke out, and unlike the majority of spy films, concentrated on espionage of Austrian and not German provenience.[54]

Spy films perfectly suited to a popular taste that, from the very beginning of the war, preferred plain entertainment and "the usual fare that had been popular before the war."[55] Feature films with war themes "were the crude and sensationalist fruits of savage competition among film companies. Superlatives of terror, baseness,

---

51 Cit. *Silent Witnesses. Russian Films 1908-1919/Testimoni silenziosi. Filmi russi 1908–1919*, ed. Paolo Cheerchi Usai et al. (Pordenone: Edizione Biblioteca dell´Immagine/British Film Institute, 1989), 236.

52 Jahn, *Patriotic Culture*, 163.

53 See: *Proektor*, no. 11-12 (June 15, 1916): 8.

54 *Kine-zhurnal*, no. 15-16 (Aug. 23, 1914): 10–11.

55 Jahn, *Patriotic Culture*, 154.

brutality, and schmaltz advertised artistically weak and overhastily lubok farces, patriotic spy and detective movies, nationalist love affairs and melodramas, and thrilling and apocalyptic 'terror films.'"[56]

While, in 1915, the Skobelev committee praised itself for a realistic depiction of war in its documentary films,[57] escapism increased as the war dragged on.[58] The retreat of the Russian army as a result of Austro-German victories in 1915 left its marks on the Russians. It was perceived as a disastrous and disgraceful defeat, destroying the vision of a glorious victory. Patriotism "became more differentiated, simultaneously reflecting separate and even disparate loyalties within society."[59] This development as a matter of course affected Russian film production, too. According to Denise J. Youngblood from "1 August 1914 to the end of the year, nearly half of films made (50 to 103) concerned the war, but in 1916 the figure was only 13 titles out of a total of 500. This startling fact reflects in large part the extreme disaffection of the public from the government and the war effort—as well as the

---

56 Ibid., 168.

57 Sumpf, "In Szene gesetzt," 339–343; *Ekran Rossii*, no. 1 (1916): 23. On the problem of "authenticity" see also: David Williams, *Media, Memory, and the First World War* (Montreal: McGill-Queen's University Press, 2009), 110; Horst Tonn, "Der Erste Weltkrieg im amerikanischen Film," in *Der Erste Weltkrieg in der populären Erinnerungskultur*, ed. Barbara Korte, Sylvia Paletschek, and Wolfgang Hochbruck (Essen: Klartext, 2008), 169–180.

58 The fact that Russian movie-goers preferred plain entertainment interested also Soviet "experts" for cinema. See for example: K. Shutko, "Imperialisticheskaia voina i dorevoliucionnoe kino. Obzor kinozhurnalov 1915–1917," in *Sovetskoe kino*, no. 8 (September 1934): 31–34.

59 Jahn, *Patriotic Culture*, 171.

government's inability to organise cinematic propaganda."[60] Peter Kenez comes to similar conclusions, considering the absence of a centralized propaganda institution: "The outbreak of the war made a difference in the character of the Russian feature film not as result of the purposeful intervention of the government, but because the filmmakers shared the momentary enthusiasm for war, and because they believed that their audiences would pay to see patriotic films."[61] But, as soon as the enthusiasm faded, and it became clear that the war was not going to become a short and glorious combat, Russian film production turned to more promising genres.

In the period between the two Revolutions of 1917 not only the Skobelev committee was preoccupied with its reorganization;[62] the whole film and cinema business was seeking re-orientation: "Ideology entered Russian cinema with the Fall of the Romanov dynasty in February 1917. A brief look at titles of some of the films released in that year is sufficient to grasp the anti-monarchist and radical public mood: *Dark Forces: Grigorii Rasputin and his Associates*; *In the Clutches of Judas*; *Governmental Deception*; *The Revolutionary, The Bourgeois, Enemy of the People*."[63] The *Kine-zhurnal* in June 1917, for instance, announced the production

---

60 Denise Youngblood, "A War Forgotten: The Great War in Russian and Soviet Cinema," in *The First World War and Popular Cinema*, ed. Michael Paris (New Brunswick, N.J.: Rutgers University Press, 2000), 172–181,173; Denise Youngblood, *Russian War Films: On the Cinema Front, 1914–2005* (Lawrence: University Press of Kansas, 2007), 14.

61 Peter Kenez, *Cinema and Soviet Society*, 18.

62 *Kine-zhurnal*, no. 5-6 (1917): 22 and 23; Richard Taylor, *The Politics of The Soviet Cinema 1917–1929* (Cambridge: Cambridge University Press, 1979), 21.

63 David C. Gillespie, *Russian Cinema* (Edinburgh: Longman Publishing Group, 2003), 103.

about the last Tsar and his "bloody reign."[64] However, 1917 was more a caesura for film producers than for the audience itself, who still preferred entertainment films.[65]

There was a noticeable uncertainty in regard to the future of Russian film production. By the end of 1917, rumors about Bolshevik plans to nationalize Russian cinematography alarmed, as the *Kine-zhurnal* stated, everyone who was in some way involved in the production or distribution of movies.[66] Starting in May 1918, the Bolshevik newsreel *Kino-Nedelja* from time to time recalled the World War by showing "remains" of the conflict: for example, German and Austro-Hungarian POWs departing or homecoming Russian POWs.[67] After the October Revolution, the exodus of film companies started. Nonetheless, the box office results in 1917 "broke previous records" and improved "by 33 percent 1916, which was itself also a banner year."[68]

---

64 *Kine-zhurnal*, no. 5-6 (March 30, 1917): 24–25.

65 Taylor, *The Politics of The Soviet Cinema*, 15–25.

66 *Kine-zhurnal*, no. 17-24 (1917): 48.

67 The "Austrian Film Museum" has published its flagship online video project: "Kino-nedelja - Online Edition." 14 of the original 43 issues of the early Soviet newsreel series "Kino-nedelja" (Kino-Week) survived in the Austrian Film Museum's collection. The newsreels, which date from the years 1918 and 1919, are not merely significant for their depiction of life in the young Soviet Russia during the civil war, but also because they represent Dziga Vertov's first contribution to cinema. See: Filmmuseum, accessed March 12, 2016, https://www.filmmuseum.at/sammlungen/special_collections/sammlung_dziga_vertov/kinonedelja_online_edition.

68 Denise J. Youngblood, *The Magic Mirror*, 14.

The Interwar Period

After 1918–19, the collapsed Russian film industry was reborn as Bolshevik cinema. The production of films on revolutionary topics replaced those on usual war themes that anyway had reached only a decreasing audience since 1915. Denise Youngblood, Karen Petrone, and Alexandre Sumpf, in their studies on Russian and Soviet Commemoration of World War One, have also examined the role the Great War played in Soviet interwar film productions.[69] Sumpf, for instance, refers to Soviet montage films like Esfir Shub's *The Fall of the Romanov Dynasty* (1927) or Evgenii Iakushin´s *The World War* (1929).[70] Significantly, in *The Fall of the Romanov Dynasty*, the assassination of Archduke Franz Ferdinand was not even mentioned, while concentrating especially on the social consequences of the conflict.[71] According to *Sovetskii* Ėkran, the enemies of Russia in "The World War" simply appeared as "imperialists." The audience, however, was confronted with an elephant from a "German zoo" who had to replace a railroad engine.[72]

Denise Youngblood emphasizes "the extremely tangential role the Great War played" in revolutionary films like, for example, Eisenstein´s famous *October* (1928). She stresses that many of the revolutionary films included only some references to World War One, "but by no stretch could they be labelled 'war films' in

69 For comparison see for instance: Claudia Sternberg, "Der Erinnerungsdiskurs im Spielfilm und Fernsehspiel," in *Der Erste Weltkrieg und die Mediendiskurse der Erinnerung in Großbritannien,* ed. Barbara Korte, Ralf Schneider, and Claudia Sternberg (Würzburg: Königshausen & Neumann, 2005), 243–342.

70 Sumpf, "Film/Cinema (Russian Empire)."

71 Ibid.

72 *Sovetskij Ekran*, no. 30 (July 30, 1929): 4.

the sense that European and American directors were making films about the world war that focused on the trials of soldiers at the front and in the trenches."[73] The only important Soviet film of the 1920s "in which Word War One battle time occupies significant screen time" is, as Youngblood states, Aleksandr Dovshenko's film *Arsenal* (1929).[74] In regard to productions of the 1930s that were dealing with the war, she concentrates on an analysis of Boris Barnet´s *Okraina* (1932).[75] Aleksandre Sumpf, beyond *Okraina* and *Arsenal*, quotes other Soviet interwar feature films "wholly or partially about the Great War." Among those are: *Comrade Abram* (1919), *Enemies* (1924), *Women of R´iazan* (1929), *God of War* (1929), *Her Way* (1929), *Merchants of Glory* (1929), *Cities and Years* (1930), *Doomed* (1930), *Sniper* (1931), *Quiet Flows the Don* (1931), *Three Soldiers* (1932), and *The First Platoon* (1933).[76]

Karen Petrone is convinced that "World War I memory was an integral part of Soviet culture in the 1920s, even if the war was often viewed as mere prelude to the Revolution."[77] The fact that, between 1919 and 1933, the Soviet film industry produced at least

73 Youngblood, *A War Forgotten*, 175.

74 Ibid., 176.

75 The title is translated by Youngblood as "Borderlands" and by Sumpf as "Outskirts."

76 Sumpf, "Film/Cinema (Russian Empire)." 2014, some of these films were shown in the course of a scientific conference in Moscow that was dedicated to the commemoration of the First World War in Russian/Soviet movies. See: "Первая мировая война в зеркале кинематографа," *tvkultura.ru*, accessed Aug. 3, 2015, http://tvkultura.ru/article/show/article_id/120085.

77 Karen Petrone, *The Great War in Russian Memory* (Indianapolis: Indiana University Press, 2011), 243.

twenty-one fictional and documentary films[78] is an endorsement of Petrone's assessment in this regard.

It is obvious that the majority of those Soviet films quoted above were produced at the same time, when films like *Westfront 1918. Vier von der Infanterie* (1930, directed by G.W. Pabst) or above all the American film adaptation of Erich Maria Remarque's novel, *All Quiet at the Western Front* (1930),[79] excited and provoked the audiences in Europe.

Again, there is the question of whether there are any traces of Austria-Hungary's participation in the war in Soviet films on the First World War of this period. Not surprisingly, neither Sumpf and Youngblood nor Petrone are interested in identifying the "enemy" in the respective productions either as Germans or as Austrians/Hungarians. They, more or less, "silently" accept that Soviet films concentrated on the Germans, often portrayed as proletarian comrades, abused by imperialism and nationalism and eventually "enlightened" and purified by experiencing communist solidarity. Obviously, only in *Te, kotorye prozreli* (*Those who were enlightened*, 1930) is the audience confronted with soldiers from the Habsburg monarchy. According to a short plot description, the film deals with the events on the Western front in March 1917, ending in friendship between Russian and Hungarian soldiers. The film,

78 In his article on war disabled on the screen Sumpf refers to the "production of at least 21 Soviet fictional and documentary films" between 1919 and 1933; Alexandre Sumpf, "War Disabled on Screen: Remembering and Forgetting the Great War in the Russian and Soviet Cinema, 1914–1940," in *First World War Studies* 6, no. 1 (2015): 57–59, here: 58, DOI: 10.1080/19475020.2015.1047889.

79 Verena Moritz, "Krieg," in *Kampfzone Kino: Film in* Österreich *1918–1938,* ed., Verena Moritz, Karin Moser, and Hannes Leidinger (Vienna: Filmarchiv Austria, 2008), 255–276, here: 265–269.

with its alternative titles *Janosh vernëtsja domoj* or *Janosh priedet zaftra* (*Janosh is coming home [tomorrow]*) is, it seems, a more than rare example of the Danube monarchy's "life after death" in Soviet interwar film productions.[80]

In sum, in many Soviet films on the First World War, there is, as A.M. Belogor′ev points out, an absence of "the enemy." [81] Cinema was not able to make comprehensible what World War One was about. The First World War more and more became "an ahistorical symbol of imperialist" and, finally, "fascist, war."[82] Nevertheless, the "imperialists" are Germans rather than Austrians, and in regard to "fascists," the connotation is obvious. Moreover, it has to be taken into account that due to Germany's role concerning Lenin's return to Russia and its intransigence in regard to the peace negotiations, the anti-German climate

80 *Repertuarnyi ukazatel′ dejstviiushchego fonda kinokartin: 1. Spisok khudozhestvennykh kinokartin na 1 marta 1940 g.*, (Moscow: Goskinoizdat, 1940), 58; *Repertuarnyi ukazatel′: Kinorepertuar. Pod redakciei P. A. Bljachana. Sostaviteli: A. I. Kacigras i A.S. Rozhdestvennskii* (Moscow: Gosudarstvennoe izdatel′stvo khudozhestvennoj literatury, 1934), 90; and a description in: "Те, которые прозрели," *my-hit.org*, accessed Jan. 2, 2016, https://my-hit.org/film/400411/; "Те, которые прозрели," *kino-teatr.ru*, accessed Nov. 26, 2015, http://www.kino-teatr.ru/kino/movie/sov/13701/annot/print/.

81 A. M. Belogor′ev, "Pervaia mirovaia voina v zerkale otechestvennogo kinematografa," in *Istoricheskaia Ekspertiza,* no. 1-2 (2015): 143–157, here: 153.

82 Aaron J. Cohen, "Oh, That! Myth, Memory, and World War I in the Russian Emigration and in the Soviet Union," in *Slavic Review* 62, no. 1 (Spring 2003): 69–86, here: 79. See also: Aaron Cohen, "Commemoration, Cult of the Fallen (Russian Empire)," in *1914-1918-online: International Encyclopedia of the First World War*, ed. Ute Daniel et al. (Berlin: Freie Universität Berlin, 2014), DOI: http://dx.doi.org/10.15463/ie1418.10421.

in revolutionary Russia even increased, whereas the Habsburg monarchy appeared as a more or less moderate contingent that was ready to accept compromises. This perception continued to exist and, as a result, dominated Soviet Russia's attitude towards "Germans and Austrians," too. Furthermore, the filmic concentration on the Germans as adversaries in the conflict shown corresponded to the Bolsheviks' constant interest in German politics and developments, while the Habsburg Empire had ceased to exist and the Austrians had turned into citizens of a small and weak state in the heart of Europe. Germany still played an important role in European politics and in Moscow's plannings; Austria and its mediocre Communist Party were only third-rate.[83] It did not match with Bosheviks' "didactic" understanding of cinema to restore to life a "dead enemy," instead of dealing with an existing danger.[84] Based on the films seen by the authoress of this article and due to the characterization of the films in Soviet journals, there can be no doubt that Austria-Hungary in Soviet interwar feature films with references to the First World War has either completely vanished or left only vague traces. Furthermore, the remembrance of the First World War in general began to fade and then disappeared. Films that picked up the issue of World War One were considered to be behind the times and therefore needless.

Already at the end of the 1920s, the Communist Party attempted "to bring political order to Soviet cinema and direct it along a secure ideological path." Film productions had to answer Communist demands in regard to an adequate entertainment of the masses:

---

83 On the interwar relations between the Soviet Union and Austria see: Verena Moritz et al., *Gegenwelten: Die* österreichisch-sowjetischen *Beziehungen 1918–1939* (St. Pölten: Residenzverlag, 2013).

84 Youngblood, *A War Forgotten*, 185.

"Acknowledging the public's love of action, adventure and comedy, which they had become accustomed to through popular Soviet films and imported American and European films, it was stressed that movies should provide communist enlightenment, but in a form 'intelligible to the millions.'"[85] Finally, the Kremlin more and more insistently wanted cinematography to respond to the demands of the armed forces and defense, too. Since 1926/1927, the fear of imminent military attack strongly influenced Soviet perception of the world. Against this backdrop, Soviet authorities claimed the production of military feature films preparing the audience for a defensive warfare.[86] Cinematography abroad, asserted the journal *Sovetskiy* Ėkran had already begun its "war" against the USSR.[87] In 1930, in the journal *Kino i zhizn′* (*Cinema and life*), there were complaints about the passiveness of Soviet cinema in regard of themes like "the defense of our country."[88] Soviet cinema had to become one of the strongest organizers of the Red Army's future victory.[89] Facing the threat of a future

---

85 Jamie Miller, *Soviet Cinema: Politics and Persuasion under Stalin* (London: Palgrave Macmillan, 2010), 16.

86 M. Korol′, "Voennokhudozhestvennaia kinoproduktsiia," in *Proletarskoe kino*, no. 4 (April 1932): 35–42, here: 35; "Privet pervomu vsesoiuznomu soveshchaniiu rabotnikov voennooboronnoi kinemtografii: Vnimanie oborone - na pervoe mesto," in *Proletarskoe kino*, no. 8 (1932), 1–10; Mikhail Korokhin, *Oborona SSSR i kino. Zametki o kino kak orudii proletariata v voine budushchego* (Moskva, 1930).

87 "Kak vooruzhaiut kinematografiiu protiv SSSR," in *Sovetskij Ekran*, no. 8 (Feb. 18, 1929): 14. "Obzor pechati," in *Sovetskij Ekran*, no. 30 (July 30, 1929): 9.

88 "Kino i oborona," in *Kino i zhizn′*, no. 16 (June 1, 1930): 7.

89 M. Sychev, "Kino na sluzhbe oborony SSSR," in *Sovetskij Ekran*, no. 30 (July 30, 1929): 5.

conflict, cinema was called upon not to copy Western pacifism or neutralize the German-Soviet antagonism on behalf a proletarian solidarity, as Boris Barnet for *Okraina* was criticized.[90] Even more abrasively attacked than Barnet was the director of *Sniper*, Semëon Timoshenko, whom M. Korol′ in the journal *Proletarskoe kino* accused of having totally ignored whether his interpretation of the war was compatible with Lenin's doctrine in regard to warfare. Korol's comments on Timoshenko and his work were crushing. He argued that Timoshenko′s mindset in fact had nothing to do with Marxism-Leninism and its attitude towards questions of peace and war. *Sniper*, he alleged, was an example of Western "Remarquism," completely neglecting the importance of class conflicts.[91] Lewis Milestone's film adaptation of *All Quiet on the Western Front* was not shown "publicly" in the Soviet Union,[92] but in a hypertrophic manner the movie served as example of Western mendaciousness in regard to pacifistic films. The Soviet people had to be indoctrinated that the only country that really wanted peace was, of course, the Soviet Union.

Various factors are responsible for the marginalization and, finally, the disappearance of World War I-related films from the Soviet screen in the 1930s. Karen Petrone in this connection refers to "many bureaucratic and ideological forces and economic constraints within the Soviet Union pushing against continued emphasis on

90 Youngblood, "A War Forgotten," 185; "Fi′lma i oborona," in *Proletarskoe kino,* no. 13 (October 1932): 3–5; V. Plonskij, "Zadachi teoreticheskoi raboty po voenno-oboronnoj fil′me," in *Proletarskoe kino,* no. 11 (September 1932): 28–31.

91 Korol′, "Voennokhudozhestvennaia kinoprodukciia," 36.

92 Karen Petrone, *The Great War in Russian Memory*, 230.

World War I."[93] Propagandistic efforts to make Soviet people aware of future conflicts have to be taken into account in particular. World War One obviously was not suited for creating an unconditional readiness for war among Soviet people. The "imperialistic" conflict of the past could not give positive example of patriotic duty as it was required by the communist fatherland in the 1930s. When Soviet cinema made the transition to sound in this period, encapsulating and cutting off from the Western cinema, it was instructed to abandon the avant-garde practices of the 1920s and to accept the guidelines of socialist realism. Cinema had to create positive heroes and obedient citizens to support the course of the Communist Party and to defend the motherland against invaders. The most famous example of films that had to convey an optimistic type of patriotism was E. Dzigan's *Esli zaftra voina* (*If War Comes Tomorrow*), released in 1938.[94]

---

93 Ibid., 291. See also: Jamie Miller, "The Purges of Soviet Cinema, 1929–38," *Studies in Russian and Soviet Cinema* 1, no. 1 (2006): 5–26, accessed April 1, 2016, http://dx.doi.org/10.1386/srsc.1.1.5_1. On the perception of the First World War without a special hint at Soviet cinema between 1941 and 1945: "Space for history opened wider during World War II as the country mobilized to fight a people's war. The First World Imperialist War suddenly became World War I, the enemy was no longer international imperialism but German imperialism, and commemorative articles outlined the communalities between past German behavior and Nazi expansionism"; Cohen, "Oh, That!," 83.

94 Jamie Miller, *Soviet Cinema*, 16–19; A.V. Fediuk, "Sovetskaia sistema kinemtografa 1930gg.: Rol′ chudozhestvennogo kino v agitacionno-propagandistskoi rabote Stalinskogo rezhima," in *Problemy rossijskoj istorii*, Vypusk 10 (Moscow: Magnitogorsk, 2010), 294–311, here: 294–296; S.V. Dobrashenko, *Russkii sovetskii chudozhestvennyi fil′m v 1930–1934 godach (na materiale zvukogo kino)*, Avtoreferat dissertatsii, predstavlennoi na soiskanie uhenoi stepeni kandidata iskusstvovedceskikh nauk (Moscow 1952), 5.

1945–2014

"The cataclysm of World War II forever changed the meaning and also the name of World War I in the Soviet Union as in the rest of Europe. In the last years of Stalin's reign, the overwhelming task of rebuilding the country despite the loss of perhaps as many as twenty-seven million people overwhelming eclipsed the remembrance of World War I."[95] In fact, after 1945, attention to World War One was only sporadic. Soviet cinema was not an exception. As Alexandre Sumpf shows, only very few films, for instance, *Agoniia* (*Agony*, 1975, directed by Elem Klimov), referred to the Great War but did not put it in the center of interest.[96] In addition, A.M. Belogor'ev quotes the TV drama *Zhizn'* Klima *Samgina* (*Life of Klim Samgin*), a 1986 adaption of Maksim Gor'kii's novel, *Bumbarash* (1971), told along with one of Arkadii Gaidar's early literary works; or *Skorbnoe beschuvstvo* (*Mournful Unconsciousness*, 1986, directed by Aleksandr Sukorov), a high-grade experimental adaption of George Bernard Shaw's play *Heartbreak House*, which because of its intransigence of (non-)narration probably met with no response among a broader audience. Besides, in 1987, Aleksandr Muratov adapted for screen a novel by Valentin Pikul'. According to Belogore'ev, *Moonzund* is the only film in the period between 1945 and the dissolution of the Soviet Union that really focused on the First World War, by showing the situation of the Russian navy at the Baltic Sea. Furthermore, Belogor'ev points to the film adaptations of Mikhail Sholokhov's *Tikhii Don* (*And Quiet Flows the Don*, 1957–1958 by Sergei Gerasimov and 1986–1992 by Sergei Bondarchuk) and Aleksei Tolstoi's *Khozhdeniia po mukam* (*Life of suffering*, 1957–1959 by Grigorii Roshalem and 1977 by Vasilii

95 Karen Petrone, *The Great War*, 282.

96 Alexandre Sumpf, *La Grande Guerre oubliée: Russie, 1914–1918* (Paris: Perrin, 2014), 457.

Ordynskii). In these films—rarely enough—Austrian soldiers and officers appear. The concept of the enemy however differs very much. In both adaptations of *Tichii Don*, the Austrian soldier who is killed by one of the central characters is more or less a victim of the circumstances,[97] whereas in Roshalem's version of Tolstoy's novel the Austrians are characterized as tormentors of Russian prisoners of war.[98]

In the 1990s, Russian cinema turned to various themes and started to rethink also the Soviet past. Nikita Mikhalkov's *Utomlënnye solntsem* (*Burnt by the Sun*, 1994), for instance, depicted the fate of a senior Red Army officer and his family during the "Great Purges," and *The Thief* (1997, directed by Pavel Chukhrai) showed a young mother and her son's everyday struggle for survival in the late 1940s through the early 1950s. Finally, Russian cinema and TV discovered history before Russia had become communist. In doing so, Russian films followed the official course of a gradual rehabilitation of the Tsarist Empire, as well as its sovereigns and "servants"—if only so they could be introduced as patriots. Putin had "recognized the enormous potential of cinema" and, of course, also of TV "for nation building purposes"[99] and for his patriotic campaign. As a result, history before the Bolshevik Revolution was integrated in a "patriotic re-interpretation" of Russian history as a whole.

---

97 Already in 1931, Olga Preobrazhenskaia had been criticized to blur the characters of the Austrian officer and Grigorii as well as of the Cosacks in general in her film *Tichii Don* (1931); See: J. Iukov, "Tichii Don," *Proletarskoe kino*, no. 10 (November 1931): 16–21.

98 A. M. Belogor´ev, "Pervaia mirovaia voina," 148–149.

99 Jasmijn Van Gorp, "National Identity in Post 9/11 Transnational Cinema: The Case of the Russian Blockbuster *9th Company*," in *Postcommunist Film - Russia, Eastern Europe and World Culture: Moving Images of Postcommunism*, ed. Lars Kristensen (London: Routledge, 2012), 13–23, here: 15.

A lot of persons engaged in the cultural sector did and do support Putin's course. Nikita Mikhalkov, as one of Russia's lead filmmakers, contributed to the new approach to Russia's past, too. In his work, he addressed Russia in the turbulent period between the 1870s and 1930s. His "love of the military as a key producer of collective subjectivity" is manifested, for example, in *Sibirskiy Tsiriul'nik* (*The Barber of Siberia*, 1998), dedicated to "Russian officers, the pride of the Fatherland."[100] The positive image of Tsarist officers replaced their damnation in the Soviet era. The restoration of Tsarist army's reputation was no longer taboo.

In 2005, Russian TV produced *Gibel' imperii* (*The Fall of the Empire*), a television series with 10 episodes, depicting the struggle of Tsarist military intelligence in the First World War and the role of intelligence officers after the caesura of 1917. German antagonists and, in very rare cases, Austrian spies and traitors figure only on the very margins of six episodes. The main characters, Russian intelligence officers and their families, are patriotic heroes and, finally, victims of unpatriotic evil, criminal revolutionaries and brutalized soldiers. *Gibel' imperii* brings a rehabilitation of Tsarist officers, insinuating that former social order was not that false: Officers do know what has to be done, soldiers don't, and beautiful middle -class women are morally and intellectually superior to superstitious and featherbrained house maids. The audience is confronted with a stirring drama of Russia's downfall and a tragic struggle of super-patriots to protect their home country from alien invaders and then, in 1917, from traitors to their own country. Andrei Kravchuk in the *Admiral* (2008) gives a similar interpretation of the war by presenting Admiral Kolchak as a superhero. The costly action film on Kolchak's fate made it quite

100 Nancy Condee, *The Imperial Trace: Recent Russian Cinema* (Oxford: Oxford University Press, 2009), 91–92.

plain that the "white Admiral" was a real patriot who served Russia until his death.[101]

Batal'on''. Pervii Zhenskii. Bessmertnyi (*Battalion*, 2014, directed by Dmitrii Meshkiev), however, is the most impressive example of the Russia's recent interpretation of World War One. The film, produced by Fëdor Bondarchuk, was supported by official Russian authorities, including the Russian Military Historical Society. The latter had been reconstituted in 2012 by the President of Russia, "with the goal of consolidating the resources of the State and the Society for the study of Russia's Military-Historical past, facilitating the study of national military history and counteracting attempts to distort it, as well as to popularize the achievements of military-historical study, encourage patriotism, and raise the prestige of military service."[102]According to this characterization by the Society itself, the film obviously had to correspond with the aims cited. Its Chairman, the ministry of culture, Vladimir Medinskii, on the occasion of the production of *Battalion*, said that WWI "has always been badmouthed." "We hope," he added, that the film "will restore some honor in the minds of the people about their motherland."[103]

The story of *Battalion* is based on real events during WWI. It depicts the establishment of a battalion of female soldiers in the era of the Provisional Government by Maria Bochkareva. Facing chaotic

---

101 See: Karen Petrone, "'Now Russia returns its history to itself': Russia Celebrates the Centenary of the First World War," in *Remembering the First World War*, ed. Bart Ziino (London: Routledge, 2015), 207–222, 129–145, and 139.

102 Official site of the "Russian Military-Historical Society," accessed Feb. 7, 2016, http://histrf.ru/ru/rvio/rvio/English.

103 "Why is Russia Commemorating WWI With a Propaganda Film?", accessed Feb. 7, 2016, http://www.indiewire.com/article/why-is-russia-commemorating-wwi-with-a-propaganda-film-20140730.

demobilization and the breakdown of the Western front, Bochkareva aimed to "save the motherland," left alone in its struggle for survival by soldiers "blinded by notions of false freedom."[104] Members of the military and administration in 1917 "were enthusiastic about the idea of a unit consisting of women, believing that female soldiers would have powerful propaganda value. They thought it would revitalize the downtrodden and fatigued male soldiers, shaming them into resuming combat duties."[105] In fact, the battalion's impact on Russian warfare between February and October Revolutions was marginal. Still, the message of the film is obvious: To protect one's motherland is a "sacred duty," notwithstanding the prospects of success. Interestingly, most of the men shown on the screen, irrespective of whether they are Russian or German, are either cruel or primitive or cowardly and depraved. So, one can reason, the ideal "creature" of current Russian patriotic self-concept is half man half woman, and above all loyal.[106] Putin's

104 M. Norris, "Dmitrii Meskhiev: *Battalion* (*Batal'on*, 2015)," *kinokultura*.com, accessed Feb. 6, 2016, http://www.kinokultura.com/2016/51r-batalion.shtml.

105 "Why is Russia Commemorating WWI With a Propaganda Film", accessed Feb. 7, 2016.

106 "Russia's women soldiers are repeatedly shown to be patriotic, they are willing to defend their motherland, they have the proper hatred for Russia's enemies, and they have the Orthodox faith. The male imperial officer class is divided, but ultimately patriotic too, particularly when several officers disobey the Soviet Military Committees by tearing off their epaulettes and joining the women. The Provisional Government, Kerensky in particular, is largely shown to be ineffective but relatively benign. The villains are the nasty German soldiers who employ chemical weapons and subterfuge and also, most significantly, the brutish, dirty, defeatist Russian soldiers who no longer want to fight. In the end, though, they too are redeemed somewhat by the patriotism of the Women's Battalion"; M. Norris, "Battalion."

various statements on his understanding of patriotism, "as well as the patriotic education program documents, make clear that among the major indicators of loyalty to the state are military service and a pledge to defend the state."[107]

In *Kino-Kultura*, Stephen M. Norris wrote very critically about *Battalion*, which had disposed a budget of about ten million dollars. He highlighted the propagandistic mission of the production and the use of history as a, in fact, replaceable setting without any expedient information for the audience: "Meshkiev's *Battalion* does not delve into anything that might offer nuance or detract from its overall patriotic mythistory. We do not learn much about the Great War, why and where the Women's Battalion fought, or much about Bochkareva's backstory."[108] So, it could not be a surprise that, once more, it was not of much importance for the filmmakers who fought against whom and for what reason. Nevertheless, the Germans are brutal and act perfidiously. It becomes evident that differences between the depiction of Germans in World War One and Germans in World War Two in Russian cinema dissolve. Austria-Hungary, however, is not even mentioned in *Battalion*.

As Stephen M. Norris, referring to Larisa Maliukova´s review in the *Novaia gazeta*, concludes: The film "uses the past to bang out a message to contemporary audiences. *Battalion* is not a movie to watch if you want to 'see history' and learn anything about the Women's Battalion of Death in 1917. It is a movie to

---

107 Valerie Sperling, "Making the Public Patriotic: Militarism and Anti-militarism in Russia," in *Russian Nationalism and the National Reassertion of Russia*, ed. Marléne Laruelle (London: Routledge, 2010), 218–276, here: 258.

108 Norris, "Battalion."

watch if you want to see how contemporary patriotism gets articulated and mapped onto the past."[109]

To restore the Tsarist army's honor, and to show that there is reason for Russian people to be proud of its performance until the uprising of October 1917, was also a goal of various documentary films that were released on the occasion of the 100th anniversary of the outbreak of the Great War.

Of course, these films do not get along without explaining the role of Austria-Hungary, especially in regard to the outbreak of the conflict. But, generally, the Habsburg state remains a dim something. Its army enters the scene only for some select moments. While, for instance, several Germany's military leaders are introduced by characterizing them as able, but also terrifying adversaries (for instance General August von Mackensen), the Austrian Chief of the General Staff General Franz Conrad von Hötzendorf is not even mentioned. Sporadically, soldiers of the Habsburg forces appear as POWs. The "great retreat" of Russian troops in 1915 as a result of German-Austrian offensive appears as "national tragedy."[110] All the more, in those episodes of the production *Istorija Rossija XX veka* that are dedicated to the First World War, the filmmakers are above all interested in showing how bravely the Russians fought. The patriotic officers of the Tsarist army are cast as victims of unpatriotic revolutionaries. Russia's enemies were predominant only because of their technological and economic superiority, not in terms of the fighting spirit and the bravery of officers and soldiers as well. Western states, whether they were allies or enemies, appear as more or less morally rotten players. France and Great Britain succeed

---

109 Ibid.

110 Rossiia XX Vek. Pervaia Mirovaia Voina (Chasti 1 I 2); Pervaia Mirovaia Voina. 1914–1918 (2 DVD); Istoriia Rossii XX veka, fil´my 1–28.

because of Russian soldiers' sacrifice.[111] The Germans had ruthlessly attacked the Tsarist Empire, and the Danube monarchy is accused for having deported thousands of "Russians" (i.e., *Ruthenen* or Ukrainians) in various "death camps"—war crimes that were hushed by Western Europe until today. Actually, on the eve of World War I, the Austrian authorities had begun a wave of persecution against the Russophiles in Galicia. Hundreds were arrested and brought to camps in Austria. In the Thalerhof camp, approximately 2,000 internees died, most of them as a consequence of epidemics and horrendous living conditions. Only in recent years was the internment of so called "Russophiles" examined by Austrian historians.[112] The death toll among internees, refugees, and POWs in Austria-Hungary was immense. The reasons are complex. The makers of the above-mentioned documentary film on World War One, however, were not interested in a balanced and differentiated analysis. They imply a conjunction of the fate of "Russian" people during World War One and Nazi mass murders. Furthermore, the audience learns that the "Ukrainian people" was a propagandistic invention

111 This interpretation was widespread already during the war. Even Austro-Hungarian secret service officers reported on this topic and stressed the impression that Russia blamed its allies for defeat and the high number of dead soldiers among Russian troops; see: Albert Pethö, *Agenten für den Doppeladler:* Österreich-Ungarns *Geheimer Dienst im* Weltkrieg (Graz: Leopold Stocker Verlag, 1998), 79.

112 Hannes Leidinger et al., *Habsburgs Schmutziger Krieg: Ermittlungen zur* österreichisch-ungarischen *Kriegsführung 1914–1918* (St. Pölten: Residenz Verlag, 2014); Georg Hoffmann, Nicole-Melanie Goll, and Philipp Lesiak, *Thalerhof 1914–1936: Die Geschichte eines vergessenen Lagers und seiner Opfer* (Herne: Schäfer, 2010).

of Russia's enemies,[113] and that there is only a minor difference between the crimes of Nazi Germany in the Second World War and the oppression Russians (not Ukrainians!) suffered in the First World War. The production, which was financially supported by Russian Orthodox Church, intends to unmask a Western Europe that is only ironically called "civilized." The anti-Western and anti-Semitic tenor is unmistakable. Experts of the "Russian Institute for Strategic Studies," established by the President of the Russian Federation, present a narrative of World War One that outlines why present-day Russia must be aware of—that is the message—Western Europe's presumptuousness and contempt of Russian people. One can read this interpretation of Russia's role in the First World War as advising self-isolation and retreat to a "better," namely a "Russian," world.

In general, the remembrance of the First World War in recent Russian feature and documentary films[114] exhibits "aspects of émigré military commemorative practice," namely "the prominence of religion and the Orthodox Church," the "valorization" of the imperial army[115] and a certain nostalgia for the Romanov monarchy. This combination, however, is complemented by a mixture of Soviet paradigms and recent re-interpretations. The emphasis on Soviet-German antagonism and the alienation from the former allies, followed by a complete discord among the

113 Putin shares this statement. On occasion of the war in the Ukraine he said: "I consider Russians and Ukrainians generally to be one people"; see "Russian Orthodox Church Lends Weight to Putin Patriotism," *BBC*, accessed Feb. 8, 2016, http://www.bbc.com/news/world-europe-33982267.

114 A special approach to WWI was chosen by the makers of the documentary film *Do voiny ja byl malen'kim* (Before the War I Was Young), produced in 2006 on Russian child soldiers during World War One.

115 Cohen, "Oh, That!," 85.

former partners, undoubtedly are perseverative narratives. Today, World War I is not a "war forgotten" in Russia, but a war "transformed": defeat has been turned into victory. The current official Russian notion that "victory is tied very closely to an emerging" or already emerged and prevailing "view of the war as a heroic one in which Russian soldiers fought valiantly and demonstrated 'mass heroism'. This stands in contrast both to long-standing Western notions that the Russian soldier fought poorly in the First World War and Soviet claims that after a very brief period of chauvinistic fervour, the Russian soldier refused to fight."[116] Russian fictional and documentary films have processed these notions and generated representations of war as tools for a patriotic re-interpretation of the Tsarist Empire's last war. Lacking a plausible utility in terms of being relevant for present Russia's politics, the "deceased Dual Monarchy" in this conception can easily be neglected or even forgotten.

116 Petrone, "'Now Russia Returns Its History to Itself," 134.

THE FALL OF THE AUSTRO-HUNGARIAN MONARCHY IN SERBIAN FILMS

Aleksandar Erdeljanović

A Historical Overview

Aware of the fact that war is one of the most memorable events in the collective consciousness of nations, and aware of the spectator's desire to watch spectacular war scenes, film pioneers like Georges Méliès, James Williamson, Edwin Stanton Porter, Lucien Nongeut, and others started to capture, reconstruct, or fake actual military events for nonfiction films and newsreels respectively. Naively believing in the truthfulness of movie scenes, viewers were excited to see counterfeit scenes from Greek-Turkish, Anglo-Boer, Russian-Japanese, and other wars of the early century. Near simultaneously, viewers across Europe were able to follow staged reports about The May Coup in 1903, the murder of the Serbian King Aleksandar Obrenović and Queen Draga Mašin, massacres in Macedonia, as well as the fighting of Komit troops in the same region, always a politically unstable area. Then two bloody Balkan Wars in 1912–1913 gave Western European filmmakers the opportunity to introduce viewers to the brutal and cruel events located in "exotic areas of the Orient." However, the First World War from 1914 to 1918 was the most brutal conflict that happened to "cultural Europe" since the time of the Napoleonic wars. The use of new deadly weapons, tanks and airplanes, sophisticated guns and machine guns, trench warfare, and the usage of poison gases for the first time in history caused great slaughter. Around twenty million people were killed in warfare or died of epidemics and famine. Roughly another twenty million were wounded, many of them incapacitated for life. The war ended with the defeat of the Central Powers and the redistribution of territory, the disintegration of four empires (German, Russian, Ottoman, and Austro-Hungarian), creating new states on their ruins.[1]

Serbian film started just a few years before the outbreak of the First World War. Namely, in the summer of 1911, the Belgrade hotelier Svetozar Botorić engaged the Pathé, Hungarian-born cameraman Louis de Berry, who together with the famous actor and director of the Royal Serbian National Theatre in Belgrade, Čiča Ilija Stanojević, and in cooperation with the Association of Serbian folk recording movies, produced the first three Balkan feature films, *Ulrih Celjski i Vladislav Hunjadi, Život i dela besmrtnog Vožda Karadjordja*, and *Ciganska svadba,* also known as *Bibija*, as well as twenty documentary films. By 1914 and the beginning of military operations, three Serbian film companies (the Savić Brothers' Company, the Brothers Cvetković Company, and Djoka Bogdanović's Company) were founded.[2] Until August 1914, four

1 Aleksandar Erdeljanović, "Oh kakav divan rat ili Prvi svetski rat na igranom filmu," *Program Muzeja Jugoslovenske kinoteke* (May 2009): 11–17.

2 Cf. Petar Volk, *Srpski film* (Beograd: Institut za film, 1996); Petar Volk, *Istorija Jugoslovenskog filma* (Beograd: Institut za film, 1986); Bosa Slijepčević, *Kinematografija u Srbiji, Crnoj Gori i Bosni i Hercegovini 1896–1918* (Beograd: Univerzitet umetnosti/Institut za film, 1982); Dejan Kosanović, *Počeci kinematografije na tlu Jugoslavije 1896–1918* (Beograd: Univerzitet umetnosti/Institut za film, 1985).

feature and seventy documentary films and newsreels were produced by the Serbian cinematography. War and occupation followed. In this tragic period, around 400,000 Serbian soldiers were killed or died from injuries and diseases, and about 640,000 people were shot, hanged or died in the camps. This means that Serbia in World War I lost about twenty-six percent of the total population.

After World War I, the situation in the new state, the Kingdom of Serbs, Croats, and Slovenes (SHS), and in particular in the Serbian ethnic territories, was very difficult because of the intense destruction, the universal impoverishment, and the apathy of state administration, which was not interested in supporting local film productions. For this reason, the first Serbian feature film in the newly created state, *Kačaci u Topčideru*, was filmed in 1924, six years after the war had ended, though the film was not completed due to lack of funding. In this Kingdom, which lasted less than a quarter of a century until the German occupation in 1941, only about twenty films in the silent and sound period were produced. However, though only a few Serbian feature films were made, two of them related to the First World War and the "Golgotha of the Serbian people and Serbian country." Moreover, *Kroz buru i oganj* (1930, directed by Ranko Jovanović and Milutin Ignjačević), today lost, and especially *S verom u Boga*, (1932, directed by Mihajlo Al. Popović), were the best Yugoslav films of the interwar period.[3] Especially *S verom u Boga*—lyrical and harsh at the same time, as well as dominated by patriarchal values and cinematic modernism—is the most sincere apology for the "suffering and salvation

3 Cf. Dejan Kosanović, *Kinematografija i film u Kraljevini SHS/Kraljevini Jugoslaviji 1918–1941* (Beograd: Filmski centar Srbije, 2011); Aleksandar Erdeljanović, "Prvih pola veka srpske kinematografije 1896–1945," *Program Muzeja Jugoslovenske kinoteke* (May 2007): 23–33.

of the Serbian people" in the First World War, a unique anti-war appeal without hatred and a strong desire for a new beginning.[4]

World War II and the occupation of Yugoslavia by the Third Reich and its adherents, while at the same time ideological and military confrontations between supporters of the old royal government and the communists strengthened by the Soviet Union persisted, ended with the victory for the Allies and the establishment of a socialist state led by Josip Broz Tito. According to that, a new country as well as a new cinematography was established in line with the standards of the socialist camp. Although over 500 films were produced through the early 1990s, the number of those associated with such an important topic as the First World War was less than the number of the fingers on both hands. With the exception of the Soviet-Yugoslav co-production *Aleksa Dundić* (1958, directed by Leonid Lukov), a biographical costumed spectacle about the life of a Serbian soldier who joins the Red Army and becomes its hero, most other movies are related to the assassination in Sarajevo in June 1914. The Serbian film *Sarajevski atentat* (1968, directed by Fadil Hadžić), described the events with modest budgets but with psychological approaches focusing on the young Gavrilo Princip and his comrades from the secret organization Young Bosnia. The Croatian version of the same event, *Atentat u Sarajevu* (1976, directed by Veljko Bulajić) had unmindful screenwriting, but scores with a spectacular

4 Aleksandar Erdeljanović, *Sa verom u Boga / In God We Trust* - tekst za DVD digitally remastered (Beograd: Jugoslovenska kinoteka, 2015). Moreover, a Czech-Yugoslav production, "A život teče dalje," should be mentioned here. This movie from 1935, directed by Carl Junghans, F.W. Kraemer, and Vaclav Dryak, centered on a touching story of a WWI-returnee from captivity finding his wife remarried with his best friend.

reconstruction of the historical incidents and the participation of famous international movie stars such as Christopher Plummer, Maximilian Schell, and Florinda Bolkan. Related also to this topic, the film *Belle Epoque* (1990, directed by Nikola Stojanović), made at the time of the dissolution of the State Union, linked the 1914 plot with the work of regional film pioneers like the Sarajevo cameraman Anton Valić, who captured the arrival of the imperial couple in Sarajevo just a few minutes before the assassination. The latest production of the Serbian cinematography on this subject is also noteworthy. This movie, *Branio sam Mladu Bosnu* (2014, directed by Srdjan Koljević), deals with the unknown and forgotten lawyer Rudolf Cistler, the defense counsel of Gavrilo Princip at the trial of the Sarajevo assassins. On the other hand, Srdjan Dragojević's *Sveti Georgije ubiva aždahu* dealt with the topic of Battle of Cer, presenting an impressive reconstruction of a month of bloody fighting and the defeat of Austro-Hungarian troops at the beginning of the war.

Apart from that, the most successful film regarding the First World War in Tito's Yugoslavia was a colored war spectacle entitled *Marš na Drinu*, released on the occasion of the fiftieth anniversary of the Battle of Cer in 1964. There was a very positive response to the film, especially from the spectators. Some comments allude that the script for the second part of the film—many say the better of the two—never passed political censorship, probably because of the patriotic topic and a kind of self-censorship in the minds of the creators. Any reference to "liberation wars" and the warfare of Serbia in the First World War could thus stimulate emotions of "national unity" and "brotherhood" through "blood and suffering."[5]

5 Aleksandar Erdeljanović, "Oh kakav divan rat ili Prvi svetski rat na igranom filmu," *Program Muzeja Jugoslovenske kinoteke* (May 2009): 11–17.

Finally, there is the question concerning the mutual perspective of Serbs and "the others" in the First World War. Adverse opinions about occupiers from 1914 and 1915 were automatically transferred from memories and history textbooks directly to the "art of film." There are two productions with different approaches to the theme: *Besa* by Srdjan Karanović from 2009 is a subtle and delicate chamber drama that speaks about tempted relations between Serbs and Albanians during the Austro-Hungarian occupation of Serbia since 1915. The feature film *Pukovnikovica* (*Colonel´s Wife*) is particularly interesting. It is unique among the Yugoslav cinematography because it deals with the end of World War I on the Serbian front from the viewpoint of the vanquished Austro-Hungarian soldiers. Therefore, it should be an object of further research and analysis in this text too.

Pukovnikovica, or the View from the "Other Side"

When the movie *Pukovnikovica* was released in 1972, a trademark of the Serbian cinematography from the beginning of the sixties and late seventies, the so-called "black wave" films, had already receded into background, after Tito's political clash with representatives of the Croatian mass movement and Serbian liberalism. The respective purge affected the culture of national filmmaking. Its prominent Serbian proponents who had chosen an open and uncompromising way of dealing with the "dark sides" of the "socialist self-management system" of former Yugoslavia perished. The work of Živojin Pavlović, Dušan Makavejev, Želimir Žilnik, Miroslav Antić, Mića Popović, and others were replaced by a so called "white wave," a collection of impersonal films presenting a perfect political system that stressed the "eternal rule of Josip Broz." Against this backdrop, for instance, Aleksandar Petrović, the author of the celebrated *Skupljači perja* (1967), who turned to a filmic adaptation of Bulgakov's novel *Majstor i Margarita*, left the domestic cinematographic scene—and with him left a source of uncompromising critique of Stalinism and any other totalitarianism.

Then arose *Pukovnikovica*, a memory of the last days of the First World War focusing on the Austro-Hungarian/Serbian northern front. This movie was directed by the renowned art critic and director, Djordje Kadijević, after the success of his first two WWII-themed productions, *Praznik* (1967) and *Pohod* (1969). The plot is very simple: In the last days of autumn 1918, an Austro-Hungarian regiment, located in southern Banat—a part of the present Serbian province of Vojvodina that belonged to the Habsburg Empire until 1918—is decimated in the course of military operations resulting in Austro-Hungarian defeat and withdrawal. Suddenly, the colonel—commander of the regiment—gets a telegram informing him that his young wife will come to the front unannounced. The surprised officer waits for her, sending two soldiers to the railway station, in case she should arrive by train. As a matter of fact, the soldiers welcome her and take her to the headquarters, while at the same time many Austro-Hungarian soldiers were killed on the river, shot by the Serbian opponents. During the fighting the colonel disappears; a Serbian swineherd resembling the Austrian officer is buried. However, the colonel reappears, dressed only in underwear. The confused soldiers kill him immediately to avoid the revelation of their mistakes. Awaiting attacks of the victorious Serbs, the regiment retreats. Two soldiers in a car take away the colonel's wife with the casket. Then they are attacked by allied planes; they seize the opportunity to rape her, and they escape. Violated, humiliated, and thrown into the grass, she is found by the arriving Serbian troops.

However, the basically interesting story did not reach the high quality of previous Kadijević films.[6] Anyway, as in his previous

6 Volk, *Istorija Jugoslovenskog filma*, 208–209.

films, there is an atmosphere that reveals the horrors of war and devastation that occurs when people—threatened by death—try to protect and "find" themselves. According to that, Kadijevic occasionally turns to a dark and naturalistic story of the swineherd and the exchange of the dead bodies, which did not exist in the original script of the film written by the famous writer Danko Popović. For Kadijević, as he remarked himself, it was important to change the scenario, thereby opposing the insatiable desire of the writer for long dialogues and unnecessary details. Because this is exactly what films do not tolerate: a kind of a lack of feeling for timing and cinematographic or "visual situations," for distinctions between literature and movies or various media in general.[7] "There was something fatally defeatist, catastrophic, which attracted me to the subject" of the film, Kadijević said.

But the desire to create a tragicomedy with elements of grotesquerie completely failed, despite impressive elements such as the exquisite Renoir impressionistic photographs and Mozart's "charming" music clashing with the deafening battle noise. Even the careful cast, with his frequent collaborators (Dušan Janićijević, Slobodan Perović, Janez Vrhovec, Slobodan Aligrudić, Ljerka Draženović), could not improve the results of his artistic endeavors. The film is still dominated by flat dialogues and psychologically unconvincing twists. All the characters in the film are one-dimensional, starting from a young woman who wants to be with her husband, followed by the autocratic officers, as well as the simple and violence-prone soldiers. There is no differentiated moral question or a more refined psychological presentation of individual feelings. The film is neither an attraction nor an intellectual challenge. The characterization of "the others" remains too

7 Cf. Dejan Ognjanović, *Više od istine - Kadijević o Kadijeviću* (Novi Sad: Orfelin, 2016).

unambiguous; individuals are only representatives of stereotypes of collectives.

Kadijević did not have the ability to make a tragicomedy comparable to earlier works by Alexander Korda, Mario Monicelli, or Philippe de Broca. That is why the famous critic Svetozar Guberinić wrote in his critical review that *Pukovnikovica*, conceived as grotesque on the topic of moral and physical destructiveness of war, is ultimately not a remarkable achievement. Its structure, Guberinić noted, ends in a series of conceptual and aesthetic questions.[8] Though the two villains of the movie are soldiers of Hungarian and Serbian nationality, the screening of *Pukovnikovica* at the local film festival in Pula (Croatia) passed without any success. In the opinion of the Kadijević: "Pula was not in the mood for a bit of anti-Croat film, because at the end Serbia wins, Serbian flags flutter, there is the collapse of the Austro-Hungarian, and thus the Croatian army. Croatian spectators in Pula did not appreciate plots like that."[9]

After that, Djordje Kadijević, the author of movies with exceptional personal sensibility and style, was excluded from Serbian filmmaking, like some other "black wave directors" from the Serbian cinema. Subsequently, he transferred to a similar medium: television. This unusual author "knew how to create multilayered visual metaphors, to coordinate the various elements of the images, to handle with visual effects and to inspire his staff. At the same time in doing so, he found refuge in the creative multitude of fascinating television films based on the basis of the rich Serbian historical tradition, folklore, myths and legends, full of horror, grotesque and tragicomic details—just to mention the

8 Svetozar Guberinić, "Staro i novo," *Magazin Sineast*, no. 19 (1972/73): 29–41.

9 Cf. Ognjanović, *Više od istine - Kadijević o Kadijeviću*.

ingenious first Serbian horror production *Leptirica* (1973), or his interpretation of the domestic literary classic Milovan Glišić, as well as the feature film *Sveto mesto* (1990), following Gogol's work *Vij*."

A Brief Outlook

All things considered, there is no indication that, after a century of controversial debate and nationalist hatred, Serbian film producers and directors turn to the "dark chapters" of 1914 to 1918, though there was one exception: *Talog* by Miško Milojević, a 2014 TV drama about a Hungarian-Serbian couple and their troubled marital relations due to the advance and occupation of Serbian territory by the Habsburg army at the beginning of the First World War. Apart from that, a lack of interest of domestic filmmakers regarding the Danube Monarchy and World War One is obvious. On the other hand, 2018 and the centennial commemorations of the end of Europe's "great seminal catastrophe" are nearing—and surprises of any kind, good or bad, are still possible.

THE REDISCOVERY OF A FORGOTTEN WAR:

THE FIRST WORLD WAR IN SLOVENE FILM AND DOCUMENTARY PRODUCTION

Karin Almasy

Introduction

Until recently, the First World War was neither a central topic in Slovene film production nor was it discussed in Slovene documentary production. That is not surprising, since First World War in general has not been really on display in Slovene remembrance culture. The First World War has been completely overshadowed by the Second World War, which polarizes the society even today. The focus of scientific research and public discussion on the First World War in Slovenia was and is on Isonzo Front; research on other aspects of the war did not really occur until recently. The big anniversary year of 2014 changed this situation and shed light on the underrepresented First World War. A documentary series for TV, *Slovenci in Prva svetovna vojna* (*"Slovenians and the Great War of 1914-1918"*) was produced, and the first Slovene feature film on that topic (produced in an Austrian-Slovene co-production), *Gozodvi so* še *vedno zeleni / Die Wälder sind noch grün* ("*The Woods Are Still Green*") was introduced to the public. Therefore, it is fitting to say that WWI has become a topic of Slovene cinematography and TV production only in the last few years. It is the main objective of this article to have a closer look at this recent film and documentary production and portray the main storylines on First World War from the Slovene perspective.[1]

A Short History of Slovene Film Production

Due to globalization, like elsewhere, today's Slovene cinemas are dominated by foreign and not domestic movies, mainly Hollywood productions. Unsurprisingly, on rankings of the most seen films in Slovenia, we find Hollywood productions.[2] The highest ranking genuine Slovene films are mainly comedies and comedy-dramas: The encyclopedia of Slovene film ranks the teenage comedy *Gremo*

---

1 Note: If not stated otherwise, all quotes from Slovene or German sources; media comments, etc. have been translated by the author herself.

2 There are different rankings of the most watched movies, which vary and whose numbers are hard to verify. According to the ranking of the most watched films between 1992 and 2009 by the national television RTV Slovenija, *Titanic* was 1st, and as highest ranking Slovene production, the Slovene romantic comedy *Petelinji zajtrk* (2007) 4th ("Lestvica gledanosti (1992-2009)," *rtvslo.si*, http://www.rtvslo.si/kultura/film/lestvica-gledanosti-1992-2009/157135). According to the "Top All Time" list from 2011, made by the big cinematographic company Cinemania, among all the American productions (again *Titanic* 1st), the teenage comedy *Gremo mi po svoje* (2010) ranked 3rd, the romantic comedies *Petelinji zajtrk* on 7th and *Kajmak in marmelada* (2003) on 11th rank ("Top All Time – Slo 2015," Cinemania, http://www.cinemania-group.si/top_all_time.asp). The ranking from the Slovene Wikipedia instead ranks the first Slovene sound film, *Na svoji zemlji* (1948), about the Resistance during Occupation, even higher than *Titanic* ("Seznam najbolj gledanih filmov v Sloveniji," *sl.wikipedia.org*, https://sl.wikipedia.org/wiki/Seznam_najbolj_gledanih_filmov_v_Sloveniji). Whatever the precise numbers might be, for the purpose of this article it is sufficient to say that the domestic Slovene film production has a hard time competing against the American movie industry, but still manages every now and then to produce a Slovene "blockbuster."

mi po svoje (*Let's Go Our Own Way*), with 205,430 viewers, as the most watched Slovene film since independence in 1991, and Marko Naberšnik's—a director we will hear about later—*Petelinji zajtrk* (*Rooster's Breakfast*)as the second.[3] But let's rather start with a closer look at the beginning of the Slovene film production.

Before 1918, there was no professional filming activity in Slovene lands. The still existing short film segments from Slovene towns made before 1918 were made by the (foreign) owners of cinematographs who enriched their program for screening with some shots from Slovene cities. The first film segments by a Slovene that survived until today were made by the lawyer Karol Grossmann (1864–1929) in 1905 in the small town of Ljutomer and show private shots of his children playing in the garden.[4] The history of Slovene feature film only began with the black and white silent films *V kraljestvu Zlatoroga* (*In the Kingdom of the Goldhorn*) (1931) and *Triglavske strmine* (*The slopes of Triglav*, 1932), both about the love for the local mountains. Since those two were the only Slovene feature movies produced in interwar Yugoslavia, the first phase of Slovene film production did not produce many films. The first sound, and therefore often considered being the first "real," Slovene movie was produced in 1948 and called *Na svoji zemlji* (*On Our Own Land*). With this epic depiction of the Partisan resistance movement in the Slovene Littoral against Italian and German occupation, the second—socialistic—era of Slovene film

3 Silvan Furlan et al., eds., *Filmografija slovenskih celovečernih filmov 1931–2010 / Filmography of Slovenian Feature Films 1931–2010* (Ljubljana: Umco Slovenska kinoteka, 2011), 762.

4 Bojan Veberič, "Die lebenden Fotografien kommen in die Stadt! Das Bild der großen, weiten Welt in den Anfängen der Kinematografie in Ljubljana," in *Stiki in sovplivanja med središčem in obrobjem: Medkulturne literarnovedne* študije, ed. Mira Miladinović Zalaznik and Tanja Žigon (Ljubljana: Znanstvena založba FF, 2014), 65.

production began. Movies from that era have always to be analyzed within the specific context of the culture scene and movie production in socialist Yugoslavia.[5] The third phase of Slovene film production started under newly changed political circumstances, with Slovenia's independence in 1991. So, between the modest beginnings and today's modern entertainment industry, are there Slovene movies on historical topics as well? Are there movies on the First World War?

An encyclopedic overview of Slovene film production from its beginnings up to 2010 lists 205 feature films in chronological order and gives an overview of their content.[6] Searching for the First World War within the Slovene filmography is a luckless enterprise, though this is not due to a lack of interest in historical topics. On the contrary, there are quite a few movies made on historical topics or telling a story embedded into a specific historical context. For example, I was able to identify fifteen films among the already mentioned 205 whose main storylines took place within the setting of Habsburg Monarchy. However, they are not "historical" by nature but mainly cinematographic adaptations of famous novels: *Samorastniki* (*Wild Growth*, 1963, directed by Prežihov Voranc), or *Na klancu* (*In the Gorge*, 1971, directed by Ivan Cankar), or biographies of famous Slovenes, such as *Pesnikov portret z dvojnikom* (Portrait of a poet with a double, 2002), on the poet France Prešeren. Another sixteen films deal in one way or the other with living conditions in socialist Yugoslavia, for example: the social consequences of the collectivization in the 1950s, *Rdeče klasje* (*Red Wheat*, 1970); the agitations

5 Ibid., 513 and 736–766.

6 All further information is taken from: *Filmografija slovenskih celovečernih filmov 1931–2010*, ed. Silvan Furlan et al. For the years 2011 until 2014 that are not covered by this encyclopedia of Slovene film, I was able to identify nineteen further films, which were mostly comedies and did not cover the topic of the First World War either. The only exception is the Austrian-Slovene co-production discussed in this article.

of the Informbiro until 1955 *Moj ata, socialistični kulak* (*My Dad, the Socialist Kulak*, 1987); or with the social conditions in Yugoslavia and specific topics such as xenophobia, *Ovni in mamuti* (*Rams and mammoths*, 1985), alcoholism, *Kormoran* (*A Cormoran*, 1986), corruption, *Odpadnik* (*The Maverick*, 1988); or youth subculture, *Outsider* (1997). Only some parts of the storyline of one film, *Dediščina* (*Heritage*, 1984) took place in 1914. However, this film was not on World War I itself but rather portrayed the life and downfall of a family.[7]

War has indeed been an important theme in Slovene film production, but only World War II: thirty-three of the 205 feature films up to 2010, an impressive number of sixteen percent, are on Partisan life, the Resistance of the Liberation Front (*Osvobodilna fronta*, OF) against occupation, on civil resistance and collaboration during World War II, or about the immediate postwar years.[8] Therefore, it can be said that WWII has undoubtedly played a decisive role in Slovene cinemas, especially in the 1950s and 1960s, and can be considered a vital theme in Slovene film production.[9] From the mid-1970s on, and specifically after 1991, Slovene movies tended to become "escapist" in high number: They did not cover political war stories anymore but were in great number apolitical, ahistorical, and entertaining or were political only by addressing social problems.[10] Returning to our initial search for WWI in the Slovene filmography up to 2010, we have to attest to its complete absence. If one judged the importance of historic events based on their reflection in the Slovene film production, it seems as if the First World War has not happened at all, or it is at least of no interest to the Slovene film industry.

---

7 Ibid., 198–199.

8 This number is my own count, based again on: Furlan, *Filmografija*.

9 See specific analyses of Yugoslav Partisan films in: *Partisans in Yugoslavia: Literature, Film and Visual Culture*, ed. Miranda Jakiša and Nikica Gilić (Bielefeld: transcript, 2015), 159–378.

10 Furlan, *Filmografija*, 548–555 and 574.

…And the Absence of the First World War

These results do not surprise at all if we compare them to the importance of WWI in Slovene collective remembrance culture in general. The First World War cannot be considered an important *lieu de mémoire*[11] for the Slovene national group identity. Proof to that claim is the fact that memorials glorifying the "heroic fight" of Slovene soldiers and monuments remembering the sacrifices, death and suffering of Slovene people can be found plenty for the Second, but only very few for the First, World War.[12]

---

11 Pierre Nora, *Zwischen Geschichte und Gedächtnis* (Frankfurt am Main: Fischer, 2005).

12 On Slovene monuments remembering victims and "heroes" of the First and Second World War, the Slovene Academy of Science (ZRC SAZU) conducted two research projects, see: "Kulturna demografija prve svetovne vojne," ZRC SAZU, http://zimk.zrc-sazu.si/sl/programi-in-projekti/kulturna-demografija-prve-svetovne-vojne#v and "Zbirka domobranskih spomenikov na Slovenskem," ZRC SAZU, http://ikss.zrc-sazu.si/sl/zbirka/zbirka-domobranskih-spomenikov-na-slovenskem#v. See further: Oto Luthar and Breda Luthar, "The Monopolization of Memory: The Politics and Textuality of War Memorials in Slovenia since 1991," in *Kulturen der Differenz - Transformationsprozesse in Zentraleuropa nach 1989*, ed. Heinz Fassmann, Wolfgang Müller-Funk, and Heidemarie Uhl (Wien: V&R Unipress, 2009), 195–206; Petra Svoljšak, "La memoria della Guerra in Slovenia," in *Esercito e popolazioni nella Grande Guerra: autunno 1917*, ed. Marco Balbi et al. (Udine: Gaspari, 2008); "The Slovenes in 1914: Between History and Remembrance," in *Znanstveni skup 1914 - prva godina rata u Trojednoj Kraljevini I Austro-Ugarskoij Monarhiji*, ed. Vijoleta Kaurić (Zagreb: Hrvatski institut za povijest, 2014); and on Slovene remembrance culture on WWI in Lower Styria as well: Karin Almasy, "'V spomin žrtvam svetovne vojne': Erinnerungskultur, Gefallenendenkmäler in der Untersteiermark und die Zäsur 1918 für die Slowenen," in *Heimatfront: Graz und das Kronland Steiermark im Ersten Weltkrieg*, ed. Werner Suppanz and Nicole Goll (Essen: Klartext-Verlag 2017, forthcoming).

After 1918, Slovenes found themselves in the newly founded Kingdom of Serbs, Croats, and Slovenes. Only shortly beforehand, they had been part of the Austrian military, being considered very loyal and *kaisertreu*, and had fought against Serbia, whereas they were now part of this new Serbian dominated state. Therefore, it is easy to imagine that Slovene (as well as the Croatian and the *prečani* Serbs) war veterans did not have the best standing within the new state; they had fought for a state that did not exist anymore, and the recently founded Yugoslav state proved unable to close the gap torn between the South Slavic people during WWI. From the new state's perspective, Slovene veterans of WWI were not only unworthy of glorification, but somehow suspicious and openly discriminated against: Until 1925, the veteran's pensions for former soldiers mutilated by war were two times higher for soldiers that fought for the Yugoslavian state than for the soldiers from the former Habsburg empire.[13] It is therefore fair to conclude that there was not room for remembrance within the first Yugoslavia, and without such memory space, there is hardly any public remembrance.[14] Within the second socialist Yugoslavia, there was no place for remembrance of World War I either: The events that took place between 1941 and 1945 were so overtly present, they blocked out almost everything else in public

---

13 Petra Svoljšak, "Nekaj utrinkov iz delovanja veteranske organizacije Zveza bojevnikov: ‚Organizacija Bojevnikov je trdna in močna, je zveza src in duš. Je temelj prijateljstva in ljubezni med narodi,'" in *Prispevki za novejšo zgodovino* XLVI, no. 1 (2006): 282–285; and an extensive overview in: John Paul Newman, *Yugoslavia in the Shadow of War: Veterans and the Limits of State Building 1903–1945* (Cambridge: Cambridge University Press, 2015).

14 Jan Assmann, *Das kulturelle Gedächtnis: Schrift, Erinnerung und politische Identität in frühen Hochkulturen* (München: C.H. Beck, 2007), 39.

remembrance culture. The remembrance cult around the Partisan movement was ritualized and became a very useful instrument to emphasize the South Slavic brotherhood between Slovenes, Serbs, Croats, Montenegrins, Bosnians, and Macedonians. According to the slogan *Bratstvo i jedinstvo* (Brotherhood and unity), there was surely no interest in emphasizing the fact that the South Slavic people fought each other during WWI. One might expect things to have changed after 1991, when Slovenia became independent and Slovenes were finally free to remember World War I. But not much has happened in this regard; the overall presence of WWII continued to overshadow WWI and has polarized the society until today. Political thinking patterns are still taking their cue from the ideological front lines: Partisans vs. *domobranci* (Slovene Home Guard) and Catholics, maintaining the traditional political partition of left and right. The First World War, instead, is basically a non-controversial historical event that does not polarize or stir up Slovene society.

WWI from a Slovene Perspective

We already established that World War I does not occupy a central position within the Slovene remembrance culture and the national "master narrative," meaning the "dominant narrative about the past."[15] Now I would like to have a closer look at how WWI is represented in the Slovene master narrative and how the story of WWI is told and interpreted from the Slovene's perspective. Concerning what of First World War is remembered and on which aspects there is

15 Konrad H. Jarausch and Martin Sabrow, "‚Meistererzählung‘ - Zur Karriere eines Begriffs," in *Die historische Meistererzählung: Deutungslinien der deutschen Nationalgeschichte nach 1945*, ed. Konrad H. Jarausch and Martin Sabrow (Göttingen: Vandenhoeck
2002), 17.

research,[16] certain central themes were given a lot of attention, while other topics do not appear much. This is not surprising because in all national master narratives, certain themes are highlighted and certain motifs strengthened; meanwhile, certain other aspects are "forgotten" or left aside.[17] For the purpose of getting a better picture of a master narrative, we can differentiate between 1) its material components (which events and people from the past are connected with each other to form the historical storyline?), 2) its

---

16 To name just some of the most important authors and their publications on WWI: on the Isonzo Front, Petra Svoljšak, *Soča, sveta reka: Italijanska zasedba slovenskega ozemlja (1915–1917)* (Ljubljana: Nova revija, 2003), on the disintegration in 1918 Walter Lukan, *Iz* črnožolte *kletke narodov v zlato svobodo? Habsburška monarhija in Slovenci v prvi svetovni vojni* (Ljubljana: Znanstvena založbe FF, 2014), on remembrance culture, Oto Luthar, *O* žalosti *niti beside: Uvod v kulturno zgodovino velike vojne* (Ljubljana: Založba ZRC, 2013), on different aspects of WWI, the collective volume, Peter Vodopivec and Katja Kleindienst, eds., *Velika vojna in Slovenci* (Ljubljana: Slovenska matica, 2005), on social and gender aspects of WWI in the Slovene Littorial, see e.g. Marta Verginella, "Ženske in prva svetovna vojna," in *Zgodovina je slastna: kulturna zgodovina hrane; 100 let začetka prve svetovne vojne: programska knjižica / 37. zborovanje Zveze zgodovinskih društev Slovenije*, ed. Branko Šuštar (Ljubljana: ZZDS, 2014). For a good overview, see also *Take vojne si nismo predstavljali (1914–1918)*, ed. Marko Štepec (Ljubljana: Muzej novejše zgodovine Slovenije, 2014) and similar publications from the aforementioned museum.

17 On the Slovene master narrative, see the excellent critical overview of Peter Štih, "Miti in stereotipi v podobi starejše slovenske nacionalne zgodovine," in *Zbornik 33: Zborovanje Zveze zgodovinskih društev Slovenije.* ed. Mitija Ferenc (Kranj: Littera picta, 2006), 25–47; and in German: "Slowenische Geschichtsmythen und Feindbilder," in *Zeitschrift des Historischen Vereines für Steiermark* (Graz: Historischer Verein für Steiermark, 2004), 59–67.

theoretical-methodical dimension (according to which line of reasoning are these material components put together to form the narrative?), and 3) its semantic components (with what kind of language, phrases, slogans, etc. are these ideas expressed?).[18] For the purpose of getting a clear impression on the Slovene view on WWI, I will now try to briefly identify the main "storylines" or "themes" of First World War from the Slovene perspective (the material components) and then search for them within the two mentioned film productions.

The central canonical theme of WWI from a Slovene perspective is undoubtedly the Isonzo Front (or *Soška fronta* because the Slovene name for that river is Soča). At this bloody frontline, where military operations lasted for twenty-nine months, specifically two events or battles stand out: Doberdob and Kobarid (Karfreit/Caporetto). The high plateau of Doberdò (or Doberdob, a small village on the same-named plateau with a mainly Slovene population in today's Italy) was one of the bloodiest battlefields since the second battle of the Isonzo in July and August 1915 and therefore became synonymous for great losses, spilled blood, and the horror of war. A semantic aspect to this material component is the song and slogan "Doberdob - slovenskih fantov grob" (Doberdob, the grave of Slovene soldiers).[19] Kobarid, in-

18 Jarausch, *Meistererzählung* 17.

19 The only Slovene war novel about World War One written by Prežihov Voranc is named *Doberdob* as well, see: Lovro Kuhar [who was publishing under the pseudonym Voranc, Prežihov], *Doberdob: Vojni roman slovenskega naroda* (Ljubljana: Naša založba, 1940) and the German translation by Karin Almasy und Klaus Detlef Olof, *Doberdo: Slowenischer Kriegsroman* (Klagenfurt: Mohorjeva, 2008/09). On this war novel in German see: Heinrich Placke, "Doberdo - Ein Roman des Slowenen Prežihov Voranc / Lovro Kuhar über den I. Weltkrieg an der Isonzo-Front," in *Erich Maria Remarque, Im Westen nichts Neues und die Folgen*, ed. Thomas Schneider (Göttingen: V&R unipress, 2014), 61–84.

stead, is remembered as the great success of Habsburg and German troops in the twelfth battle of the Isonzo, when they were able to defeat Italians troops using poison gas. The culmination of this famous and bloody event is known as "Čudež pri Kobaridu" ("Das Wunder von Karfreit" / "The miracle of Caporetto"). On the other hand, the Western and the Eastern fronts were not much on display for Slovenes and were overshadowed by the Isonzo Front completely. The attention lies clearly on battlefields where Slovene soldiers were fighting and where the Slovene civilian population was affected, as was the case on the Isonzo Front.

Moreover, the Slovene narrative on WWI neither focused solely on military aspects nor on the bigger picture of the great power politics, but mainly on civil aspects of the war and the Slovene destiny during war. Therefore, it comes as no surprise that there were other topics discussed frequently: the process of disintegration up to 1918 and the growing South Slavic political ideas, politics, and petitions fighting for more rights within the Empire, the still existing strong loyalty to Habsburg on the one hand and Vienna's mistrust and fear of expected pan-Slavic tendencies on the other (which led to a great number of arrests, especially among the Slovene national clergy),[20] the devastations and deprivations caused by the war, the growing dissatisfaction (as expressed by soldiers in acts of insurrections), and the transition into the new statehood.[21]

20 See detailed, in: Martin Moll, *Kein Burgfrieden: Der deutsch-slowenische Nationalkonflikt in der Steiermark 1900–1918* (Innsbruck: StudienVerlag, 2007).

21 This becomes obvious if we have a look at the *Kronika XX stoletja*, where WWI is discussed on only fifty-two pages: only minor parts really reflect on military aspects, most articles focus on living conditions and the transition between the two different forms of statehood; Marjan Drnovšek et al., eds., *Slovenska Kronika XX. Stoletja I.* (Ljubljana: Nova revija, 1995), 149–201.

Thanks to the 100th anniversary of the beginning of WWI in 2014, interest on that "seminal catastrophe of the twentieth century" has grown noticeably. Not only are there significantly more conferences, publications, and research on that topic, but what has especially increased is the presence of the topic in a broader public sphere. An official committee for the 100th anniversary of WWI was founded, national memorials held, and exhibitions on topics connected to the First World War were put on display.[22] The public television and radio, RTV Slovenija, was active as well: On a special website, all news segments, reports, short television documentaries, round table discussions, radio reports, event tips, and other information on WWI were collected and presented in order to attract more public interest.[23] For the objective of this article, I want to concentrate now on two outstanding productions, both released in 2014, by giving a short overview of their content, reception, and the circumstance of their production first and then analyzing them according to

22 See more detailed: Karin Almasy, "Der Stellenwert des Ersten Weltkrieges in der slowenischen Erinnerungskultur und das Gedenkjahr 2014 in Slowenien," in *Gedenken und (k)ein Ende - was bleibt vom Jahr 2014? Das Gedenkjahr 1914/2014 und sein historiografisches Vermächtnis*, ed. Bernhard Bachinger et al. (Wien: Verlag der Österreichischen Akademie der Wissenschaften 2017), 51–67. For the web presence of the National Committee, see: "Slovenian National Committee for the 100th Anniversary of World War I (2014–2018)," *100letprve.si*, http://www.100letprve.si/en/noga/slovenian_national_committee/; and for the museum of First World I in Kobarid: Kobariski Muzej, http://www.kobariski-muzej.si/.

23 See the news portal on WWI of the national television portal "RTV Slovenija," at: http://www.rtvslo.si/1sv (accessed Sept. 30, 2015).

the mentioned criteria (material component, theoretical-methodical dimension, and semantic components of the Slovene master narrative on WWI).

In February 2014, RTV Slovenija aired a high quality documentary series in five episodes named *Slovenci in Prva svetovna vojna* ("*Slovenians and the Great War of 1914-1918*"). This has been the first Slovene television documentary series on the First World War. Therefore, it is worthwhile having a good analytic look at this big project undertaken by the historian and curator of the National Museum of Contemporary History Marko Štepec and the well-known movie director Valentin Pečenko.[24] The second production worth mentioning and discussing in detail is the first feature film from a Slovene director on the First World War, namely the Austrian-Slovene co-production *Gozodvi so* še *vedno zeleni/Die Wälder sind noch grün* ("*The Woods Are Still Green*") by the popular movie director Marko Naberšnik.[25] Other recent, much shorter, TV and radio features, news segments, documentaries, etc.—although they cover interesting aspects of WWI—will not be considered in the following analysis due to the lack of space and the considerably different format

24 Valentin Pečenko and Marko Štepec, *Slovenci in 1. Svetovna vojna 1914-1918* (Ljubljana: RTV Slovenija, 2013). In all further citations mentioned in short as Pečenko/Štepec (2013). The documentary series has now also been subtitled into English. Thanks to Marko Štepec for that and further information.

25 Marko Naberšnik, *Die Wälder sind noch grün / Gozdovi sp* še *vedno zeleni* (Vojnik: Fivia, 2014). In further citations mentioned in short as Naberšnik (2014). See the official website, at: http://www.die-wälder.com/ (accessed Sept., 30, 2015).

and scale of these productions.[26] Also the only three documentary segments produced earlier than 2014 will not be considered in the following analysis for the same reason: Two of them deal exclusively with the Isonzo Front: a seven minute long contribution to the television show "Kalejdoskop" (Kaleidoscope) about the still existing traces and remains of the Isonzo Front on the mountain Rombon by Drago Kocijančič from 1967,[27] and a documentary from 1997 named *Bitka*

---

26 Most noteworthy of all the recent smaller productions is the TV documentary *V Fokusu: Ženske v veliki vojni 1914–1918* on Slovene women during WWI by Valentin Pečenko and Petra Svoljšak, who guides the thirty minutes long TV documentary. Topics discussed are: The difficult supply situation at the "home front," where mostly women had to take care of those left behind; women in hospitals and the emergence of the whole new profession of nursing; women in the arms industry and abandoned agriculture, where they were burdened in multiple ways and had to be "landlord, servant and horse all at once"; see at: "Videonovice," *rtvslo.si*, accessed Sept. 30,2015, http://www.rtvslo.si/prva-svetovna-vojna/TVinRAarhiv. Another very interesting documentary is named *Doberdob: Roman upornika* [Doberdob: The novel of a Rebel] and was produced in 2015 by Martin Turk in a co-production of Bela Film, RTV Slovenija, and RAI Furlanija julijska krajina. The documentary covers WWI in large segments by focusing on the aforementioned writer Prežihov Voranc and his novel on WWI, *Doberdob*. Voranc experienced the fighting at the Isonzo himself and deserted over to the Italians. After the war, he was one of the first, and later on even highest-ranking members, of the Yugoslav Communist Party. Due to that fact, he was forced to live under irregular circumstances and in hiding. Therefore, the manuscript of this only Slovene novel on WWI got lost and had to be rewritten several times. See footnote 19.

27 See the seven minute long video in black and white: "Sto let, odkar so soško fronto stresli prvi boji," *rtvslo.si*, accessed Sept. 30, 2015, http://www.rtvslo.si/kultura/razglednice-preteklosti/sto-let-odkar-so-sosko-fronto-stresli-prvi-boji/365741.

za reko (*Fight for the river*) directed by Igor Pediček and produced by Micom productions. The third one, *Slovenci v vojni 1914–1918* (*The Slovenes during the war 1914–1918*) was produced by Božo Grlj and Marko Štepec in 2009.[28]

Gozodovi so še *vedno zeleni / Die Wälder sind noch grün*

In striking and impressive pictures, shot at original locations on the former frontlines in the high mountains of today's Western Slovenia (at the mountain Mangart in the Julian Alps, along Soča River, at the Kluže Fortress and Strmol Castle), the film is not what one might expect from a "war movie" on WWI. As a positive critique in *The Hollywood Reporter* stated, the producers were indeed "not interested in crafting some kind of wartime action adventure."[29] The movie is surprisingly quiet, silent and unhasty, though never dull or tedious. We do not see the masses fighting, killing and dying in the trenches. Instead, the director chose an isolated and seemingly idyllic and safer outpost in the mountains.

---

28 Thanks to Marko Štepec for that information. I do not exclude the possibility that there were some other tiny news segments; however, the documentary production earlier than 2014 can basically be summed up with these three productions. For *Bitka za reko / Fight for the River*, see: *The International Historic Films Complete Online Catalog* at http://ihffilm.com/22841.html; and the Slovenian Film Center at http://www.film-center.si/sl/film-v-sloveniji/filmi/1419/bitka-za-reko/ (accessed Sept. 30, 2015). The last aforementioned segment is also available online, see: "Slovenci v vojni 1914-1918," *YouTube.com*, accessed June 6, 2017, https://www.youtube.com/watch?v=hmFCwURQfEo.

29 Elizabeth Kerr, "'The Woods are Still Green': Shanghai Review," *The Hollywood Reporter*, updated June 26, 2014, accessed Sept. 30, 2015, http://www.hollywoodreporter.com/review/woods-are-still-green-shanghai-714018.

Rather than telling the stories of many, the first Slovene (-Austrian) movie on WWI tells the story of one young soldier. Holding a seemingly safe post in late summer 1917 on the front to Italy (shortly before the "Miracle of Kobarid"), three Austro-Hungarian soldiers are isolated from the major frontline fighting in the valley. Their spot is not safe for long, however, because Italian artillery shelling strikes their observation post, kills one soldier and mutilates their commander, who loses a leg. Nineteen-year-old Carinthian soldier Jakob Lindner (Michael Kristof) is now on his own, commanded to hold the base, trying to prevent his Czech-Jewish commander Jan Kopetzky (Simon Šerbinek) from dying. They run low on water, alcohol, and food, and the help promised by the anonymous voice on the field telephone never comes. When there is no water left, he heads down to the Soča valley in order to get some and almost runs into Italian troops. In this scene, shot in the woods at night, the actor Kristof manages to convince the audience of being a frightened and overwhelmed young man, scared for his life. When he comes back to the mountain shed, his commander has died. He drinks the remaining rum; the field telephone is ringing, but he does not answer. He falls asleep and has a nightmare that is at first not apparent as one. In his nightmare, he is punished for not answering the field telephone by a strict general who is feasting at a richly set table. The general shouts at him and tells him that his disobedience caused the death of 40,000 soldiers in one night. After a strict lecture on loyalty ("Who's your father, Lindner? / Josef Lindner, a carpenter by trade. / Wrong, the Emperor is your father. / Where are you from? / Neuhaus bei Lavamünd is my home, General, Sir. / Wrong, the Empire is your home, Austria-Hungary!")[30], he is sentenced to death by the general and executed by a soldier in a gas mask with

30 Naberšnik (2014), 01:24:40.

a machine gun. When he awakes from this disturbing dream, the field telephone is ringing again. But Lindner does not answer. He makes two caskets for his dead comrades, packs his few belongings and the personal belongings of his diseased comrades, and leaves the shed. The end is left open, and the audience does not learn what happened to Lindner. Since he once mentioned that his home is just on the other side of the mountains, and he could reach his home in a day, we hope he makes it home in one piece but are left with uncertainty. In a final scene, we see today's Kluže Fortress and in a museum's glass cabinet the personal belongings shown in the movie, among them the (fictive) diary of Lindner.[31] Even though the director and screenplay writer Naberšnik was inspired by original sources, mainly letters sent home by soldiers from the frontlines—the title of the film itself is a line taken from such a letter—the portrayed characters are purely fictitious.[32]

"Finally a Movie on WWI that We Can at Least to Some Extent Call Our Own"

How were the public opinion and the reviews on *Gozdovi so* še *vedno zeleni*? For this purpose, I had a look at Slovene reviews and press statements about the movie. The film was very well received, and won some prestigious prices, for example at film festivals in Shanghai, Jagran, Cottbus, and Ljubljana.[33] What is somehow very specific to the Slovene reviews on this film is the repeated discussion of its "Sloveneness" and whether this co-production

31 Naberšnik (2014), 01:40:44.

32 As Marko Naberšnik explained in a TV interview, to be seen at: http://www.rtvslo.si/prva-svetovna-vojna/TVinRAarhiv [30.09.2015] and Izak Košir, Intervju z Markom Naberšnikom: Prva svetovna vojna je bila drugačna od druge, 16.10.2014, in: https://www.dnevnik.si/1042684670 [30.09.2015].

33 See die-wälder.com.

can be considered a *Slovene* cinematic achievement at all. What maybe sums up this opinion best is the following film review on one of biggest Slovene news portals: After explaining the very tight financial situation of the Slovene film industry, which constantly relies on subventions due to the market's smallness,[34] director Marko Naberšnik "had no other choice than making his third feature film, the war drama *Gozodovi so* še *vedno zeleni/Die Wälder sind noch grün* in collaboration with our Northern neighbors. [...] With Austrian support, we Slovene people finally got a movie on WWI that we can at least to some extent call our own, since we cannot consider it our own entirely."[35] In another review, the national television obviously felt the need to point out the genuine Slovene contribution to this co-production between the Austrian producing studio Artdeluxe Films and Perfo Productions, in "which Perfo from Ljubljana acts as junior partner. Nonetheless, the Slovene team plays a pretty important role, since alongside director and co-producer Naberšnik there is the actor Simon Šerbinek, the director of photography Miloš Srdić, the production designer Miha Ferkov, and the editor Jan Lovše, if we only name the ones with the most important roles."[36] What

34 The Slovenski filmski center [Slovenian Film Center] is the public agency of the Republic of Slovenia to co-finance Slovene film productions, on whose funding Slovene film productions rely heavily, see: "About," Slovenian Film Center, accessed Sept. 30, 2015, http://www.film-center.si/en/about/.

35 Klemen Černe, "Ocena filma: Gozdovi so še vedno zeleni," last modified Dec. 9, 2014, accessed Sept. 30, 2015, http://www.siol.net/scena/film/recenzije/2014/12/gozdovi_so_se_vedno_zeleni.aspx.

36 MMC RTV SLO, *Gozdovi so* še *vedno zeleni* [film review on the occasion of the 25th International Film Festival in Ljubljana], last modified Nov. 15, 2014, accessed Sept. 30, 2015, http://www.rtvslo.si/kultura/liffe/gozdovi-so-se-vedno-zeleni/351214.

is particularly striking is who they fail to name: the main actor Michael Kristof, widely praised for this film debut as a frightened young soldier. Kristof, a Carinthian Slovene who attended the Slovene high school in Klagenfurt/Celovec and has a diploma from the Slovene Academy for theater, radio, film, and television (AGRFT) in Ljubljana,[37] where he was a student of Naberšnik, is *not* considered a Slovene actor by this critique, which tells us a lot about narrow—national—thinking patterns. Cutting this argument at this point without contributing any further to this discussion on "how Slovene" the film is, I simply wanted to point out that this was a largely debated dimension of *Gozodvi so* še *vedno zeleni*. Obviously, it is still valid today, when the authors of the Slovene filmography stated that "the 'peculiarity' of Slovene film lies in the fact that it was conceived as a national 'Thing.'"[38] The international European film production *No Man's Land* (2001) on the war in Bosnia, shared the same destiny: Even though it was shot and co-produced in considerable parts in Slovenia, "not even an Oscar win could make the Slovene audience perceive it as an 'also Slovene' film."[39]

The main reasons for not being considered a "real" Slovene movie are most likely: 1) the soldiers in the film speak German to

---

37 "Gozdovi so še vedno zeleni," *kolosej.si*, accessed Sept. 30, 2015, http://www.kolosej.si/filmi/film/gozdovi-so-se-vedno-zeleni/.

38 Furlan, *Filmografija*, 513.

39 Ibid., 572. *No Man's Land* is not listed in this cited *Filmography*; we will see whether a future edition will name *Gozdovi so* še *vedno zeleni*. If we have a look at Wikipedia's list of Slovene films and perceive this list as an even more democratic and representative mirror of Slovene public (self-)perception, it says a lot about that topic that the film is not (yet) named there either, see: "Seznam slovenskih filmov," *sl.wikipedia.org*, accessed Sept. 30, 2015, https://sl.wikipedia.org/wiki/Seznam_slovenskih_filmov.

each other; 2) the initial idea came from the Austrian co-producer and co-writer Robert Hofferer, who invited Naberšnik to shoot an intimate portrayal on WWI; and 3) it was financed without Slovene governmental subventions but mainly by private (Austrian) funds. Naberšnik was asked on several occasions why the film was shot in German and whether this constituted a problem for him. He replied that he did not consider it a problem at all; being from Lower Styria, he is accustomed to German language and learned it in school. Moreover, he argued that the film would have been unauthentic in Slovene, because the language of command and "lingua franca" in the Austrian military was in fact German.[40] This statement shows that the producers obviously endeavored to make their film historically accurate. Also concerning other historical details, the film team was advised by historians, scientists, and others in order to create an authentic imagery. The equipment was manufactured based on historical models, and even original loan objects from private collectors were used.[41] Therefore, the film portrays a very convincing picture of these events. Finally, another aspect of the film that has been stressed by the reviews is its message for peace by demonstrating the horror of war. Probably because it focuses on one single soldier instead of the big anonymous masses of men, the film succeeds in delivering that message to today's audience. Following the popular bottom-up approach of history studies of telling the big story (of WWI) through the small story, *Gozodvi so še vedno zeleni* lets us empathize with all the horror even more.

---

40 All this information given by Marko Naberšnik, at: "Videonovice," *rtvslo.si*, accessed Sept. 30, 2015, http://www.rtvslo.si/prva-svetovna-vojna/TVinRAarhiv.

41 See: "Die Wälder sind noch grün," *filmneweurope.com*, accessed Sept. 30, 2015, http://www.filmneweurope.com/festivals/item/108405-die-waelder-sind-noch-gruen-english-title-the-woods-are-still-green.

A Television Documentary Series in Five Episodes

The television documentary series *Slovenci in Prva svetovna vojna* (*"Slovenians and the Great War of 1914-1918"*), on the other hand, is definitely a Slovene production and unique of its kind: It took three years to produce it and was shot at original sites of the First World War, therefore showing interesting shots from Galicia in today's Ukraine, and Poland, Vienna, Trieste, Sarajevo and of course Slovene locations. What makes it unique and very interesting for historians are the rich historical filmic, photographic, and printed sources used in this multimedia documentary: From the very first private amateur film by Grossmann and first film segments of Slovene towns at the beginning of the twentieth century to official Austro-Hungarian and Italian film reports on the war and rich photo material from the Slovene lands, from newspaper reports to diary entries of soldiers, etc. Quite a few documentaries and movies show World War I from the British, German, or French perspective—from the perspective of big nations. However, one from a Slovene perspective, meaning from a small nation's view, was missing so far. According to the producers, this was their motive for making a Slovene documentary on WWI: to show the narrative from a Slovene perspective by also using Slovene sources.[42] The main narrator leading through the documentary is the historian and producer Marko Štepec himself, always reporting in front of the historical site under discussion. Other excellent national and international historians give their expertise on certain topics as well (for example, Petra Svoljšak, M. Christian Ortner, Janez Cvirn, Peter Vodopivec, Jože Pirjevec, Marco Mantini, and Janez Švajncer). The different visual and auditory elements are

---

42 See this interview with Štepec, at: Gorazd Utenkar, "Prva vojna, totalna in nepredstavljiva," *delo.si*, accessed Sept. 30, 2015, http://www.delo.si/zgodbe/nedeljskobranje/prva-vojna-totalna-in-nepredstavljiva.html.

put together, forming a complex collage on WWI, using experts' interviews as well as reports and testimonies by contemporaries read by an off-screen voice, taken from sources such as letters, newspapers, and postcards, while these written sources are shown as well as the sites of former frontlines. All these elements mix with historical filmic and photographic material. By combining this multitude of sources[43] into one documentary production, the audience gets a precise feeling of the material, emotional, and scenic world during 1914–1918, already a hundred years away from our own experience.

After these general remarks on the documentary series, I want to have a closer look at the chosen topics. This allows interesting conclusions on the material components of Slovene's gaze on World War I. The five episodes of the documentary series tell the story of WWI in chronological order, and the single episodes are named as follows:

1. *Zatišje pred viharjem* (*"Calm Before the Storm"*)
2. *Krvave galicijske poljane* (*"Galician Planes in Blood Bath"*)
3. *Doberdob, slovenskih fantov grob* (*"Doberdob, the Grave of Slovenian Lads"*)
4. *Preboj pri Kobaridu* (*"The Breakthrough at Kobarid"*)
5. *Propad* (*"The Collapse"*)

---

43 The shown printed and photographic archival material was contributed by Slovene, Italian, and Austrian archives, such as: Muzej novejše zgodovine, Ljubljana; Heeresgeschichtliches Museum, Vienna; Kobariški muzej, Kobarid; Museo centrale del Risorgimento, Rome; Musei Provinciali di Gorizia; Museo Storico Italiano della Guerra, Rovereto; Vojni muzej Logatec etc. The archival film material was contributed by La Cineteca del Friuli, Gemona; Filmarchiv Austria, Vienna and Dokumentacija TV Slovenija, from the documentary series *Svet v letih 1900–1939*, a production of TV Zagreb from July 1977, see Pečenko/Štepec (2014), Part 4, 00:43:00.

The first episode gives an excellent overview of the living conditions under Habsburg rule in the late nineteenth century, on economic, cultural, educational, and national circumstances and developments and reflects on historical events back to the revolutionary year 1848, the *Ausgleich* in 1867, and explains alliance policies in Europe, the national "awakening" of Slovenes as well as national rivalries and tensions between Germans and Slovenes. Even though the bigger picture of the political situation in Europe is briefly mentioned, the main focus is on events and developments in the lands co-inhabited by Slovenes. Only after the first half hour is the assassination of Archduke Franz Ferdinand and his wife Sophie in Sarajevo that led to WWI explained. This first episode is mostly dedicated to the cultural, political, and social life of Slovene people under the Habsburg rule on the eve of WWI; that is, before 1914.

The second episode of this documentary series on the "bloody battlefields of Galicia" is maybe the most surprising one of all, because it puts the Eastern Front and the fight against the Russian army on display—a topic that was not at all in the focus of the older Slovene historiography, even though most Slovene soldiers lost their lives in Galicia and not along the Isonzo River.[44] The precise numbers of losses in the bloody summer of 1914, the following battles in the winter of 1914–15 and the siege of Przemyśl

---

44 Already during and also after the war, the events on the Eastern Front were less visualized than the Western and the Isonzo Front, which probably influenced that asymmetrical remembrance; see on that subject: Hannes Leidinger, "Visualisierung des Krieges: Die Ostfront in österreichisch-ungarischen Fotografien und Filmproduktionen," in *Jenseits des Schützengrabens: Der Erste Weltkrieg im Osten. Erfahrung - Wahrnehmung - Kontext*, ed. Bernhard Bachinger and Wolfram Dornik (Innsbruck: Studien-Verlag, 2013), 464.

is not known, but it is clear that ninety percent of all Slovene soldiers were called to Galicia.[45] Therefore, more Slovene soldiers lost their lives there than on any other battlefield during World War I.[46] Nevertheless, the narrative of episode two does not focus solely on military aspects, but also on the horror of this frontline, the exhaustion, fatigue, illnesses, and the plenty deaths by freezing or sickness. It compares the euphoric marching into war with the reality of the Galician front lines, which was not what most soldiers naively expected a war to be like.[47]

The third episode deals with the opening of the frontline against Italy along the river Isonzo/Soča and the bloody battles of 1915–16. After the Gorlice-Tarnow offensive in October 1915, when Austria was able to push back the Russian front in Galicia, the Eastern frontline became rather static. Most of the Slovene soldiers were ordered back because the new frontline with Italy opened up in May 1915, and contingents were urgently needed. In the Treaty of London, Italy was promised South Tyrol, the Austrian Littoral, and Dalmatia for joining the Entente. This "bitter betrayal of Italy" was strongly condemned in Austrian and Slovene newspapers. From this time onwards, the diction of newspaper articles became much more emotional than it was before.[48] This new frontline ran in its lower part almost complete-

---

45 Pečenko/Štepec (2014), 00:11:05.

46 Cf. as well Marko Štepec trying to raise awareness for the Eastern front publicly, as in: Utenkar, "Prva."

47 In accordance with that, the exhibition, curated by Štepec on WWI, that was on display until May 2015 in the National Museum of Contemporary History featured the title "Take vojne si nismo predstavljali" [We never imagined such a war], a line taken from autobiographical memories of surviving soldier Ivan Matičič.

48 Petra Svoljšak, in: Pečenko/Štepec (2014), Part 3, 00:05:13.

ly through territories populated by Slovenes, the most precious conquest targets in this area being the cities of Trieste and Gorizia. More than 100,000 civilians had to be evacuated from the area and were brought to Carniola, Carinthia, and Styria and from there to other parts of the monarchy. The inhabitants of Trieste, Gorizia, and Kobarid, though, stayed in large numbers, it is said, because of their strong attachment to their hometowns, stressing their bravery.[49] For the Slovene soldiers in all battles along the River Isonzo, it is also said—and this is an important topic for Slovenes during WWI—that they were known for their relentless bravery and persistence.[50] They had to defend their own homeland. If the frontline fell, their own hometowns would fall, which encouraged them a lot. Though episode three focuses on military maneuvers and strategy, it does not lack mention of the horrendous consequences of war for civilians in the cities, as well as for regular soldiers caused by diseases, starvation, freezing, and poor equipment.

Episode four starts by explaining the extensive supply system in the hinterland of the Isonzo front and the big efforts necessary to supply the troops on a daily basis by exploiting the remaining civilian population, the military resources, and the many thousands of Russian prisoners of war. It was in 1917, covered by this part of the documentary series, when the discontent and exhaustion

49 Pečenko/Štepec (2014), 00:08:47.

50 In the fifth episode, General Svetozar Boroević is quoted saying in a speech at Postojna that Slovene soldiers are the most reliable of all, and he would always choose them over all others and will spread this praise among the highest military leaders. This was documented by the priest Andrej Ažman, who was present for that speech, in his parish chronicles. Due to strict censorship, this praise never made it to the newspapers; see Pečenko/Štepec (2014), Part 5, 00:04:45.

of the troops grew exponentially. Acts of desertion had been much rarer among Slovenes than among other nationalities—or in comparison, among Slovenes much lower than on the Eastern battlefields. Many of those who deserted to the Italian side did it because of their pan-Slavic or other beliefs. The most scandalized example of a Slovene deserting was Commander Ljudevit Pivko, who was charged with high treason, and his family at home was incarcerated for their presumed assistance.[51] The latter half of part four deals extensively with the so-called "Miracle of Kobarid," the twelfth battle of Isonzo, when in October 1917 Austrians, with the support of German divisions, were able to change course of events and pushed the Italian troops all way back to the River Piave. Episode four is, together with episode three, the most military-focused part of this documentary series, dealing precisely and mainly with events on the Isonzo Front. Extensively discussed is, for example, the question of whether it was really mainly the use of poisonous gas that helped the Austrian and German troops succeed in Kobarid, ergo, the Italian press was exaggerating and thereby defending the Italian defeat, or whether it was indeed as well caused by the unpreparedness and low morale of the Italian troops.

Episode five deals with—as the title *Propad* (*"The Collapse"*) already reveals—the last year of war, 1918, the collapse of the Habsburg Empire, and the founding of the new state of the South Slavs (SHS). Even though there were some successes to be celebrated, like the reconquest of Gorizia, the situation was generally bad for the Austrian troops: The supply of weapons and food ran very low. In this respect, the uprising of frustrated and nationally thinking soldiers is mentioned, among them the ones in May in Judenburg, Murau, and Bad Radkersburg (the one in Judenburg

51 Pečenko/Štepec (2014) Part 4, 00:24:08.

being the biggest in the Austrian hinterland) and directly behind the frontlines at the River Piave in October 1918.[52] The horrible supply situation is also named as the reason for the ultimate defeat, because army commanders such as General Boroević overestimated the strength of their own already severely weakened troops. In September 1918, the monarchy was at its end; in October, Emperor Karl tried to prevent the collapse until the last minute with his Manifest. The famous answer of Anton Korošec, Reichsrat member, soon to be president of the National Council and undoubtedly the most important Slovene politician of this time and the interwar period, supposedly was: "It's too late, Your Majesty."[53] The latter half of this last episode concentrates on the founding of the provisional State of Slovenes, Croats, and Serbs and the unification with the already independent Kingdom of Serbia. Very suddenly, people forgot that they had been loyal subjects of the Austrian Emperor until very recently. This is also the time when the ideological slogan of *Völkerkerker* was enforced.[54] The documentary series ends by mentioning the painful territorial loss of the Littoral (*Primorska*) and Lower Carinthia, as well as the missing official remembrance for the Slovene fallen soldiers and veterans. It finds an abrupt end, as the Habsburg Empire itself did in 1918.

52 Pečenko/Štepec (2014), Part 5, 00:14: 20 and 00:20:05. More detailed on the uprising in Judenburg, see: Karin Almasy, "'V spomin žrtvam svetovne vojne' - Erinnerungskultur, Gefallenendenkmäler in der Untersteiermark und die Zäsur 1918 für die Slowenen," in *Heimatfront: Graz und das Kronland Steiermark im Ersten Weltkrieg,* ed. Werner Suppanz and Nicole Goll (Essen: Klartext-Verlag, 2017).

53 Pečenko/Štepec (2014), Part 5, 00:20:05, and in all detail: Feliks Bister, *"Majestät, es ist zu spät": Anton Korošec und die slovenische Politik im Wiener Reichsrat bis 1918* (Wien: Böhlau, 1995).

54 Pečenko/Štepec (2014), Part 5, 00:26:50.

Drawing Conclusions

If we want to sum up the most important "material components" of the Slovene narrative on WWI presented in these two productions, it is fair to state the following: The Isonzo Front is (and obviously will remain) the dominant theme above all other frontlines or military aspects. The first, and so far only, Slovene feature film takes place on the Isonzo front and two out of five episodes of the documentary series deal mainly with events along the river Isonzo/Soča. Nevertheless, the documentary series does not neglect to mention lesser known sites of Slovene involvement in World War I: In episode two, for example, the stationing of one division from Celje in Boka Kotorska and later in Serbia on the Balkan frontline in order to fight Serbia. Meanwhile, some Yugoslav-orientated Slovenes already fought for Serbia against the Habsburg troops. Even though only a few in number, this is also the situation of Slovenes fighting against Slovenes. Other not well known Slovene involvements include a sea battle against Italy on the coast of Ancona in May 1915, mentioned in episode three, and the bloody battles in the Dolomites mountains at Monte Chiesa and Asiago in May 1916, mentioned in episode four, where still today one valley is called *Dolina degli Sloveni*. What is not really discussed instead is the Western front, the *Kriegsschuldfrage* (Question of war guilt); the Russian revolution and the politics of the Great Powers is only mentioned where it is necessary, probably because, from a Slovene perspective, others made the big decisions, and they were just pawns in the game between the Great Powers of Europe. The documentaries portray the picture of a small nation within the Habsburg Empire on its way to a new statehood due to war. Localities most mentioned in the documentaries next to Ljubljana were Trieste and Gorizia, Doberdob, Kobarid and Judenburg, Przemyśl, and Sarajevo. Only few "heroes" are mentioned in these documentaries: General

Boroević, the Emperor(s), among politicians first and foremost Anton Korošec, alongside "traitors" such as Ljudevit Pivko, and "insurgents" such as Anton Hafner (the leader of the Judenburg uprising). Most names mentioned are "small" and historically unimportant Slovene soldiers, who left diaries or letters and give an idea of WWI from the viewpoint of privates. A comparison of the "material components" of this Slovene documentary series in five episodes to one German[55] and one British[56] documentary production offers interesting insights. What they all have in common is that they stay mainly within their own national perspective; that is, at the same time, why they differ considerably in the regarded topics and sites. The Slovene storylines on WWI, meaning the

---

55 The exemplary German production in five episodes, *Der Erste Weltkrieg*, aired on ARD in 2004. Their episodes were named as follows: 1. "Mythos Tannenberg" ["The myth of the battle of Tannenberg"], 2. "Gashölle Ypern" ["The poisonous inferno of Ypern"], 3. "Alptraum Verdun" ["The nightmare of Verdun"], 4. "Schlachtfeld Heimat" ["The home front"] 5. "Trauma Versailles" ["The trauma of Versailles"]. This documentary series was analyzed by Silke Fengler and Stefan Krebs, "Das Schöne und der Krieg: Zur filmischen Ästhetisierung des Ersten Weltkrieges gestern und heute," in *Jahrbuch für Kommunikationsgeschichte* (Stuttgart: Franz Steiner Verlag, 2007), 196–210.

56 *The First World War*, a documentary series in ten episodes, based on the book by Hew Strachan and produced by Channel 4 in 2003 and aired again by the BBC in 2014, focuses on the British perspective and interpretation of historical events but offers a broad overview on different regions of the Commonwealth and their involvement in WWI, therefore this series features comparatively "exotic" side stages of the Great War, such as the Ottoman Empire in episode four, "Jihad," or Africa in episode three, "Global War," etc. See further: "The First World War," *bbc.co.uk*, accessed Sept. 30, 2015, http://www.bbc.co.uk/programmes/b00jz8g2/episodes/guide.

"theoretical-methodical dimension" (according to which line of reasoning are these material components put together to form the narrative?), differ considerably from the British and German ones. The geographic focus is much smaller, and world politics of the Great Powers is not much mentioned. It seems, and this appears to be a positive aspect, that in the Slovene narrative, WWI is much more presented from a bottom-up perspective, meaning from the point of view of "ordinary people," of little soldiers, and in a collective sense, from the viewpoint of a small nation.[57] This is obviously true for *Gozdovi so* še *vedno zeleni*, but it is also a valid point for the documentary series that strongly relies on historical sources like diaries and letters from soldiers and other contemporaries, thereby portraying the war more from a socio-historical, and not solely military or politically strategic, perspective. On the other hand, one could argue that the Slovene documentary series fails to (or, due to its different guiding question, never attempts to) connect the dots of the bigger picture of Europe's Great Power politics, but rather stays within the regional frame of events in the Slovene lands.

The "semantic components" of the Slovene narrative on WWI have been on display especially in the documentary series, even present in the titles of the single episodes, especially three *Doberdob, slovenskih fantov grob* ("*Doberdob, the Grave of Slovenian Lads*") and four *Preboj pri Kobaridu* ("*The Breakthrough at Kobarid*"). Even though the series mentions nationalistic and ideologically one-sided slogans, it critically reflects upon them and explains the context of their emergence. For example, while it was still quite

57 Unfortunately, most international encyclopedic publications on WWI still neglect the small nations and their destinies, see: Walter Lukan, "Zgodovinopisje o Prvi svetovni vojni," in *Velika vojna in Slovenci*, ed. Peter Vodopivec and Katja Kleindienst (Ljubljana: Slovenska matica, 2005), 34.

possible to read about the ideologeme of *Völkerkerker* ("Prison of people's nations"), an idea reinforced after the disintegration in 1918 to make nostalgic feelings of belonging to the Austro-Hungarian Empire disappear, in older Slovene historiography, such stereotypes cannot be found in this documentary.[58] In *Gozdovi so še vedno zeleni*, a particularly quiet war movie, I would argue that the "semantic component" is characterized by the speechlessness of the protagonists in front of the overwhelming war experience. Only in the mentioned nightmare, soldier Lindner is confronted with the ideological phrases of fatherland and the father figure of the Emperor.

* * *

Recapitulating Slovene film production on WWI in general, I would argue that until recently it did not really exist, but that the productions under discussion in this article prove to be a very valid and solid powerful thrust in this direction. Both productions discussed at length made great efforts in order to be historically accurate and portray a realistic—neither naïve nor romantic nor nationalistic—picture of the specific situation of Slovene people during the First World War. Since a small but very committed circle of historians and movie producers is trying to raise awareness for WWI in Slovenia, we can expect more such excellent productions in the future. Especially for the year 2018, commemorating the 100th anniversary of the turning point, 1918, in Slovene history, one can expect some more research and TV productions on that topic. Even though WWII is not going to dominate public perception any less, the view on WWI is not completely blocked anymore.

58 Pečenko/Štepec (2014), Part 1.

POSTSCRIPT:

A CINEMA OF LIMINALITY

Thomas Ballhausen

I do dream you
Allow me to believe you are the real me
I see you breathing under water
See you on both sides of a door

–John Frusciante, "Away and Anywhere"

In 1916, retrospectively regarded as a temporal turning point of the First World War, the reprint of a report from the *Reichenberger Zeitung* is found in the journal *Kinematographische Rundschau.* In the reproduced text, the soldier Hans Kasper von Starken reports of his military-instilled, even military-molded, experiences with the medium of film and the performance context of mobile field cinema. Among other things, the text negotiates the question of whether or not civilians are at all capable of fully experiencing the cinematic art per se. The author finds here reason for doubt, due to the extensive receptive experience:

You must have lain for three weeks in a trench, waded through mud and heard the American ammunition Yankee Doodling. Only then can one come to an accurate understanding of this cinematic achievement. Even the pacifist has no idea what cinema is

.... Become a soldier!—a field-grey soldier. I advise you well, just to learn to see cinema properly. All at once you will be opened up to completely new concepts ... The cinema is for us warriors the only art institution. Therefore we are learning to fully enjoy, nuance and dissect it. Where do we see a well-dressed woman? Only in the cinema. Where do we see merriment, lunacy, humor? In the cinema. Where do we see coquetry, love play, flirtation? In the cinema [...] We see and experience every movement: we haven't had such things put in front of us for such a long time. We are thirsty for it. This is why we can also really take delight in the fun of it and the large lit up eyes. We take the film personally. [...] We will be totally removed from the steady beat of the war machine, we are suddenly in another land, together with people, who don't move in the same gear as we do. That does us well. The cinema is the shore of oblivion for us, and therefore a point of rest. The nerves relax. By purely seeing, one is in a kind of opium dream—yes, one dreams whilst conscious and has no hangover afterwards.[1]

The editorial staff of the *Kinematographische Rundschau* were likely pleased with this assessment, which after all has the air of a military-political commissioning of a hotly-contested medium and speaks of the in/as of 1916 more easily traceable exchange between (so-called) fictional and (so-called) documentary examples of Austrian film propaganda.

A productively adapted use of the term "border" is necessary for the comprehension of these at-hand explanations, which are aimed at the First World War and Austrian film history up until 1938. This concerns not only the aforementioned incorporation of documentary-enlightening elements of feature films, or the likewise implied integration of feature film-like episodes in newsreels or special films. The framings of (re-)constructive

1 *Kinematographische Rundschau*, no. 418 (1916): 10.

gestures of boundary should be, in my opinion, significantly more pronounced. That is, through closer observation of the "inner" cinematic phenomenon of blurring borders (for example, the insertion of intertitles or the application of supposedly robust genre definitions), formal conception (for example, the predetermination of patterns of perception through fixed frame or montage), content-related design/standardization (for example, portrayal of gender relations or the natural elements), and subsequent periodization attempts. In order to avoid the threat of arbitrariness, a focus on the construction-impulse of the corporeality of the cinematic and of cinematic physicality should lie within this deliberately short attempt—one which shares, I presume, the mentioned underlying problems. The production of things documentary-related is hereby addressed, which at least with regard to the negotiated source pool is subject to essentially narrative imperatives, but also to aspects such as the fictional foundation of historiographic designs or the (mis-)use of "depots," which, along with the "border," presents another case of semantic polymorphism. In order to express the links and splices of a diligent analysis (or rather, reflection) into the period under examination with at least a semblance of communicability (as well as a boundary)—without altogether simultaneously forgetting the tense relationship that is part of the creation of memorable images or the aspiring narrative potential of war—here follows a contextualizing sketch of Austrian film propaganda between 1914 and 1918, comments on the relevant thematic variety of the feature film *The Hands of Orlac* (1925) and concluding (if not hopefully also enlightening) remarks on the "archive" as a model for theorization.

Film History Guidelines

The belligerent parties made use of mass media during the First World War to an until then unprecedented extent. Namely, propaganda was not transported through one sole primary medium. Rather, its intense utilization was achieved through an existing and namely more interconnected media system. Even the Austrian war press bureau—which had to deal with extensive tasks in a large geographic area—worked with the already existing entwinement of different media, and consequently established an early form of inter-medial, information-oriented warfare. The history of Austrian cinematic war reporting during the First World War can be, as previously noted, divided into two large periods: one phase until around 1916, in which the presentation of technology was of importance, and the time period of the final war years, in which a stronger integration of narrative elements within cinematic propaganda is apparent. Common within the periods is the complex interconnection with other media forms.

The question of the social-political motivated legitimization of violence depiction has been, and is chosen for the most part, as the means to approach this topic exclusively from the side of violence. It is necessary for this approach to point out that the tradition of media pedagogical guidelines can be considered long and not particularly cheerful or even constructively critical. It is an approach that accepts in principle the dubious legitimacy of violence and that perpetuates the myth of state legitimized violence.[2] In regard to a larger concept, this can also be said of politically motivated propaganda, i.e. for image-specific war reporting and the corresponding presentation environment. This legitimization of militarization and military violence bases its arguments on the historical-political development and the development of national organizational structures. This extensive legitimization also

2 Cf. Burkhard Liebsch, "Gewalt und Legitimität," in *Handbuch der Kulturwissenschaften. Bd. 3: Themen und Tendenzen*, ed. Friedrich Jaeger, Jörn Rüsen, and Jürgen Straub (Stuttgart: Metzler, 2004), 503–520, here: 503.

reached into the field of entertainment, which in times of crisis was just as exposed to state and political exertions of influences as were existing mediums—mediums that were constantly having to redefine their stance with regards to not only their socially public anchorages but also their internal, historical as well as technical, development processes of discussion on entitlement and rights. The aforementioned connection between these two fields will now be illustrated by using the self-trained cinema system and its accompanying media (supposed) experiences as an example. The illustration and portrayal of violence on the basis of its conception and origin was anything but foreign to film as a medium, whose potential as propaganda instrument had already been recognized early. The audience was quite familiar with the theatrical structure of Vaudeville entertainment, exhibition techniques, display modes, and entertainment possibilities of pre-cinemagraphic time. Therefore, on the basis of this media socialization, the entire entertainment offering could be militarily shaped without a problem. In doing this, the film serves not only the depiction of violence, but also the mould of its typical power structures. If one assumes that the propaganda has been successfully implemented, the cinematic medium, as a contested field, mirrors the planability and orderliness of war. And, therefore, also the inevitable violence which comes with it: "The film [. . .] recasted the catastrophic-chaotic initial occurrence of war into a civilizatory event, and gave it a visually narrative and moral order, which does not occur in war per se. In this way, the war film, in all of its forms, contributes to the always new illusion of planability of war."[3]

3 Gerhard Paul, "Krieg und Frieden im 20. Jahrhundert: Historische Skizze und methodologische Überlegungen," in *Krieg und Militär im Film des 20. Jahrhunderts*, ed. Bernhard Chiari, Matthias Rogg, and Wolfgang Schmidt (München: Oldenbourg, 2003), 3–76, here: 7.

On a formal level, solutions to two communication problems could already be offered with the new medium of film, even in its infancy: the overcoming of geographic distance to the place of occurrence and the politically effective communicability of time limited conflicts. However, the fabricated forgery of events was more quickly available and often also had a more successful effect on the public than the actual report. The just now mentioned reconstruction of occurrences was quite normal and ranged from feigned battle scenes to reshot earthquakes. Furthermore, the question of usability of material for propaganda purposes was constantly being questioned, in regards to whether these limited representation possibilities on the reality of war actually could and can be reproduced. The alleged approach to the reality of war was and remains, to a great extent, a deception. War reporting and hence its communication is, in the case of party participation in a military conflict, never free of instrumentalization. Quite on the contrary, the chasm of accepted actuality would be in fact widened because of the alleged approach to reality. The tendencies for visualization and simulation are therefore also always orientated to a particular media socialization standing: "Images of modern warriors and war technologies, of death, killing and extermination, stretched over the frame of a canvas or screen, and released for consumption under the general conditions of consumption of reproduced images on a mass scale, will be admitted into a reception-spectrum, which is in itself formed after a long-term process through the media."[4] The described instrumentalization of the gaze, which will appear later in more focus, is therefore already perceptible in early cinema history and is clearly

4 Bernd Hüppauf, "Kriegsfotographie," in *Der Erste Weltkrieg: Wirkung - Wahrnehmung - Analyse*, ed. Wolfgang Michalka (München: Piper, 1994), 875–909, here: 875.

comprehensible through a changing relationship between world and image. The world was already beginning to be captured by visual portrayals in the early modern era. In the late nineteenth century, this undertaking led finally to the attempt at depicting the world as an image. In the case of war reporting, an increasing overlap of arranged reality though projections (in relation to imagination and cinematography) is the direct consequence and is still even perceivable today: "The analogy of cinema and catastrophe has masked, perhaps even alleviated, our horror, but we can no longer escape this film. More so, every event accelerates the cinematographization of the world. The accurate image in the cinema barely cares about how much reality and falsity is contained within it. In the cinema-world, it seems only logical that onto an image which portrays reality as if it were a cinema dream, a fake image follows, which absolutely seems to be real. It is therefore not simply the image anymore, which will turn into the world (even if the transformation of horror into propaganda is achieved precisely through this). The world becomes its own image."[5]

Seams and Scars

The moment of image-creation is also central in Robert Wiene's screen adaptation, *The Hands of Orlac.* In a contemporary critique, which also mirrors the expectations of the film, the plot twist rich story is summarized as follows:

A piano virtuoso is robbed of the use of his hands in a railway disaster. The doctor treating him surgically gives him the hands of an executed robber and murderer. From here, informed by a

5 Georg Seeßlen and Markus Metz, *Krieg der Bilder - Bilder des Krieges: Abhandlung* über *die Katastrophe und die mediale Wirklichkeit* (Berlin: Ed. Tiamat, 2002), 29.

stranger, the artist fears that he will be driven to crime by the hands of the dead man, and is soon caught up as a suspect in the murder of his own father. It is only now explained that the crime was carried out by a friend of the executed man, who also committed the crime that the innocent man was accused of. The subject has an extremely thrilling exposition and holds tension until the very last scene, executed by an excellently assembled ensemble, with Conrad Veidt at the helm, who presents it in its best light. The directing is firm and careful, especially in the extremely realistic scenes of the railway catastrophe, the presentation tasteful, the plot events effectively underscoring. The photography is in every regard competent. It is a domestic film which matches up to the best foreign productions.[6]

The disruptive shock of the train crash afflicts not only the hands of the pianist, but even more so the mind of this peculiar homecomer. The scene of the crime is staged as a battlefield, which stands at the interface between expressionist horror and psychological thriller. Along these lines, the inner life of the main character is staged as a fissured landscape—a circumstance that begins to yield negative results for the protagonist:

Orlac becomes even more the victim of intrigue than of his own imaginings, so to speak falling prey to his own image, embodied in the film's own expressionistic way, and comes close to his own demise. Whereas Fritz Lang's criminal in the sound motion picture MABUSE farewells himself sarcastically from expressionism [...], Orlac distances himself from it in an inner fight to the death. A psychological branch has begun with *The Hands of Orlac*, which above all opens up new opportunities for the actors. Horror will no longer merely be experienced as a possibility for eeriness

6 "Orlac's Hände," *Paimann's Film-Liste: Wochenschrift für Lichtbild-Kritik,* no. 441 (1924): 181.

in image form, but rather also as a subjective sensation within humans.[7]

The shapes spring into motion through a combination of cutting—almost irrespective of straight movement by hand or sideways movement through imaginative space—and segmented parts. The opposite can easily arise from the overlapping security of form and contour. The mutilated and then re-mended bodies are not any more recognizable through form/norm as are the detached limbs and organs. In accordance with the technical cinematic advances of cutting techniques, a corresponding film tradition at a contextual level also developed—one which, along with the deconstruction of form, also demonstrated a constant increase of chaotic conditions.[8] Not at least because of this, the dramatic (action) prelude of the film results in hysteria, loss of confidence, and crime. In *The Hands of Orlac*, the criminal investigation is finally set against the outbreak of the First World War—a rational mingling of explanation and interpretation that leads to the construction of a happy ending. If we were, however, to travel back to the plot development in a linear manner, we would experience the main character Paul Orlac as a traumatized man. In view of the narrative circumstances, it doesn't seem surprising that Wiene compresses Maurice Renard's figure-rich novel to a harmonious, sparsely populated thriller/melodrama with fewer protagonists, with only one remarkable exception: the train crash. Differing from the quasi-documentary filming from the time of the First World War (which transforms the classic battlefield image of war into that of an empty dead zone), the inter-war period film draws

7 Georg Seeßlen and Fernand Jung, *Horror: Geschichte und Mythologie des Horrorfilms* (Marburg: Schüren, 2006): 116.

8 Cf. Eberhard Nuffer, *Filmschnitt und Schneidetisch: Eine Zeitreise durch die klassische Montagetechnologie* (Potsdam: Polzer, 2002), 51–60.

from the experiences of irreversibly mechanized, revved-up conflict, and transforms them at every level:

> There are images of claustrophobic and liminal rooms, of subjectively distorted dimensions, panoramas of emptied, abstract landscapes, images of invasion, aggression and violence. The experience of the battlefield—shock and disorientation—is in conflict with simple narrativization based on cause and effect. That is why many post-war films seem so abrupt, illogical, and confusing. Whereas the war films of around 1930—more than a decade after the end of the war—tried to narrate trauma, the early films of the Weimar Republic radically bring shock and disorientation on a formal level to the forefront. They break up every simple and linear narration and shift the experience of the battlefield, in its divided and violent form, into formally aesthetic questions. These films (*The Cabinet of Dr. Caligari*, *The Nibelungs*, *Metropolis*, *M*, and many others) are pervaded by images of archetypal scenes, which function as fragments of memory of the bygone war, as traces and compulsively re-occurring elements of a traumatic experience.[9]

In this way, Orlac is caught up in an (aesthetic) minefield of expressionism. Concerning the design of the film, this is not to be understood as a rigid condition, but rather as a constantly changing system of newly arranged components. That is, an expression of an archive-specific aesthetic of horror. This is how *The Hands of Orlac* can and should be assessed as the continuation of "expressionist tradition,"[10] it being the first of many adaptations of

---

9 Anton Kaes, "Schlachtfelder im Kino und die Krise der Repräsentation," in *Schlachtfelder: Codierung von Gewalt im medialen Wandel*, ed. Steffen Martus, Marina Münkler, and Werner Röcke (Berlin: De Gruyter, 2003), 118–128, here: 128.

10 Peter Hutchings, *Historical Dictionary of Horror Cinema* (Lanham: Scarecrow Press, 2008), xii.

Renard's original novel and particularly as a "stylish horror thriller."[11] One of the constant factors of the film is certainly the body, which becomes the venue of the dialectic dilemma of Having and Being and, if you like, also becomes the discursive battlefield. The accident as paradigmatic framework of modernity clearly shows the significance of the fragility (or to be more precise, vulnerability) of the medialized body and the repercussions of inscription and the use of medical and criminological practices. At this point, the dense discourse of the Archive, the Horror, and the Wounding unite: "The archive is in this way understood a symbolic formation (a collection of signs) and may be so maintained in that it is again and again reproduced in a similar/the same way (repetition), in that it is bounded, it has an outside."[12]

Thinking the Archive

The full leap of establishing the "archive" as hypothesis can only be realized by simultaneously considering potentially ambiguously understood critique—something like the ability to take criticism or the worthiness to be criticized. This mode is accompanied by an expression of this critique. Let us turn back to the supposed end and to the actual beginning of the topic at hand, taking into consideration the ambiguous assumption, borrowing from Heidegger's categories of assumption, i.e. to the expectations, the hypotheses, and the acceptances.[13] That is, the misunderstanding of film as pure illustration or undisturbed portrayal of so-called reality obscures our view of the cinematic expressions of mediality.

11 Ibid., 336.

12 Ulrike Kadi, "Archiv: Schmerz, Dokument," *texte,* no. 4 (2007): 39–55, here: 40.

13 Cf. Martin Heidegger, *Zollikoner Seminare* (Frankfurt am Main: Klostermann, 2006), 5ff.

The renewed (or maybe even new) placement of the archive as hypothesis opens our eyes to the, not least of all, material images into which history disintegrates. Deliberately repeated word-for-word, that means: The archive should be applied on the one hand as a trio of institution, collection, and practice, and on the other hand—having recourse to David L. Martin—with regard to the audio-visual source as a discursive troika of collection, body, (also in the sense of a physical makeup of the respective sources), and medial cartography that makes possible a progressive critique of linear-progression historiography.[14] In this regard, the collection can be used to break this down. The analogue film material is also always the starting point, for instance, for the availability on online platforms, restorations, re-use, and possible productive reception. The ordering archive serves as a register of the historiographical and as an option of reflection on how we give sense to a senseless history, and to what degree. This moment of foundation is, however, not to be thought of as a uniquely set and subsequently embraced hermeneutical practice, but rather more as necessity, which is competent—but also skeptical—to incorporate sources again and again (and always new) with readings and contextualizations. Even this is a part of the incessantly cyclical, to-be-communicated work on the archive—as work on the archived. The limiting view of film as illustration and vividness must be additionally opposed to the emphasis of cinematic mediality. An in this way expanded view detaches the particular instances from the entirety of the collection and is conscious not only of its historicity, but also of the present moment. The outlook on the subsequent future (as well as on the film in its variations and adaptations) manifests itself constantly anew as a provocation

14 Cf. David L. Martin, *Curious Visions of Modernity: Enchantment, Magic, and the Sacred* (Cambridge, MA: MIT Press, 2011).

to ethical attitudes toward an obligation to be responsible concerning collection and the general public. The intellectual as well as logistic achievement of the archive (or the archivers) allows not only for the questioning of sources, but also for the development of resistances. The horizon of this endeavor is—in all its ambiguity—a critique of the archive itself.[15]

15 Cf. Thomas Ballhausen, *Signaturen der Erinnerung: Über die Arbeit am Archiv* (Wien: Edition Atelier, 2015).

SELECTED BIBLIOGRAPHY

Karin Almasy. *Wie aus Marburgern 'Slowenen' und 'Deutsche' wurden: Ein Beispiel zur beginnenden nationalen Differenzierung in Zentraleuropa zwischen 1848 und 1861.* Graz: Pavlova hiša - Pavelhaus, Wissenschaftliche Schriftenreihe des Pavelhauses 16, 2014.

-------, "Der Stellenwert des Ersten Weltkrieges in der slowenischen Erinnerungskultur und das Gedenkjahr 2014 in Slowenien," in: Bernhard Bachinger, Richard Lein, Verena Moritz, Julia Walleczek-Fritz, Stefan Wedrac, Markus Wurzer, eds., *Gedenken und (k)ein Ende – was bleibt vom Jahr 2014? Das Gedenkjahr 1914/2014 und sein historiografisches Vermächtnis.* Vienna: Verlag der Österreichischen Akademie der Wissenschaften, 2017, 51-67

------- with Tanja Žigon und Andrej Lovšin. *Vloga in pomen prevajanja učbenikov v 19. stoletju: kulurnozgodovinski in jezikovni pogledi.* Ljubljana: Znanstvena založba Filozofske fakultete, 2017

Barbara Artymys, Leszek Artymys, and Wiesław Stradomski, *Historia filmu polskiego*, vol. 2, 1930-1939. Warsaw: Wydawnictwa Artystyczne i Filmowe, 1988

Thomas Ballhausen. "Between Virgo and Virago: Spatial Perceptions and Gender Politics in Austrian Film Production, 1914-1918," in *Gendered Memories: Transgressions in German and Israeli Film and Theater*, ed. Vera Apfelthaler and Julia B. Köhne. Vienna: Turia + Kant, 2007, 147-159

---------- and Günter Krenn. "Kriegs-Bilder und Bilder-Kriege: Die kinematographische Kriegsberichterstattung Österreich-Ungarns während des Ersten Weltkriegs," in *KINtop: Jahrbuch zur Erforschung des frühen Film.* Frankfurt am Main, Nr. 12 (2003): 143-150

---------- and Günter Krenn. "(Re)Telling War: Austrian Newsreels of the First World War Between Presentation and Representation," *Journal of Film Preservation* 10 (2003): 7-9

Banal Militarism: Zur Veralltäglichung des Militärischen im Zivilen, ed. Tanja Thomas, Fabian Virchow. Bielefeld: Transcript Verlag, 2006

Martin Baumeister. "L'effet de réel: Zum Verhältnis von Krieg und Film 1914 bis 1918," in *Krieg und Militär im Film des 20. Jahrhunderts,* ed. Bernhard Chiari, Matthias Rogg, and Wolfgang Schmidt (Beiträge zur Militärgeschichte 59). Munich: R. Oldenbourg Verlag, 2003, 245-268

Besetzte Bilder: Film, Kultur und Propaganda in Österreich 1945-1955, ed. Karin Moser. Vienna: Verlag Filmarchiv Austria, 2005

Kees Boterbloe., "Chto delat'?: World War I in Russian Historiography after Communism," *The Journal of Slavic Military Studies* vol 25, no 3 (2012):393-408, DOI: 10.1080/13518046.2012.705655 (last accessed Feb. 1, 2016)

Gian Piero Brunetta. "L'immagine della prima guerra mondiale attraverso il cinema," in: *Operai e contadini nella Grande Guerra,* ed. Mario Isnenghi. Bologna: Cappelli, 1982

--------. *La guerra lontana: La prima guerra mondiale e il cinema tra i tabù del presente e la creazione del passato.* Rovereto: Zaffoni, 1985

Elisabeth Büttner and Christan Dewald. *Das tägliche Brennen: Eine Geschichte des österreichischen Films von den Anfängen bis 1945.* Salzburg: Residenz, 2002

Gianfranco Casadio. *Il grigio e il nero. Spettacolo e propaganda nel cinema italiano degli anni Trenta.* Ravenna: Longo, 1989

-------. *La guerra al cinema: I film di guerra nel cinema italiano dal 1944 al 1996*, vol. 1. Ravenna: Longo, 1997

Český hraný film - Czech Feature Film, 6 vols. Prague: Národní filmový archiv, 1995-2010

James Clarke. *War Films.* London: Virgin Books, 2006

Milutin Čolić. *Jugoslovenski ratni film* ½. Belgrade: Institut za film / Užice: Vesti, 1984

Nancy Condee. *The Imperial Trace: Recent Russian Cinema.* Oxford: Oxford University Press, 2009

Robert von Dassanowsky. *Austrian Cinema: A History* Jefferson, NC: McFarland & Company, 2005

------------. "Finis Austriae, vivat Austria: The Re/Vision of 1918 in Austrian Film," in Österreich 1918 und die Folgen*: Geschichte, Literatur, Theater und Film. Austria 1918 and the Aftermath. History, Literature, Theatre, and Film*, ed. Karl Müller and Hans Wagener. Vienna: Böhlau, 2009, 179-196

László Deák-Sárosi. *A szimbolikus-retorikus film: The symbolic-rhetorical Film - Szőts, Jancsó, Huszárik, Mundruczó, Tarr and modernisms.* PhD dissertation, Budapest, 2016)

Alfréd Deésy. *In the circus ring, on the stage, on movie screen: Recollections.* Budapest: Magyar Filmintézet, 1992

James Der Derian. *Virtuous War: Mapping the Military-Industrial-Media-Entertainment Network.* Boulder: Westview, 2001

Pier Marco De Santi. *1914-1918: Una guerra sullo schermo.* Rome: Rivista Militare, 1988

------------. "La Grande Guerra nel cinema italiano," in *La Grande Guerra degli artisti*, ed. Nadia Marchioni. Florence: Polistampa, 2005

Aleksandar Erdeljanović. "Prvih pola veka srpske kinematografije 1896-1945, Program Muzeja Jugoslovenske kinoteke," in *Jugoslovenska kinoteka.* Belgrade: maj 2007, 23-33

------------. "Oh kakav divan rat ili Prvi svetski rat na igranom filmu, Program Muzeja Jugoslovenske kinoteke," in *Jugoslovenska kinoteka.* Belgrade: maj, 2009, 11-17

Der Erste Weltkrieg im Film, ed. Rainer Rother, and Karin Herbst-Messlinger. Munich: edition text + kritik, 2009

Alessandro Faccioli. "La guerra al cinema," in *Gli Italiani in guerra: Conflitti, identità, memorie dal Risorgimento ai nostri giorni*, ed. Mario Isnenghi, Vol. 3. Turin: Utet, 2008

--------. "Pellicole sul fronte: il cinema e la guerra," in *Dizionario storico della prima guerra mondiale*, ed. by Nicola Labanca. Bari: Laterza, 2014

--------. "Il cinema italiano e la Grande Guerra," in *A fuoco l'obiettivo! Il cinema e la fotografia raccontano la Grande Guerra*, ed. Alessandro Faccioli and Alberto Scandola. Bologna: Persiani, 2014

A.V. Fediuk. "Sovetskaia sistema kinematografa 1930gg.: Rol′ chudozhestvennogo kino v agitacionno-propagandistskoi rabote Stalinskogo rezhima," in *Problemy rossijskoj istorii*, Vypusk 10. Moscow, 2010, 294-311

The First World War and Popular Cinema: 1914 to the Present, ed. Michael Paris. New Brunswick, NJ: Rutgers University Press, 1999

Enrico Gaudenzi and Giorgio Sangiorgi. *La prima guerra mondiale nel cinema italiano: Filmografia 1915-2013*. Ravenna: Longo, 2014

Daniel Gethmann. *Das Narvik-Projekt: Film und Krieg*. (Literatur und Wirklichkeit 29). Bonn: Bouvier Verlag, 1998

Manuela Gheorghiu-Cernat. *A Concise History of the Romanian Film*. Bucarest: Editura ştiinţifică şi enciclopedică, 1983

David C. Gillespie. *Russian Cinema*. Edinburgh: Longman Publishing Group, 2003

Gianfranco Miro Gori. *Patria diva: La storia d'Italia nei film del ventennio*. Florence: La casa Usher, 1988

Gothic Crime: Essays und Materialien zu Orlac´s Hände, ed. Armin Loacker and Thomas Ballhausen, Vienna: filmarchiv austria, 2013

The Great War in Post-Memory Literature and Film: Media and Cultural Memory/Medien und kulturelle Erinnerung. Vol. 18, ed. by Astrid Erll, Ansgar Nünning. Berlin: De Gruyter, 2014

Svetozar Guberinić. "Staro i novo," in *Magazin Sineast* no. 19 (1972/73): 29-41

The Habsburg Legacy: National Identity in Historical Perspective, ed. Ritchie Robertson, Edward Timms (Austrian Studies V). Edinburgh: University Press, 1994

Lutz Haucke. "Rumänische neue Welle?" in *Nouvelle vague in Osteuropa? Zur ostmittel- und südosteuropäischen Filmgeschichte 19601970.* Berlin: Rhombos, 2009, 424437.

Jule Hillgärtner. *Krieg darstellen.* Berlin: Kulturverlag Kadmos, 2013

Andrew Hoskins and Ben O´Loughlin. *War and Media: The Emergence of Diffused War.* Cambridge: Polity Press, 2010

Marilena Ilieşu. *Povestea poveştii ⊠n filmul românesc (19122012).* Bucarest: Polirom, 2013

Information.Macht.Krieg., ed. Gerfried Stocker and Christine Schöpf .Vienna: Springer, 1998

Mario Isnenghi. "L'immagine cinematografica della grande guerra," in *Rivista di storia contemporanea* vol. 7, no. 3 (1978)

Hubertus F. Jahn. *Patriotic Culture in Russia During World War I.* Ithaca, NY: Cornell University Press, 1995

Anton Kaes. *Shell Shock Cinema: Weimar Culture and the Wounds of War.* Princeton: Princeton University Press, 2009

Peter Kenez. *Cinema and Soviet Society, 1917-1953.* New York: Cambridge University Press, 1992

Ivan Klimeš. *Kinematografie a stát v českých zemích 1895-1945.* Prague: FF UK, 2016

Barbara Korte, Ralf Schneider, and Claudia Sternberg. *Der Erste Weltkrieg und die Mediendiskurse der Erinnerung in Großbritannien: Autobiographie - Roman - Film 1919-1999.* Würzburg: Königshausen & Neumann, 2005

Dejan Kosanović. *Počeci kinematografije na tlu Jugoslavije 1896-1918.* Belgrade: Univerzitet umetnosti / Institut za film, 1985

Dejan Kosanović. *Kinematografija i film u Kraljevini SHS/Kraljevini Jugoslaviji 1918-1941.* Belgrade: Filmski centar Srbije, 2011

Hannes Leidinger. "Visualisierung des Krieges: Die Ostfront in österreichisch-ungarischen Fotografien und Filmproduktionen," in *Jenseits des Schützengrabens: Der Erste Weltkrieg im Osten. Erfahrung - Wahrnehmung - Kontext*, ed. Bernhard Bachinger and Wolfram Dornik. Innsbruck: StudienVerlag, 2013, 451-465

---------. "`Die vaterländische Pflicht an der visuellen Front`: Bildberichterstattung und Bildpropaganda in Österreich-Ungarn unter besonderer Berücksichtigung der `östlichen

Kampfschauplätze` 1914-1918," in *Erster Weltkrieg: Globaler Konflikt - lokale Folgen. Neue Perspektiven*, ed. Stefan Karner and Philipp Lesiak. Innsbruck: StudienVerlag, 2014, 321-332

----------. *Der Untergang der Habsburgermonarchie.* Innsbruck: StudienVerlag, 2017

Václav Macek and Jelena Paštéková. *Dejiny slovenskej kinematografie.* Martin: Osveta, 1997

Franz Marksteiner. "Where is the War? Some Aspects of the Effects of World War One on Austrian Cinema," in *The First World War and Popular Cinema. 1914 to the Present*, ed. Michael Paris. New Brunswick, NJ: Rutgers University Press, 1999, 247-260

Jamie Miller. *Soviet Cinema: Politics and Persuasion under Stalin.* London: Palgrave Macmillan, 2010

Marco Mondini. *La guerra italiana: Partire, raccontare, tornare. 1914-18.* Bologna: Il Mulino, 2014

Karin Moser. "`Visuelles Erinnern` - der Erste Weltkrieg im österreichischen Film- und Fernsehschaffen," in ed. Hannes Leidinger, Verena Moritz, Karin Moser, and Wolfram Dornik, eds., *Habsburgs schmutziger Krieg: Ermittlungen zur österreichisch-ungarischen Kriegsführung 1914-1918.* St. Pölten: Residenz, 2014, 235-253

-----. "Zwischen Fiktion und Realität: Filmische Repräsentation und Leerstellen," in *Virtuelle Ausstellung "Der Erste Weltkrieg und das Ende der Habsburgermonarchie"*, http://ww1.habsburger.net/de/themen/zwischen-fiktion-und-realitaet-filmische-repraesentation-und-leerstellen (last accessed No. 30, 2014)

------. "Mythische Helden: Filmquellen als Träger, Bewahrer und Vermittler von Idealen und Propaganda," in *Virtuelle Ausstellung "Der Erste Weltkrieg und das Ende der Habsburgermonarchie"*, http://ww1.habsburger.net/de/themen/mythische-helden-filmquellen-als-traeger-bewahrer-und-vermittler-von-idealen-und-propaganda (last accessed Nov. 30,2014)

Verena Moritz, Karin Moser, and Hannes Leidinger. *Kampfzone Kino: Film in Österreich 1918-1938*. Vienna: filmarchiv austria, 2008

Carlo Moos. *Habsburg post mortem: Betrachtungen zum Weiterleben der Habsburgermonarchie*. Vienna: Böhlau Verlag, 2016

Dominique Nasta. *Contemporary Romanian Cinema: The History of an Unexpected Miracle*. New York: Columbia University Press, 2013

Österreichische Spielfilme. *Vol. 1: Spielfilme 1906-1918*, ed. Anton Thaller. Vienna: filmarchiv austria, 2010

Dejan Ognjanović. *Više od istine - Kadijević o Kadijeviću*. Novi Sad: Orfelin, 2016

Gerhard Paul. "Krieg und Film im 20. Jahrhundert: Historische Skizzen und methodologische Überlegungen," in *Krieg und Militär im Film des 20. Jahrhunderts*, ed. Bernhard Chiari, Matthias Rogg, and Wolfgang Schmidt. Munich: Oldenbourg, 2003, 3-78

----. *Bilder des Krieges - Krieg der Bilder: Die Visualisierung des modernen Krieges*. Paderborn: Ferdinand Schöningh/Wilhelm Fink, 2004

Ante Peterlić and Momčilo Ilić. *Filmska enciklopedija ½*. Zagreb: Jugoslovenski leksikografski zavod 'Miroslav Krleža', 1986

Karen Petrone. *The Great War in Russian Memory*. Bloomington: Indiana University Press, 2011

Łukasz A. Plessnar. *100 filmów wojennych*. Cracow, 2002

Siegbert Salomon Prawer. *Between Two Worlds: The Jewish Presence in German and Austrian Film, 1910-1933*. New York: Berghahn Books, 2005

Georg Seeßlen and Markus Metz. *Krieg der Bilder - Bilder des Krieges: Abhandlung über die Katastrophe und die mediale Wirklichkeit*. Berlin: Edition Tiamat, 2002

Silent Witnesses: Russian Films 1908-1919/Testimoni silenziosi: Filmi russi 1908-1919, ed. Paolo Cheerchi Usai, Lorenzo Codelli, Carlo Montanaro, and David Robinson. Pordenone-London: Edizione Biblioteca dell'Immagine/British Film Institute, 1989

Bosa Slijepčević. *Kinematografija u Srbiji, Crnoj Gori i Bosni i Hercegovini 1896-1918*. Belgrade: Univerzitet umetnosti / Institut za film 1982

Renáta Šmatláková. *Katalóg slovenských celovečerných filmov 1921-1999*. Bratislava: Slovenský filmový ústav, 1999

Pierre Sorlin. "Tre sguardi sulla Grande Guerra: I film di finzione in Francia, Germania e Italia," in *La Grande Guerra: Esperienza, memoria, immagini*, ed. Diego Leoni and Camillo Zadra. Bologna: Il Mulino, 1986

Philipp Stiasny. *Das Kino und der Krieg: Deutschland 1914-1929.* Munich: edition text + kritik, 2009

Richard Stites. *Russian popular culture: Entertainment and society since 1900.* Cambridge: University Press, 1992

Alexandre Sumpf. *La Grande Guerre oubliée: Russie, 1914-1918.* Paris: Perrin, 2014

István Szőts. *Szilánkok és gyaluforgácsok.* Budapest: Osiris Kiadó, 1999

-----., "In Szene gesetzt: Der Erste Weltkrieg im russischen und sowjetischen Kino," in *Osteuropa* vol. 64, no. 2-4 (2014): 339-350

-----. "War disabled on screen: remembering and forgetting the Great War in the Russian and Soviet cinema, 1914-1940," in *First World War Studies* vol. 6, no. 1 (2015): 57-59, DOI: 10.1080/19475020.2015.1047889

Richard Taylor. *The Politics of the Soviet Cinema 1917-1929.* Cambridge: Cambridge University Press, 1979

Horst Tonn. "Der Erste Weltkrieg im amerikanischen Film," in *Der Erste Weltkrieg in der populären Erinnerungskultur*, ed. Barbara Korte, Sylvia Paletschek, and Wolfgang Hochbruck. Essen: Klartext, 2008, 169-180

Marian Țuțui. *O istorie a filmului românesc/A history of Romanian cinema.* Bucarest: Balkanski Proiect, 2004

Velikii kinemo: Katalog sokhranivshikhsia igrovykh fil´mov Rossii 1908-1919. Moscow: Novoe literaturnoe obozrenie, 2002

V. Vishnevskii. *Dokumental´nye fil´my dorevoliutsionnoi Rossii 1907-1916 gg*. Moscow, 1996

Petar Volk. *Istorija Jugoslovenskog filma*. Belgrade: Institut za film, 1986

----. *Srpski film*. Belgrade: Institut za film, 1996

Denise J. Youngblood. *The Magic Mirror: Moviemaking in Russia 1908-1918*. Madison: The University of Wisconsin Press, 1999

Davis Zima. "Interpretace první světové války v československé meziválečné kinematografii," in *České, slovenské a československé dějiny 20. století IX.*, ed. Tomáš Hradecký, Pavel Horák, Pavek Boštík a kol. Ústí nad Orlicí: Oftis, 2014, 181-196

LIST OF AUTHORS

Karin Almasy is a historian and translator and is currently finishing her PhD at the university of Graz on ideological steering through translations in Slovene school readers (1848-1918) and is part of the FWF-funded research project "Postcarding Lower Styria. Nation, Language and Identities on Picture Postcards (1885–1920)." Research interests: Austrian and Slovene history of the 19th century, translation history, national differentiation, and the role of language in nationalization, Slavs in Habsburg monarchy, postcard studies.

Thomas Ballhausen is an Austrian writer, literary scholar, lecturer at the University of Vienna and head of the Press Collection at the *Literaturhaus Wien*. He studied Comparative Literature, German Philology, Philosophy and Language Arts in Vienna. His current research topics include comparative media studies, critical heritage studies, aesthetics and theories of the archive. Among his most recent book publications are *Gespenstersprache* (2016), a study on literature and historiography, and *Mit verstellter Stimme* (2017) - his most recent collection of poems.

Francesco Bono is an Associate Professor of film history at the University of Perugia. His primary field of research is Italian, German and Austrian cinema between the two world wars. His books include *Casta Diva: Percorsi nel cinema italiano fra le due guerre* (2004); *Kino: Il cinema in Germania dopo la riunificazione* (2006); *Willi Forst: Ein filmkritisches Porträt* (2010); as well as (as co.editor) *Tenöre, Touristen, Gastarbeiter: Deutsch-italienische*

Filmbeziehungen (2011); and *Morte a Venezia: Thomas Mann/ Luchino Visconti* (2014).

Enikő Dácz received her first degree in German and English Language and Literature at the Babeş-Bolyai University in Cluj-Napoca in Rumania, a second MA in Central European Studies at the Andrassy Gyula German Speaking University Budapest and her PhD in German Literature at the University of Szeged in co-operation with the University of Rostock. She worked as a research associate at the Andrassy University and has served since 2014 as a research associate at the Institute for German Culture and History of Southeastern Europe at Ludwig-Maximilians-Universität München.

László Deák-Sárosi has been an associate of the Hungarian National Digital Archive and Film Institute for seven years, and is currently a librarian at the National Széchényi Library. He studied classical guitar in Székelyudvarhely, Budapest, and Luxemburg, and mathematics for a year in Timisoara. He graduated in Budapest from ELTE BTK in Hungarian language and literature, film theory and film history in 2007 and PhD in ELTE Linguistics Doctoral School in 2016. He is a member of the Hungarian Writers' Association (*Magyar Írószövetség*), József Attila Kör Literary association and the Hungarian Society of Semiotics, and a co-editor of the literary journal *Hazanéző*.

Aleksandar Erdeljanović graduated at the Faculty of Political Science of Belgrade University and has been employed at the *Jugoslovenska Kinoteka* (Yugoslav film archive) since 1995. Since 2001 he is head of the Film Archive of the Jugoslovenska Kinoteka. He is the author of the book *Nitrate Film Catalogue* in (2005) and co-author of the books *Karadjordje or the Life and Deeds of the*

Immortal Karadjordje (2004), *The first Slovenian film star Ita Rina* (2007) and *Lifka and Lifke* (2011). He is author of more then 300 articles on movie history published in daily newspapers, film journals and professional publications.

Márton Kurutz is working at the National Film Archive in Budapest since 1988 as a researcher of the Hungarian film history between the two World Wars. His interests also cover Hungarian mass culture. In this connection he was a developer of several cultural online databases. His most important aim is to share the knowledge and the cultural heritage of Hungary.

Hannes Leidinger serves as a Visiting Professor and Lecturer at the University of Vienna, Associated Researcher at the University of Berne, Switzerland, Lecturer at the University of Salzburg and the Andrassy University of Budapest. He is member of the commission for military history and military monuments of historical importance at the Austrian Federal Ministry of Defence, head and member of various research projects, curator and collaborator of several exhibitions on historical topics, editor of DVD-boxes presenting filmic sources on Austrian history, author of numerous publications on Austrian history and the development of Central and Eastern Europe especially in the 19th and the 20th century.

Verena Moritz is head of the FWF (Austrian Science Fund)-project "POWs in Austria-Hungary" at the Austrian State Archives, Lecturer at the Universities of Vienna and Salzburg, member of the Austrian-Russian Commission of Historians, since 1998 head and collaborator of several research projects on the history of Russia and the Soviet Union, the history of Austria 1918-1955 and film history, author of numerous publications.

Karin Moser is a historian, researcher, lecturer in film history, consumption history and contemporary history at the University of Vienna and at the University of Innsbruck. She also works as a historical and dramatic consultant, scriptwriter, and co-director of TV-documentaries; she is the author of numerous publications and DVD-editions on Austrian history of the 20th century, film and media history, propaganda film, national identity construction, East-West stereotypes/Cold War, film censorship, film policy, commercials and industrial films. Her recent publications are: *Film in the Interwar Period: Popular Mass Culture- Tradition, Ideology, Propaganda and Modernity* (2015), *Music and Commercials - pure sensuality and practical utility* (2016).

Václav Šmidrkal is an Assistant Professor of Contemporary European History at the Charles University, Prague, Czech Republic, and a project researcher at the Masaryk Institute and the Archives of the Czech Academy of Sciences. His research focuses on the social and cultural history of war, and the military and violence in 20th Century Central Europe.

Piotr Szlanta is a historian and political scientist specializing in the 19th and 20th century history, especially in the history of international relations, colonial policy and the First World War. He is Professor at the Department of History, University of Warsaw; he also serves as a regional editor of 1914-1918-online. *International Encyclopedia oft he First World War* and holds a scholarship of the Humboldt Foundation.

INDEX

SYMBOLS

A

B

C

D

E

F

G

H

I

J

K

L

M

N

O

P

Q

R

S

T

U

V

W